Making It Home

Making It Home

MEMOIRS OF J. ANGUS MACLEAN

J. Angus MacLean, P.C. O.C. D.F.C.

with the assistance of
Marian Bruce

RAGWEED
THE ISLAND PUBLISHER

Author cover photograph: MacNeill Photography
Edited by: Jane Billinghurst
Printed and bound in Canada by: Friesens

*Ragweed Press acknowledges the generous support of
The Canada Council for the Arts.*

Published by:
Ragweed Press
P.O. Box 2023
Charlottetown, PEI
Canada   C1A 7N7

Canadian Cataloguing in Publication Data

MacLean, J. Angus, 1914-

Making it home

Includes index.
ISBN 0-921556-75-6

1. MacLean, J. Angus, 1914- 2. Prime ministers — Prince Edward Island —
Biography. I. Bruce, Marian. II. Title.

FC2625.1.M32A3   1998   971.7'04'092   C98-950170-1
F1048.M32   1998

*I dedicate this book
to the many brave people
who made my escape from
Nazi-occupied Europe
possible.*

Acknowledgements

First, I would like to thank all the people who encouraged me to write my memoirs: they convinced me that an audience was waiting to read my life story. Thanks also to the people who helped me prepare this book: Marian Bruce, who worked closely with me for many months, helping me put the events of my life in perspective and then on paper; Louise Fleming and Sibyl Frei at Ragweed Press, for all their assistance making this book come to life; and Horace Carver, Ed MacDonald, Dennis Wallace and the late Jim MacNeill, who all generously agreed to read an early draft of my memoirs and give me the benefit of their expertise. A special thanks to Jim MacNeill, who suggested the title.

My longtime secretary and friend, Rosemary Trainor, helped me remember many events that I may otherwise have overlooked. My family, especially my wife Gwen, have been a constant source of support in my life and I am grateful for their patience and encouragement while I was writing my memoirs.

Foreword

I grew up in Charlottetown in a family that took an intense interest in politics (as it seems most families in Charlottetown did). In the case of my family, my paternal grandfather was the Liberal Speaker of the provincial legislature in the 1920s. He was a representative of the Liberal side of our family; the other side was solidly Tory.

I learned early on that J. Angus MacLean was someone special, for when he decided to run in the federal dual riding of Queens, the Liberals in our family split their votes to vote for both the Tory Angus and whoever was running for the Liberals at the time. It was explained to me that, as a war hero, Angus MacLean deserved our support, despite his party. It is clear from the election results of the day that the Liberal representatives of our family were not the only people on the Island to feel this way. Later on in Angus MacLean's political life, I was fortunate enough to watch him in action from the parliamentary press gallery. It seemed he was continuing his tradition of attracting support from people in parties other than his own, for I quickly learned that his integrity, wisdom and self-effacing humour had won him the respect of members on all sides of the House.

The dictionary defines a hero as "1. In mythology and legend, a man, endowed with great courage and strength, celebrated for his bold exploits, and favoured by the gods. 2. A person noted for feats of courage, especially one who has risked his life: soldiers and nurses who were heroes in war. 3. A person noted for special achievement in a particular field." By all of the definitions listed above, J. Angus MacLean is a hero.

Meeting him today on the family farm at Lewis, Prince Edward Island, it is hard to imagine that this quiet man is not just a military hero, but a political leader whose integrity, common sense and loyalty set a standard to be aspired to by politicians of the current generation.

Making It Home describes MacLean's personal and political life from his birth on the family farm to his retirement there sixty-nine years later. It includes both social and political commentary, and high adventure.

Today's generation of Islanders and visitors to our province will marvel at MacLean's vivid description of life on an Island farm in the early days of this century. His picture of those days before the arrival of the automobile, the radio, the telephone or electricity is thoughtful and revealing.

For those who love adventure, MacLean has a gripping personal drama to tell. The heart beats faster as a young airman bails out of a crippled bomber over Holland. We hold our collective breaths as, helped by members of the Resistance but initially hindered by his inability to ride a bicycle, he makes the tense 72-day journey across occupied Europe under the noses of the Gestapo before getting to safety. We are in the audience at Buckingham Palace as King George VI presents the young war hero with the Distinguished Flying Cross; we are taken through the decision-making process as the young MacLean decides to follow in his father's footsteps and seek elected office.

MacLean may be a war hero, but Prince Edward Islanders are not easily convinced that they should elect a Tory in a traditionally Liberal riding. Finally, after two close calls, the voters succumb, and MacLean makes it to Ottawa, going on to become the most elected Islander ever.

Making It Home moves from adventure story to political drama as MacLean gives us an insider's view of Prime Minister John Diefenbaker's troubled government. As minister of Fisheries, MacLean has a seat in the cabinet in which Diefenbaker and his ministers struggle with issues such as the Avro Arrow and nuclear armaments.

As MacLean reflects on his life in politics, the most important political leaders of the past half-century — John Diefenbaker, Louis St. Laurent, Lester Pearson, Pierre Trudeau, Joe Clark and Brian Mulroney — all come under his critical gaze. In particular, MacLean makes it clear that he viewed the rise of Liberal Pierre Trudeau with dismay, but he is also clear that he believes that Tory politicians did not always serve Canada well. He is blunt about Joe Clark's short-lived government, and his judgement of Brian and Mila Mulroney is severe.

MacLean reveals that he supported a Quebecer, Claude Wagner, for the Tory leadership in 1976, and he speaks fondly of Quebec's first separatist premier, René Lévesque. MacLean believes that our Constitution should reflect Quebec's unique place in Canada, and he offers his most trenchant political insights when he dissects Pierre Trudeau's patriation of the Constitution. By the time of the constitutional negotiations in 1981, MacLean had returned to Prince Edward Island and been elected premier of the province. From this vantage point, he takes us behind the scenes at 24 Sussex Drive when Trudeau and his rival, Lévesque, meet with the other premiers in private on the Constitution.

Trudeau was contemptuous of Lévesque and refused to treat the separatist leader with elementary courtesy. MacLean believes this hostility killed any chance of a constitutional agreement and created a rift that bedevils the nation to this day.

MacLean is a social commentator not just for his time but also for today. He was a visionary who saw the adverse impact decisions about the Charter of Rights, the Constitution, economic development, and Island projects such as the fixed link could have on generations to come. He states his dissenting position on political decisions that at the time garnered widespread support. He also argues strongly that when we throw away our traditions without seriously considering the consequences, we risk losing what made Canada great.

Angus MacLean brings a critical, well-informed point of view to the Canada of today. From the farm to the military, to the top of Canadian political life, it is all here, told in a straightforward, engaging manner. The book is not only highly informative, it is a pleasure to read. Enjoy.

Mike Duffy
Editor-in-Chief
CTV Sunday Edition

Table of Contents

Part Three: Federal Politics

Part Four: Provincial Politics

Part Five: Retirement

Growing Up in P.E.I.

CHAPTER ONE

Childhood

My earliest memory is of a late-winter's day in 1917, when I was nearly three years old. Our family had gathered in the dining room of our farm home in Lewis, Prince Edward Island. One of the adults lifted me up so that I could see inside a small white coffin, lying on a table. In the coffin I could see my baby brother, Malcolm, very still. He had died of an infection at the age of 10 months. At that time, my parents, George and Sarah MacLean, had been married 15 years — years filled with hard work and with the whole gamut of emotional experience, from joy to crushing sorrow. Sometimes it must have seemed to them that they had more than their share of the latter.

My father had inherited the family farm in Lewis, a Scottish-Presbyterian community amid the rolling hills of eastern Prince Edward Island, about eight miles inland from the Northumberland Strait. It was a 200-acre mixed farm, bigger than normal for those days, with about 100 acres cleared. In 1902, he married his second cousin Sarah MacLean, a schoolteacher from the neighbouring community of Culloden. He did most of the farm work alone, with the help of three part-Clydesdale horses, Maude, Prince and Dick; she did all the inside work, looked after the large family that eventually arrived and ran the local post office for a while. The young couple also took on the task of supporting and caring for my father's aged parents.

My grandfather became an elder in the Caledonia Presbyterian church soon after it was established in 1880. For a while, his oldest son, Murdoch, was the Precentor for the Gaelic singing, reading out the songs and then leading the congregation in singing them line by line. (I suppose having a Precentor in Gaelic singing arose because the congregations could not read Gaelic.) My uncle Murdoch did not stay a presenter for long, however. In 1885, he left to study medicine in California. There were no old-age pensions in the early part of this century, and the custom was that the son or daughter who inherited the farm assumed the responsibility of caring for its former owners until they passed away. In Murdoch's absence, this responsibilty fell to my father. My grandparents lived with my parents until my grandfather died in July 1906 and my grandmother in March 1913, more than a year before I was born. Three generations in one home was the general rule in those days.

Eight children, four girls and four boys, all of us spaced one or two years apart, were born in that house. Margaret, the eldest, was born in 1903; Catherine arrived a year later; and then the rest of us came a couple of years apart — Duncan, Mary, Effie, Murdoch, Angus and Malcolm. By the time little Malcolm died, my parents had already suffered a devastating blow. In the winter of 1911, they had lost Duncan, their first-born son. At the time, he was also their only son and the apple of my father's eye. That winter, my father had made a little wooden sleigh for Duncan. He loved it and jealously guarded it from his two older sisters, Margaret and Catherine. One wet day in March, he pulled his sleigh to the eastern boundary of the farm and covered it with snow to hide it from the girls. The next day he was sick with a bad cold, which quickly developed into pneumonia. In spite of desperate efforts by my parents and whatever medical help was available, he passed away on March 24, about two months before his fifth birthday. My parents grieved deeply for Duncan. For years, they kept mementoes of him, including the sleigh, which my father found later that spring when the snow melted. I remember that a large portrait of Duncan hung in the living room when I was growing up. I do not recall hearing my father talk about him; I think it was too painful a subject. My mother felt that my father never fully recovered from the awful shock of watching helplessly while their only son died.

This sort of experience, of course, was by no means rare in those days. Pneumonia and tuberculosis devastated many a family in Prince Edward Island. Many families on the Island, including mine, were descended from immigrants from the Hebrides. Perhaps because of the isolation of the Hebrides, those settlers and their descendants were vulnerable to certain diseases. Young adults were the most common victims of tuberculosis — or consumption, as it was called in those days — and pneumonia killed people of all ages. There were no effective remedies for either illness.

Both my parents were descended from Scots from the small island of Raasay, which lies between the Isle of Skye and the mainland of Scotland. My father's grandparents, Murdoch MacLean and Margaret MacLeod, landed in Prince Edward Island in 1832. Their son Duncan — my grandfather — was born a few weeks after they reached the shores of the Island. My mother's father, Murdoch MacLean, was about four when he sailed from Scotland with his parents and grandmother about five years later. That family settled in a log cabin in upper Belle River, then known as Burnt Woods. (A forest fire had swept through the area a few years before; according to local tradition, it had been started by sparks from an open fire built by a pioneer woman who was trying to do the family wash.)

My maternal grandfather's memories of Scotland were naturally few, but all his life he remembered people weeping on the shore as his family boarded the vessel bound for Prince Edward Island, never to be seen again by the friends and relatives they were leaving behind. My grandfather also remembered seeing his grandmother in tears in the new home. "Why are you crying?" he asked his grandmother in Gaelic. His mother warned him never again to ask that question: in this strange and lonely wilderness, the elderly woman was weeping for her beloved Raasay and the friends she would never see again.

The immigrant families helped each other as much as they could in those early days. Once, a distant relative, Alexander MacLean, walked five miles through the woods from his home in Eldon to give a sheep and a lamb to his poorer relatives, my great-grandparents. (This line of sheep continues to this day on my farm in Lewis.) The new settlers also found comfort in their language, their music and their religion. The immigrants and their descendants kept their cultural traditions alive for generations. When I was a child, Gaelic was still the social language of the community, although my parents did not speak it to us at home. At that time, people had the notion that speaking Gaelic gave their children an undesirable accent in English. My mother even remembered being made to stand in the corner at school for the crime of addressing her teacher in Gaelic — even though Gaelic was also the teacher's native tongue. But my parents did speak Gaelic with their neighbours, and, until about 1925, the service in the Presbyterian church in Caledonia, two miles from our farm, was in the ancient tongue every second Sunday.

My father had inherited the dark hair and blue eyes unique to a certain Celtic type; my mother had the typical Nordic look of many Hebrideans — fair hair and blue eyes. Both of them maintained the Scottish reverence for learning. My father's formal education had not gone beyond grade 10 at the local school, but he was a well-read, intelligent man, and there were always books and magazines and newspapers in the house. My mother loved music. She sang in the church choir, and when she had a rare free moment, she used to play hymns and favourite songs in the parlour on her beloved reed organ, an instrument she had brought with her when she came to the house as a bride.

Our family, like all farm families of that time, was closely knit. As soon as children were able, they were expected to help with the farm chores and family duties. When I was about two my oldest sister, Margaret, who was 13 at the time, became my babysitter for as long as I needed one. We played together and sang together around the reed organ. Ada Trainor, a schoolteacher who taught in the local school and boarded at our home, taught Margaret to play the reed organ. All the family read books and the daily and weekly papers.

Lewis in those days was a close-knit and practically self-sufficient community. Every farm was occupied, usually by large families. The community had a small store, a large saw mill, a post office and a one-room school. In Caledonia, the next district, there was a larger store beside the church where you could buy most of the necessities of life, from cod-liver oil to caskets. On the farm, the neighbours exchanged labour and shared machinery. They produced their own vegetables, fruit, flour, oatmeal, meat and sometimes maple syrup. They built their homes from the forests they owned. They made their blankets and some of their clothes and linens from wool and flax grown at home. When people in the district had sick or injured animals, they often called on my father. He would apply the veterinary skills he had learned from his father, thus carrying on a family tradition dating at least as far back as the last decade of the 18th century, when Duncan MacLeod and Duncan Matheson, two of my father's great-grandfathers, had worked in partnership to provide practical veterinary services to their neighbours in the Hebrides.

The social life of the times consisted mainly of visiting the neighbours, exchanging small talk after church and attending the odd house party or, at election time, a political meeting in a nearby hall. On weekday evenings, young people gathered at Stewarts' store in Caledonia; on Sunday evenings, they scouted out prospective mates next door, in the church. Once or twice a summer, they would hold an outdoor square dance, with old Scottish tunes such as "Lord MacDonald's Reel" supplied by a local fiddler. Communities also organized events such as ice-cream festivals. For this event in Caledonia, an outdoor square dance would be organized, and ice cream would be obtained from Montague and sold with cold drinks as a modest fundraiser. Ice cream was a rare treat as there were no domestic refrigerators, although for some years our farm had had an ice house. It was insulated with sawdust and filled with ice harvested from the local mill pond every winter.

My brother and sisters and I had the run of the farm. Our playground encompassed the fields and forests, and our playmates included the farm animals. One of our young horses, Dick, was a special pet. My sisters used to visit him in the pasture when he was a foal; they taught him to come when they whistled by rewarding him with lumps of sugar. One summer day when I was about nine, I was roaming around a fenced-in part of the woods that was connected to the horse pasture. I became disoriented, and I was not sure how to get back to the field. I whistled for Dick and stayed where I was. He came cantering over to me; I got on his back and rode out to the back gate.

As a rule, nobody strayed far from home. Occasionally, a farmer would haul a horse-drawn load of potatoes to the wharf in

Montague or Murray River, where a schooner would be loading for Newfoundland. My parents took the train to Charlottetown three or four times a year, and some of the young people ventured even farther afield to find work, usually to the New England states. But when I was a child, my world extended only about five miles in any direction — the distance you could comfortably travel in an afternoon in a horse and wagon. There were no telephones in our community. Nobody had a car or a radio. Our news of the outside world came from the newspaper, which arrived every evening on the train from Charlottetown.

The big news in my early childhood was the war in Europe. Many of our young neighbours had gone overseas in uniform, so naturally, the grown-ups talked among themselves about the war, the Germans and the new tank weaponry. I listened to all this talk and vaguely understood some of it. One day in the summer of 1918, when I was four, I was playing in the farmyard when I heard an unearthly clattering roar. I looked up to see a huge black machine lumbering up our lane. I was terrified. I knew that it had to be a German tank. I scurried off and hid behind the woodshed. Then, as I peeked around the corner, I saw my father open the gate, so I guessed that the monster must be friendly, after all. When the machine reached the yard, a man dismounted. I learned later that he was driving an automobile — the first one I had ever seen. It was a Gray Dort touring car; he was a salesman from Charlottetown named Rodd. He sold Empire cream separators, for which my father was the local agent. The salesman gave my mother, Murdoch and me a ride to Charlottetown in the Gray Dort that summer to visit my mother's older sister Katie, who, with her husband, Donald MacKay, had recently moved to Charlottetown from Hartsville. That was the last car I saw for another year or so.

A few months after the appearance of the Gray Dort, the war ended. We learned about it in a strange way. On November 11, 1918, the train on its evening run to Murray Harbour blew its steam whistle almost continuously, all the way from Charlotte-town. As it passed our neighbourhood, my parents concluded that the war must have ended. When the mail arrived in the post office, the news was confirmed. It was a great relief to everybody, especially to people with relatives in the army. And there were many such people in our little neighbourhood. In four years, eight families from the Caledonia church had lost sons.

The end of the war coincided with other changes in our small world. A few people acquired radios; cars became a more common sight on the red clay roads. By the time I was about 10, my brother and sisters and I used to amuse ourselves by counting the cars in the churchyard during the Sunday evening service. Sometimes there would be as many as nine or 10 parked beside the horse-drawn wagons.

Things were slowly changing on the farm, too. Just after the war, my father ploughed a couple of acres of "new land" on our farm. It was the last piece of land cleared for cultivation on the farm. This was in line with the general farming trend. The number of acres of cultivated land on the Island peaked in 1911 and from then on declined. The reason for this was the difficult transition from small-scale subsistence farming to large-scale commercial farming. Self-sufficient farming meant hard labour, but it also gave families a sense of fulfilment and of control over their own destinies. The old-style farm not only produced almost everything a family needed, it also produced energy in the form of firewood and feed for the horses. In contrast, the new commercial farm placed farmers at the mercy of market forces over which they had no control, and they often found themselves competing with other farmers from faraway places — people who had better growing climates, for instance. The new farms required ever-increasing amounts of land to support one family. The result was that people started leaving the land to look for work in the cities, and the number of farms declined.

The post-war years brought two memorable events to our immediate family. The first happened in 1923, when I was nine and I got my first taste of politics. My father was a mild-mannered, rather reserved man, but he also had many friends and a talent for public speaking. He had been the local Conservative poll chair for several years; that year, he was persuaded to run as a candidate for the Conservative Party in the provincial election. I witnessed my first political meeting that year. It was a thoroughly entertaining, all-candidates' gathering with rousing partisan speeches, lots of jokes and friendly heckling from the crowd. My father lost the election by fewer than two dozen votes, which was a good showing for a Conservative in the riding in which he was running. The party, however, was elected and the leader, J. D. Stewart, a Charlottetown lawyer, became premier. Then in 1927, the Conservative government was defeated, electing only six members to the Liberals' 24. Again, my father made a good showing but was not elected. He also ran in 1928, 1931 and 1935. He always did well in a strong Liberal riding but never quite won; nonetheless, he was highly regarded by the electorate.

The second event was a traumatic one. The year I was 11, my parents suffered the agony of knowing they might lose a third son. In late November, I became ill with pneumonia. For days, I hung between life and death. Our family doctor, Lester Brehaut, drove to the house several times. "I'll come again in two days if I'm still needed," he would say as he walked out the door. I was hallucinating part of the time and too sick to be frightened, but I was aware that my parents were very distressed, especially when my skin started to turn a ghastly shade of blue. Between visits from the doctor, my mother and the neighbour women placed hot poultices on my chest every couple of hours. That care and concern apparently pulled me through. By Christmas, I was on the road to recovery. By March, I was well enough to go back to school. It was my first brush with death, but it was by no means my last.

Education

In our home, it was taken for granted that we would get a good education. That was partly because of the Scottish love for learning and partly because of family tradition. My mother was a role model for my four sisters, who all became teachers; on the other side of the family, my father's brother, Murdoch, had put himself through medical school by driving streetcars in San Francisco by day and studying by night.

The local one-room school in Lewis was only a couple of hundred yards from our land. I knew I would be starting school the September after my fifth birthday; however, my parents and the teacher, Christina MacPherson, thought it would be a good idea for me to be initiated into the routine by attending school for the month of June. I felt betrayed, but eventually forgave my parents and teacher when I discovered that school was a pleasant experience. I attended the local school for nine grades with such teachers as Jim McTague, Pat Bolger and Anna MacKenzie. As well, my sister Catherine taught in our school for three years.

For my grade 10 year, I moved to West Kent School in Charlottetown. By that time, the Depression had begun and money was scarce. Fortunately, my oldest sister, Margaret, who was married, lived in Charlottetown, and I was able to board with her. I could have taken my grade 10 year in Lewis, but at the end of grade 10, one had to take a provincewide examination that would determine whether one could go on to higher learning. As the quality of education in Lewis depended on the ability of the current teacher, which varied greatly, my parents felt that I would get a better grounding for my future education in the city.

When I was in grade 10, I started a relationship with the military that, although I did not know it at the time, was to lead me to the greatest adventure of my life. The year was 1931 and I was 16. One of my teachers was Dan Bell, a tall, physically fit man who happened to be a veteran of the First World War. He was also a popular teacher. The students found him approachable, but at the same time he commanded our respect. He ran the school's army cadet corps, so naturally most of us senior boys joined up.

It was through the army cadet corps that I took my first trip off the Island. Being in the cadets gave young men the chance to join one of the local militia units. I joined the Charlottetown Company of the Reserve Signal Corps. In the summer, we took a boat from Charlottetown to Pictou, Nova Scotia, and then travelled by train and truck to a two-week summer camp at Aldershot, near Kentville. It was a wonderful experience for a young boy from the farm. Not only did I learn how to shoot on the rifle range and how to send messages by Morse code and semaphore, I also made lifelong friendships with some of the other boys. Most of these fellows served in the forces in the Second World War and later became business people and lawyers in Charlottetown. I earned $1.10 a day, which would buy a meal in a restaurant in those days, and I found out what the world was like on the other side of the Northumberland Strait.

The next year, with the Depression well under way, I stayed home and worked on the farm. Then, instead of going back to Charlottetown to take grades 11 and 12, I decided to speed up my university-preparation years by taking grade 11 at Mount Allison Academy in Sackville, New Brunswick. When I passed grade 11 in the spring of 1933, I was qualified to enter university; however, as money was so tight, I worked on the farm another year. In the 1934-35 school year, I took grade 12 at the newly established Summerside High School. This qualified me to enter the second year of a four-year bachelor's program at university.

In those days, aspiring to a university education was a lofty ambition indeed. I remember a story my Aunt Jessie told us about a young schoolteacher from the Murray Harbour area, where she lived. His name was Jordan, and he was determined to get a degree from Dalhousie University in Halifax, Nova Scotia. When he was still a year away from graduating, his money ran out. His parents mortgaged the farm to help pay for his final year. Everything was riding on his passing the exams. The day the marks were posted, his parents received a telegram from him. All it said was, line so-and-so in hymn such-and-such. Since hymns are not usually considered lighthearted literature, it was with great foreboding that the family looked up the reference. Imagine their relief when they read: "Sorrow vanquished, labour ended, Jordan passed."

Like young Jordan, I began my university career with support from my family. It was 1935, in the depths of the Depression, and I could not have hoped to go to university at all without help from my older sister Catherine, who now had a good job with the Canadian Red Cross Society. I entered Mount Allison University, planning to get a bachelor of science degree, majoring in chemistry. My best marks in school had been in science and mathematics, and industrial chemistry was considered a good career choice.

I had no desire to escape from the farm. I had a great love for the land, and my university years only deepened that attachment. In university, my courses in elementary biology increased my appreciation for the magnificence of nature — I learned about the development of plants and animals over the centuries, the intricate systems by which their lives are regulated and their amazing ability to find antidotes to threats to their existence. Working with nature on the farm seemed to me an interesting and honourable occupation; however, at that time it was not a practical alternative. Farm prices were so low it was impossible to make a profit on anything. All we could do was to try to keep our family farm going in hopes of better days to come. In the meantime, we young folks looked for employment elsewhere, as Islanders have had to do for generations.

The next year, I had a chance to study at the University of British Columbia, having won a scholarship that paid all my tuition costs for a year. This did not go unnoticed by *The Guardian* in Charlottetown, which printed a small article congratulating my parents and lauding my debating skills, "which talent is looked upon by his Belfast friends as being hereditary." I had joined the debating team at Mount Allison and before that had had some experience in making political speeches, which the newspaper duly noted. "Those who had the privilege of hearing Mr. MacLean on the platform in Iona hall a few years ago feel the above honour is truly merited," the article added, referring to a speech I had made at a Conservative rally during an election in which my father was a candidate.

Although I did not have to worry about tuition fees, I still had to solve the problem of travel costs to Vancouver. Luckily, Willie MacLean, a young man from Bellevue, Prince Edward Island, who had settled in California, happened to be visiting his mother, who was one of our neighbours. He was planning to drive to California and would be travelling alone from Boston to Oakland, across the bay from San Francisco. He said he would very much like to have a travelling companion who could help with the driving. I jumped at the chance. I took the train to Saint John and a boat to Boston, and we set off for California.

On our way through Minnesota, we stopped at the Mayo Clinic in Rochester, where a couple of our former neighbours, Phemie and Margaret McGowan from Kilmuir, were working as nurses. Aside from that, our trip was fairly uneventful until we arrived in Oakland, with Willie at the wheel. We were driving in rush-hour traffic when a car went through a red light and slammed us into a truck. Willie was taken to hospital in an ambulance, where he soon recovered. Miraculously, I was unhurt. A police officer asked me to try to drive the wreck out of the traffic jam, which I did, gingerly. When I found a suitable place to stop, I got out my address book, looked at the street names and numbers nearby and concluded that my Aunt Katie, my father's sister whom I had never met, lived only three blocks away. I drove to her house, where I received a hug and a warm welcome, and spent a couple of days getting over the trauma of the accident before moving on to Vancouver.

Vancouver, with its spectacular mountains, soft climate and lush greenery, was quite a contrast to the environment I was used to, but I soon felt quite at home because I had relatives in the city. I found a place to board in Point Grey, near the university gates, and I joined the Canadian Officer Training Corps on campus, which gave me a bit of military training every week.

At the end of my year at UBC, I was faced with the problem of getting back across the continent. Luckily, I found a couple from Toronto who were returning home by train and needed someone to drive their car back to Ontario. The couple put me in touch with two young women who wanted a ride to Sarnia. The three of us set out for Ontario by way of the northern United States — this was years before the Trans-Canada Highway. We headed for the border crossing at Blaine, Washington. I thought we would get through customs with just a routine check. Not so. "Park your car over there and give me your keys," one of the customs officials ordered. Then he ushered the young women into an office, one at a time. When one of the women reappeared, she was seething with rage. The second one came out, wiping away tears. Then it was my turn to be interrogated. I found out that the border officials were trying to crack down on a ring that imported prostitutes into the States, and they suspected that I might be one of the drivers. I finally convinced them that we were headed for Canada and that my mission was simply to deliver a car. I thought the border officials were particularly inept in view of the real identity of my passengers: members of a religious sect heading to Ontario to train as missionaries.

I spent the summer of 1937 on the farm and I decided to join the Mizpah Masonic Lodge at Eldon. My father had been a member for a number of years, and my brother, Murdoch, had joined the previous summer. That fall, I was back at Mount Allison University for my final year. In the spring of 1938, I was still two courses short of a degree because I had taken my junior year at UBC, so I took one course at summer school. It was German, a language I had been studying since grade 12, mostly because I found it easier to get my tongue around than French.

One day in 1938, as I sat in the common room of one of the university residences, listening to the radio, a news broadcast came on. The announcer was reporting on British prime minister Neville Chamberlain's negotiations with Hitler. Hitler had invaded Austria that spring and seemed to have territorial ambitions elsewhere in Europe. Britain was ill-prepared for war. In making concessions to Hitler, Chamberlain was promising "peace in our time." One of the professors walked into the room and listened to the radio with me. He was a Jewish refugee from Nazi Germany, and he was skeptical about Chamberlain's assurances.

I hoped Chamberlain was right. But in the meantime, I had to deal with practical matters at home. That fall I went back to Lewis to work on the farm. My parents were alone because my brother, Murdoch, had just left to join the Royal Canadian Mounted Police; he was now in the Musical Ride. Over the winter, I completed my one remaining university course by correspondence, graduating in May of 1939 with a bachelor of science degree in industrial chemistry. I was hoping to get a job as a chemist in a factory. As it turned out, the next few years prevented that from happening. Those years also led me to believe that I should look for a more humanitarian career.

PART TWO

The War Years

Taking to the Skies

It was a sunny morning in September 1939. I was seeing the city of Halifax for the first time, and, for a few moments, from a rather unusual vantage point — upside down, hundreds of feet above the trees and houses, suspended by a harness attached to the open cockpit of a biplane. This was my first experience in an aircraft.

I had taken the train to Halifax the day before to start flying instruction with the Royal Canadian Air Force (RCAF). I had seen an advertisement in a flying magazine indicating that the Royal Air Force (RAF) was about to grant two short-service commissions to Canadians to train in England as pilots. War was in the air, although nothing was for sure. This would be employment if war did not come; if war did break out, it was taken for granted that everyone would do his or her duty. My parents, therefore, did not object to my joining the air force. For my part, I figured that it would be better to be in at the start. I applied and was given a medical examination. A letter of acceptance soon arrived, saying that I was to acquire, among other things, a tuxedo, and should be ready to sail in early September on the liner *Athenia*. I bought the tuxedo but did not get to wear it for a while. On September 3, 1939, Britain declared war on Germany, and hours later, a German U-boat claimed its first victim. The *Athenia*, bound for Montreal from Belfast with 1,000 passengers on board, was torpedoed and sank.

Shortly after that, I received a message from the Eastern Air Command of the RCAF asking whether I would accept a short-service commission in the Canadian force instead of the RAF. It would be for 10 years, six on active service and four on a reserve list. The pay would be $4.75 a day and at the end of my active service, I would get an additonal $500 for each year I had served.

On September 9, the day after I joined up, Canada declared war. My father drove me to the train station, and from there I went to Halifax to get my first 50 hours of flying training with a Halifax flying club, one of many pressed into wartime service. The next morning, I took a streetcar to the landing field, then located on the outskirts of the city. To my amazement, one of the instructors, Henry Gates, immediately told me to climb in the back seat of a Gypsy Moth. "I'm taking you up for a familiariza-tion flight," he informed me. The airplane looked very fragile to me. It had two seats in open-air cockpits with dual controls. It had folding wings, which were held in the flying position with spring-loaded pins, and a skid (a steel strip that slid along the ground) instead of a tail wheel. Gates flew over the city for about half an hour, throwing in some loops and slow rolls for my amusement. I do not remember being afraid, but I did find it an exhilarating experience, to say the least.

The speed at which we recruits were initiated into flying was a forerunner of things to come. The armed forces were under great pressure to churn out fighting men. That fall, Halifax quickly changed into wartime mode, with convoys of ships forming in Bedford Basin. During our training, we had to meet the same standards as in peacetime, but faster. There were eight of us in the class at the Halifax flying club. One of the men was George Hill, who had gone to Mount Allison with me. He had a distinguished flying career during the war, and then he studied and practised medicine after the war. The other men were new recruits from Nova Scotia.

From the Halifax flying club, we were transferred to ground school in Trenton, Ontario. When we arrived in Trenton, we were joined by four or five other groups of eight, who had had their initial 50 hours of flying training at other flying clubs. The atmosphere was definitely full of tension — war had been declared and it was inevitable that a difficult period lay ahead for everyone. We did not have much time for socializing — we were all fully occupied with an intense course in the theory of flight, mathematics, Morse code as well as a gruelling exercise regimen. We were up early marching and running across the airport before breakfast every day. We all looked forward to our 48-hour breaks. Everything moved fast, and at the end of the course we all went off in different directions.

After a few months of ground training in Trenton, our class was posted to Camp Borden, also in Ontario, for intermediate flying training on the airspeed Oxford, a two-engine airplane made in Britain. At Borden we were joined by a few members of an air force reserve squadron who had had some flying training there. They included Hartland Molson, who with a few others was posted overseas early and took part in the Battle of Britain. (He became a senator in 1955.) Most of the class passed their wings test and all received their wings; the few who did not pass their flying tests became administrative officers. I had six hours of dual instruction before my first solo flight. Four days later, after 30 minutes of instruction in an Avro Anson, I took it up alone. In April, I received my pilot's wings. In my final exam, I was rated "above average." Three days later, I was back at

Trenton, flying Oxfords in advanced training, which included cross-country flying, air-to-ground gunnery practice, formation flying and high- and low-level bombing. I graduated on May 15, 1940, my 26th birthday, and again was rated "above average" as a pilot. In June I began training as a flying instructor. I graduated in late July, with a rating as an average instructor. While on a 48-hour leave pass, I went to Toronto, and while I was there I bought myself a Masonic ring.

While I was in Trenton that summer, the war in Europe began in earnest. The Germans overran Belgium, Holland and much of France, and the British evacuated France of most of their forces at Dunkirk, with the assistance of ships of every sort. From then on, from the Allies' point of view, the war effort became much more urgent, as only the British Commonwealth stood against Hitler and his war machine. An RAF exchange officer on the staff, who was from Devon, England, was worried that the invasion of Britain might occur at any time.

The British Commonwealth Air Training Plan, which involved setting up military training posts outside of Britain, was now in effect, and Camp Borden became the No. 1 Service Flying Training School. I joined the staff as an instructor, flying mostly Oxfords, Ansons and Yale aircraft. Then I was posted to No. 4 Service Flying Training School in Saskatoon. That September, another pilot and I, along with mechanics to service the aircraft, were dispatched to Toronto to ferry two Ansons to Saskatoon. During that trip, I made one of those apparently inconsequential decisions that turn out to have a profound effect on one's life.

We made an overnight stop in Winnipeg. I checked into my room at the hotel, weary and looking forward to going to bed early. One of the officers knocked on the door. He was going dancing with a nurse friend and two other young women from the hospital staff. Another pilot was going along, but they needed a third man. "Will you join us?" he asked. Luckily, I decided to go. One of the women was Gwen Burwash, a pretty young dietician from the hospital, whom I found quite fascinating. When I danced with her, I was delighted to find out that she was from Saskatoon and was going back there soon. I asked whether I might look her up. On arrival in Saskatoon, I learned that my mother had had a stroke, and I was immediately given two weeks' compassionate leave to return home and visit her. When I returned to Saskatoon and was settled in, I discovered that Gwen lived within easy walking distance of my rooming house, so I saw her often during my few months there, and we formed a very special friendship. It was not until several years after the war that our paths crossed again, although we did correspond on and off by letter throughout the war years.

In January 1941 I had to leave. I was posted to the No. 7 Service Flying Training School at MacLeod, Alberta, and became the officer commanding "C" flight there. At MacLeod, there were always three classes at various stages of training, and most of the time two of the three classes were made up of Australians. All of the students were the elite, in the best sense of that term. Most were university graduates with excellent physiques and perfect eyesight — the cream of their generation. The students who came to us had 50 hours of flying training on small, single-engine training airplanes. At first, the twin-engine Ansons we flew at MacLeod, with many more controls and instruments, were daunting to most of the students. Those who had experience with machines such as tractors in civilian life took to the Ansons more quickly than the others. One of my students who did well had been a streetcar driver in Vancouver. Another, an Australian, adjusted to the Anson with the greatest of ease. I asked whether he had ever flown in a twin-engine before. "No," he said, "I guess I just inherited the gift from my parents. My father is a switcher in the railway freight marshalling yard in Sydney and my mother plays the pipe organ."

My stint at MacLeod ended in January 1942, when I was posted overseas. Squadron Leader A. J. Shelfoon, who was also from Prince Edward Island, was at the Central Flying School in Trenton and gave me an instructor's recategorization test. His official comment on the certificate was: "Flight Lieutenant MacLean is an above-average instructor who imparts knowledge in an excellent manner." That raised my category to A2. Before being posted overseas, I was given embarkation leave, which I was looking forward to spending with my parents on the family farm. I had not been home since the fall of 1940, when I had been given leave to visit my mother. Her health had improved since then, but she had not fully recovered. When I arrived home I was saddened to find that she could no longer sing a note or play her beloved reed organ.

My parents tried hard to be cheerful during my leave, but I am sure they were haunted by memories of the First World War. The eight names on the war memorial tablet in Caledonia church were just names to me, but to my parents they were neighbours and friends who lived on in their memories. I could sense that my parents felt that they might be seeing me for the last time, and that I might become like their oldest and youngest sons — just a fond memory that always awakened heartbreak and sorrow. I also suspected that my parents were not fully aware of the risks that aircrew ran at the best of times. Although I had an inkling of the dangers in store for me, I kept my knowledge to myself.

My two-week leave was happy but far too short. I visited friends and neighbours, went to church and did some errands, including the purchase of a new steamer trunk at Moore and MacLeod in Charlottetown. When it was time to go, my father drove me to Charlottetown in our Dodge sedan. The train station had a distinctly military air, with all kinds of young Islanders in uniform waiting for the train. My father and I said our farewells and I boarded the train for Halifax, my first and only stop on my way to Europe. In Halifax, we were issued with two tags, each bearing our name, rank and military number (mine was C1107). Both went on a cord around our necks. One was to remain there; the other, which had two holes, would be nailed to our grave-markers if that's where we ended up.

Bomber Command

I was in a small group of air force officers and noncommissioned officers (NCOs) who were to travel on a ship that had just arrived in Halifax from Rio de Janeiro. The only other passengers were a small group of British citizens on their way back to England. This group included two ladies, one a young bride travelling with her husband, the other a single woman of about 35. (About a year later I met the latter by chance on the street in an English town. We were both amazed at this chance meeting, and she expressed her delight that I was still alive.) Our ship joined a slow six-knot convoy that took 18 days to travel from Halifax to Belfast, Ireland. We played cards a lot with our new civilian friends and endured two pretty violent storms. When we reached the range of aircraft from Europe, the air force personnel manned machine guns mounted on the decks in two-hour shifts, night and day. The convoy was escorted by three destroyers, which sometimes rushed around at high speed, making us wonder if we were about to be attacked by German U-boats. We never took it for granted that we would make it across the Atlantic — this was wartime and the enemy U-boats were everywhere. On reaching Belfast, we remained on board for another night, and then we took a ferry to a small port in northern England. Then it was on to Bournemouth by train via London.

During my first few days in Britain, an eye specialist gave me a night-vision test. I graded average. This considerably lowered my chances for survival in this war, because it meant that I would be posted to a night bomber squadron. Airmen with above-average night vision tended to be posted to night fighters; those with below-average night vision were usually posted to daylight flying. In both cases, survival rates were better than in the night bomber squadrons. In the meantime, however, I had more mundane matters to think about. Like other Canadians overseas, I was having a few problems adjusting to day-to-day life in wartime conditions and to the English way of doing things.

In March 1942 I was posted to No. 27 Operational Training Unit at Litchfield, between Birmingham and Derby, but before my course started, on March 17, I had a few days off. I went on an overnight sightseeing trip. In Burton-upon-Trent, I found a room in a rooming house run by a middle-aged woman. In contrast to the housing on most temporary wartime bases in England, the place was pleasantly warm, just right for a nice warm bath. I had just settled into the tub when I heard footsteps in the hall. Then someone unlocked the bathroom door. I barely had time to stand up when the landlady barged into the room. "You can't use all that hot water without paying me three shillings in advance," she said. In no position to argue, I replied, "In that case, would you be good enough to hand me my pants?" She did, I handed her three wet shillings and she left. I had learned my first lesson: warm water was a valuable commodity in wartime Britain.

Lessons of a more serious nature awaited me when I returned to Litchfield. First, we had a couple of weeks of ground school, including lectures on astro-navigation for navigators and pilots.

Our instructor was a permanent force RAF flight sergeant navigator. An excellent lecturer, he tended to be a little distant. One day, one of the other staff explained why. Earlier in the war, he had gone home to Coventry for his parents' 40th wedding anniversary party, but had been recalled from leave to go on a bombing mission. When he returned safely from the raid, he learned that a German bomb had hit the house where the celebrations were taking place. His entire family, plus other close relatives, had been killed.

The course I was on consisted of 10 crews of seven men each. About 50 of them were Australians. The rest were English, except for me, the only Canadian on the course. Under the British Commonwealth Air Training Plan most air training for all the Commonwealth air forces, including the RAF, was done in places well away from the war zone, mostly in Canada and South Africa. Only final training for operations in Europe was done in England. In England, positions in squadrons were filled by any Commonwealth personnel available at the time, regardless of their country of origin. I started my training on a Wellington 1C in April. After about six hours of dual practice, I went solo on the Wimpy, as the Wellington was called, and then flew some night circuits and did some night practice bombing. I had a grand total of about 20 hours' flying time on the Wellingtons when the chief instructor asked to see my pilot's flying log book. He discovered that I had more than 1,200 hours of flying time and was an A2 category instructor. He decided I was already well qualified. I was pulled off the course and posted to 405 RCAF Squadron at Pocklington, about 20 miles east of York. (The class I was in at Litchfield agreed to have a class reunion in York on a certain day in October. Sadly, only two of us made it to the reunion: the rest were either dead or prisoners of war.)

It was a glorious spring day when I arrived in the historic city of York. The daffodils were in full bloom along the old city wall.

I strolled around the city, and as I marvelled at the grandeur of York Minster and at a landscape bursting with new life, I thought about the threat hanging over this green and pleasant land. It seemed to me an apocalyptic tragedy that civilized people should be so vulnerable to the ambitions of lunatics like Adolph Hitler. When such people gain power, they scorn the rights of their fellow human beings and leave those in other countries only two choices: abject servitude or a battle to defend their rights — a battle that might mean the death of millions. My own role in the terrible battle that was World War Two was just beginning. Those thousands of hours of training and hundreds of hours of flying time would now be put to the test.

When I reported to 405 Squadron, I learned that a well-known Islander, O. B. "Ossie" LeFurgey from Summerside, had been a member of the squadron. In the 1930s, he had been the goalie for the Summerside Crystals hockey team during their many contests with the Charlottetown Abbies. The previous January, LeFurgey and his crew had been air-testing a Wellington when it developed engine trouble. The weather was bad and the plane crashed; the entire crew of five were killed. One of Sergeant LeFurgey's duties had been to fly the station's communications plane, a two-seater Magister. After he was killed, this duty was taken over by Squadron Leader McCormack. Just before I arrived at Pocklington, the Magister had crashed, killing McCormack and his navigator. A new one replaced it, and I was told that one of my duties would be to fly the new Magister on errands for the station.

One of those errands cropped up the first week in May. The station commander, Group Captain Brook, told me that a small group of senior Russian officers, including some generals, had flown to Wick in northern Scotland, where they had been met by a British passenger airplane. The British airplane was to take them to London for a secret meeting with government officials.

On the way to London, the airplane had crashed in Yorkshire, killing all on board. A court of enquiry — Brook, two Russian officers and I — had been appointed to investigate the cause of the crash. Two days in a row, we flew in the Magister to RAF Station Linton-on-Ouse, where the enquiry was being held. After hearing many witnesses, both technical experts and observers of the crash, we and our Russian counterparts were satisfied that the event had been an unfortunate accident. An engine part had failed, and no sabotage or other criminal act had been involved.

I started flying on bombing operations in May 1942. The first few operations were fairly uneventful. I was attached to Squadron Leader Len Fraser's crew as second pilot. We would leave after dark, about nine o'clock, and get back four or five hours later, to be debriefed by a squadron intelligence officer. The first few times, we were lucky enough to avoid being attacked, although we could see other aircraft coned in searchlights and disabled, probably by flak (gunfire from the ground), and the crews parachuting. It was always a huge relief to get out of enemy territory and over the sea to Britain. On every bombing operation, we were pretty sure that at least one of our squadron aircraft would not make it back home.

Our targets were factories in Bremen, Emden and the outskirts of Cologne, and the Krupp ironworks in Essen. We bombed Cologne on the night of May 30. All around us, RAF aircraft roared across the night skies in the first 1,000-bomber raid against Germany. Again, the German ground and air defence ignored our aircraft, and we made it back to base. Two days later, the front page of the *Daily Telegraph* carried a photograph of our crew being served tea from a YMCA van. The caption read: "The crew of one of the thousand bombers which took part in Saturday's raid on the Ruhr. Behind them is 'H for Harry,' the giant Halifax bomber in which they flew."

I was appalled by the rate of casualties in Bomber Command. Many squadrons were losing the equivalent of their entire air-crew strength — about 135 men — every six months. In our squadron, we were losing an average of three seven-member crews a month. My friends were disappearing, one by one. Six of us had the habit of having breakfast together at the same table in the officers' mess. One morning, I was shocked to find myself alone at our usual table. I learned that one of my five friends, who had been on operations the night before, was missing in action; the other four had skipped breakfast.

Although death always lurked on our doorstep, we tried not to dwell too much on our personal danger. We clung to the notion that we were not going to die. Death would always come to "the other guy." Still, most of us did a lot of praying. What frightened us most were the German night fighters. After the first couple of raids, I was of the opinion that our military authorities were overly concerned about the dangers of heavy flak and not alert enough to the threat of the night fighters. Flak no doubt damaged or destroyed many aircraft when they were flying straight and level to get their targets in the bomb sights, but many crews who were shaken up or even damaged made it back to base and could report the enemy attack. Victims of the night-fighter attacks rarely made it back home.

I suspected that the German night fighters were far more advanced than our people realized and were therefore much more deadly than flak. The RAF heavy bomber, unlike the American Flying Fortress, had no belly gun turret, so there was a blind area below the aircraft that none of the crew could easily see. The German night fighter, guided perhaps by radar, could climb below the bomber in this blind spot and bring down the aircraft before the crew even knew it was there. It was not long before I had a personal encounter with those deadly night fighters.

By this time, I had taken over Squadron Leader Fraser's crew as first pilot, with no second pilot. Our crew consisted of five Canadians and two British airmen, almost all in their early- or mid-20s. I was the old man of the crew at age 28. Jim Wernham, the navigator, a good-looking, intelligent man from Winnipeg, was about 25; Harry Olsen, the tail gunner, a warm-hearted, friendly fellow, also from Winnipeg, was 22; Bill Kerr, the wireless operator, a fair-haired, outgoing man from Saskatoon, was about 23; and G. B. Porter, the quiet mid-upper gunner from Cartier, Ontario, was the youngest of the lot at 20. The two RAF members were Bill Forbes from Liverpool, the bomb aimer, and Jock Shields, the flight engineer. Jock was tall and thin, with a mop of dark hair and a thick Lowland Scots accent that grew even thicker when he was under pressure. On those occasions, I served as the unofficial translator for the rest of the crew.

On the evening of June 8, on my sixth bombing operation, our crew met, as usual, in the briefing room. The squadron commander, J. E. Fauquier, told us we would be taking part in another raid on the Krupp works in Essen. It was to be relatively small — fewer than 300 aircraft. This news worried me for two reasons. First, I was sure that, after the destructive 1,000-bomber raid a few days before, the Germans would be making an all-out effort to strengthen the defence of the Ruhr Valley; second, we were all keenly aware that fewer bombers on a raid usually meant a higher risk for everybody. The odds of getting home for our bacon and eggs were not good.

The weather, at least, was on our side. It was a dark, moonless night, with broken overcast skies — as good a night as any for slipping unseen over enemy territory. As we flew over Germany, it seemed as though our luck might be holding out. Then, as we were about to drop our bombs, flying straight and level, someone on the ground flipped a switch. Instantly, we were caught in a cone of powerful blue searchlights. Inside the cockpit, it was as bright as day, as though we were being illuminated by continuous sheets of lightning. It was a terrifying feeling, because without a doubt, it meant that the Germans had singled us out. We were the target. And all around us, heavy flak shells were exploding.

I knew I had to do something fast. For a start, I had to make quick changes in direction and altitude. Our bomb load was still on and the bomb doors were open. That, plus the effects of the bursting shells and my probable over-reaction, caused the aircraft to stall suddenly and then go into a spin. I lowered the nose to regain safe flying speed. Then I tried to recover from the spin by righting the aircraft with the guidance of the artificial horizon on my instrument panel. After some unsuccessful attempts, I realized that the artificial horizon, which was controlled by a gyroscope, had tumbled when we turned upside down and was giving a wildly wrong reading. I then resorted to using the more primitive turn and bank indicators to get out of the spin. When we were flying more or less normally again, we had 5,000 feet of altitude to spare. In this wild ride, we had fallen nearly two miles. Our aircraft, dear old "H" for Harry, was functioning normally, except that the ailerons — sections of the wing that control banking in turns — were jammed in the left-turn position. As a result, we had to fly in large circles while a west wind blew us farther and farther into Germany. German ground defences were following us closely, firing light flak at us.

When our bomb aimer got a large building that looked like a factory in his sights, we dropped our entire bomb load and got our bomb doors closed. We had 12 enemy-recognition cartridges — flares that were designed to give the Germans the false message that this was one of their airplanes. Each time they fired light flak at us, we fired off a cartridge. The enemy fire would stop for a while, then start up again. No doubt we were the lone target, because our other bombers were now on their way home. After more than an hour of this nerve-racking ordeal, we had used up our supply of enemy-recognition cartridges. For about the 100th time, I tried with all my strength to straighten the ailerons. This time, to my amazement, I did it. Now I could fly the aircraft straight and level, although only the starboard aileron was working. Jim Wernham and I had a quick conference on the intercom. We decided it would be suicidal to fly back west through the flak defences of the Ruhr Valley. Instead, we would fly just north of the city of Münster and then set course for the nearest point in England.

As we headed north, there was peace and quiet for a time. All enemy action had stopped. Through a momentary break in the cloud cover, I could see the North Star and the Big Dipper, and I thought about my childhood on the farm in Lewis, when I had often gazed with awe at the night sky. Reflecting on that peaceful time, I wondered why humankind seems to be the only species in God's creation that deliberately sets out to destroy its own. My period of reflection was brief. As we set course for England, we began to see flares that were being fired from the ground. We suspected that night fighters were being directed to our flight path. I called up the navigator. "Should we go down to a low level, Jim?" I asked. "It might save us from being hit from below."

Jock Shields, the flight engineer, was back changing the fuel lines to different tanks. Suddenly there was a crack in my earphones. The intercom went dead. At that instant, a stream of cannon shells shot by my window, less than a foot from my head, and then veered to port, puncturing our port wing from the fuselage to beyond the port engine. All three of our gunners opened fire. Because the intercom was dead, the bomb aimer, Bill Forbes, came up to the cockpit to act as messenger. "I think we nailed the bastard," he said. I told him our port engines seemed to have lost all power. "Will you check it out with Jock?" Forbes came back a minute later. He said the flight engineer's instrument panel had been shot away. "We've lost the power in both port engines, and only one aileron is working," I said. "Tell the crew we cannot maintain our altitude. We may have to parachute."

At this point, I was facing a horribly difficult decision. I was responsible not only for my own life, but for the lives of the other six crew members, all of them fine young men. Off to our right, I could see the Zuider Zee, the North Sea inlet in northeastern Holland. Normally we would soon be across the enemy coast and out to sea and safety. But now, I thought, even if we jettisoned everything we could, and even if some of the crew bailed out over enemy territory, we could not make it to England. If we tried it, we would probably have to ditch in the sea, and since our dinghy was likely shredded, we would probably all die.

When we had lost all but 1,200 feet of altitude, I ordered the crew to bail out. While this was happening, of course, we lost a little more height. Now it was my turn. I snapped on the chest-pack parachute, left the controls and scrambled to the escape hatch — only to find that the aircraft was doing a slow roll to the left and would soon dive into a crash. So I had to scramble back to the pilot's seat, straighten up the aircraft, throttle back the two good engines and trim the aircraft into a straight glide. All of this used up several hundred feet of our precious 1,000 feet of altitude. When I dived out the escape hatch, I knew I was very low, so I pulled the ripcord immediately. The opening of the parachute had barely registered in my mind when I crashed to the ground on my back.

I was in a field, in the middle of a herd of Holstein cows. Strangely enough, they were not at all spooked by my sudden arrival. Instead, they were overcome with curiosity about what had fallen out of the heavens, and they all crowded around, sniffing me. I was afraid they would step on me, because I could not move. I was paralyzed from the waist down. I could not feel my feet or legs. As I lay on the ground, I could see the glow of the aircraft burning about 200 yards away, and I could hear the bang! bang! of ammunition and oxygen bottles exploding. There was nothing I could do but wait until someone — probably a German soldier — found me. Then a miracle happened.

A Houseboat in Holland

As I lay in the cow pasture, awaiting my fate, the feeling suddenly started coming back to my legs. Then I found I could wiggle my toes and move my legs, so I got to my feet. The cows then wandered off, apparently realizing that I was just another uninteresting human. I took off my parachute harness, folded the chute and did a brief search for one of my flying boots, which had come off on my way down. No luck. A canal ran beside the field and there was a bridge nearby. Just beyond the canal I could see a railway track and a house beside it. I hid the parachute as best as I could under the overhang at the edge of the canal and crossed the bridge to the house. Above the bridge, there was a sign in a language I did not recognize. It was neither French nor German, which confirmed my assumption that I was in Holland.

I knocked on the door of the house. I could hear someone moving inside, but nobody came to the door. Then I realized that it would be futile to try to contact anyone this close to the crash scene. I also knew that I was at least a couple of miles from my crew, so it would be hopeless to try to find them. I was very much alone. I went back to the cow pasture and started walking south across the fields, a boot on one foot and a woollen sock on the other. It was starting to break daylight, and I could see I was leaving a trail in the grass because of the heavy dew, so I rounded up the cows and drove them with me to blot out my tracks. I repeated this process with the cows in the next field and kept walking south. In my escape kit I found a rubber bag meant for drinking water. At the far end of the third field, I singled out a cow, milked a pint of milk into the water bag and drank it. Then I crawled under a small hedge and slept for a few hours.

When I awoke I could see some activity in the fields some distance away, but no sign of a search party. My left arm was quite painful, so I removed my flying suit and jacket and shirt and found lacerations from my armpit to my wrist, probably from scraping myself on the edge of the escape hatch. I consulted the silk map in my escape kit. As far as I could tell, I was now between the Maas and Waal rivers. Several canals joined them in the area, so I was in effect on an island. I would wait in my hiding place until dark. At about six o'clock in the evening, two young girls walked towards the hedge and started picking strawberries. The rows they were working on led directly to the spot where I was lying. I knew they would soon spot me, so I stepped out from my hiding place. They seemed to take in the situation at a glance. I tried out my high school German on them. *"Ich bin Englander,"* I said. This they understood. The older girl noticed my Masonic ring. "My grandfather is a Freemason," she said in German. "I will bring him here. You stay here with my sister."

A few minutes later, the girl returned with a tall, lean man of about 75, wearing a pair of wooden shoes. He gestured that I was to go with him. We set off across the field. As we came to farm houses, the old gentleman stopped to talk to his neighbours. Some of them joined us; eventually we were a party of eight or nine. This procession made me nervous, especially since I was still in uniform. One of the men spoke a little English. "It's not safe for us to be travelling so openly," I told him. He spoke to the rest of the party, and they seemed to agree. They sent a boy on a bicycle down a road we were about to cross to see whether there were any Germans about. When the boy came back, they quickly ushered me into a small farm building and shut the door behind me. Through a crack in the door, I could see the road. Two German soldiers were passing on bicycles. As they approached, I suddenly realized I was not alone. A goat in the barn with me was in a panic because of my presence and was running around, bleating loudly. Luckily the Germans paid no attention. When they were out of sight, my new friends let me out of the building, and we proceeded farther south.

At dusk, we reached an orchard. My friends indicated that I was to stay there, and someone would come in the morning with food and civilian clothes. I spent a long, wakeful night in the tall grass, covering myself with some freshly cut grass to try to get warm. About eight o'clock the next morning, two men with scythes came to continue cutting the grass. At first, they ignored me, but at noon, one of them gave me a sandwich from his lunch. A couple of hours later, they left. I did not know what to do. Maybe my friends of the previous evening had simply been delayed. But was it safe to wait any longer? Could the grasscutters be trusted, or would they report me to the Germans? I had not had any training in matters such as these. When I had been taken off the course at the operational training school and posted to 405 Squadron, I had missed some rather important lectures: what to do when you are shot down. In trying to evade the enemy, I had nothing to guide me but my own judgement.

I decided — wrongly, perhaps — to leave. I walked along the hedge row and along the bottom of a drainage canal that contained about a foot of water. After a mile or two, I took a path through a grain field and sat down in the grain to rest for a while. Then I saw an elderly man heading my way. I had to make contact with someone, so I moved back to the path and sat down. He was obviously deep in thought. He almost fell over me. But when he did see me, he reacted quickly. With sign language, he told me to wait where I was. A few minutes later, he came back with his wife. She gave me a bowl of boiled milk to drink, and he gave me a dark brown suit of clothes and what were obviously his Sunday boots. He gestured that he would burn my flying suit and uniform and my one boot. Then he and his wife went back home, taking my uniform with them.

In my new clothes, which fitted reasonably well, I was emboldened to travel quite openly along the road. From time to time, I met people who greeted me in Dutch. But I wondered how I would manage to cross the Maas River without being caught, because it seemed likely that the Germans would guard the bridges. At one point, I went up to a man working alone on the railway track and tried to find out whether this was so. He thought the railway bridge had a guard but the road bridge did not.

Armed with this information, I felt fairly confident as I walked along the sidewalk of the road leading to the bridge. Then I saw a car coming around a bend ahead of me. It was a roadster with the hood down, driven by a German officer. The moment he saw me, he slowed down. I tried to look nonchalant as he approached. I did not look around, but I could feel myself breaking out in goose pimples — I feared that the jig was up. The German officer finally accelerated and kept going, but his suspicion made me puzzled and worried. It was true that I had not shaved for three days, but surely that was not obvious from 50 yards away. Was the pain in my muscles noticeably affecting my walk? Was there something obviously wrong with my clothing? If so, I could not figure out what it was. I decided to press on.

At the first house in a small village, I saw a carpenter working in a yard, repairing a door on a couple of sawhorses. I asked him whether it was safe for me to cross the bridge. Using a combination of sign language and figures scrawled on a scrap of paper with his carpenter's pencil, he indicated that 95 percent of the people in the area would help me, but the other 5 percent could not be trusted. At the same time, he pointed to the house. A moment later, an angry middle-aged woman came to the door and started yelling at me in Dutch. She seemed to be ordering me off the premises and asking me where I was going. Having memorized the area on my silk map, I said, "Zaltbommel" and walked back in the direction from which I had come.

I had an uneasy feeling that the trap was closing in on me. Why did she want to know where I was going, if not to phone the German authorities and collect an informer's reward? As soon as I was out of sight of the village, I hid in some shrubbery. Just then, two German soldiers on motorcycles passed, travelling towards Zaltbommel. Then a truckload of German soldiers went by. About a 100 yards from my hiding place, the truck met the returning motorcycles and stopped. An officer spoke to the motorcycle soldiers, and about 20 soldiers got off the truck and fanned out in both ditches, heading towards Zaltbommel. My guardian angel was working overtime!

When the Germans were out of sight, I headed for the bridge, which turned out to be a temporary pontoon structure. When I reached it, I saw a man in uniform at the other end, inspecting identity cards. It was too late to turn back. What was I going to do? Just then, the bridge swung open to let a barge go through. While this was going on, a cluster of people accumulated on each side, waiting for the bridge to close. Just before it did, a young woman with a baby carriage arrived. I admired the baby, a cheerful little fellow about a year old, and played with him for a minute or so. Then, when the bridge closed, I pushed the baby carriage across the bridge and up the steep slope on the other side while the young mother walked beside me. Since there were about 30 people in the group, the guard stopped only two or three young men. He ignored women and older men — and the young couple with their baby.

A hundred yards from the bridge, I touched my hat, nodded good-bye to my wife of 10 minutes and headed down a side road that followed the riverbank. During our brief acquaintance, we had not spoken a word. I could not figure out whether she had instantly guessed who I was and wanted to protect me, or whether she was so slow-witted that she considered my behaviour quite normal. In any case, I was across the Maas and out of the worst danger area, and I was breathing easier.

A few hundred yards along this side road, I came to a house-boat that was tied up at the bank of a small river. On the deck, a middle-aged woman was washing clothes with a washboard in a tub. I was getting so stiff and sore, I could not go on much longer. I walked across the small gangplank and said, "*Ich bin Englander. Helpen bitte.*"

The woman dried off her right hand, shook my hand and said, "*Komm.*" I followed her into the boat. It was the home of the Pagie family — people to whom I am eternally indebted. They were Mr. Pagie, a craggy-faced man of about 60, who was retired and living on a small income; Mrs. Pagie, a stout, motherly woman with greying hair, who looked after the household; and Jane, their bright, decisive oldest daughter, who was about 21 and worked in a factory. Also living at home were Pete, about 18, and two younger daughters, Nellie and Annie, aged about 12 and 15 respectively. Jane spoke a little English, and she conveyed to me the decision of the family. They would shelter me until I could move on to some other safe place. I was shown a bedroom, which was to be mine as long I was there. Mrs. Pagie gave me something to eat, and I thankfully crawled into bed.

The next day, I told the Pagie family about the German officer in the roadster and asked why he had been instantly suspicious of me. They explained that what I had assumed to be a sidewalk was really a bicycle roadway and walking on it without a bicycle was a no-no.

For the first three weeks, I spent a lot of time in bed, recovering from my injuries. I thought a great deal about my family. I knew that by then my parents would have word that I was missing, and I wished there was some way of letting them know I was still alive. I learned much later that on the very day that I arrived at the Pagies' houseboat, J. E. Fauquier, the wing commander of 405 Squadron, had written my parents a letter confirming that I had been reported missing from operations the night of June 8. He wrote, "We can give you no further news at the moment, but I would like to assure you that immediately any fresh news is received you will be informed." A few weeks later, my mother received another letter from 405 Squadron, acknowledging receipt of a parcel she had sent me and informing her that the contents had been distributed among squadron members. "Such is the wish of the boys," the letter continued, "and this is the reason for such action."

One day Jane brought me a German newspaper. Allied fortunes were at or near their lowest point in the war. The exuberant headlines no doubt kept Nazi morale high. Roughly translated one read, "Africa Corps Approaching Alexandria, Now at El Alamein." There were also glowing reports of German advances on the Russian front. I told my hosts about the growing strength of Allied forces in the United Kingdom and that the power of American forces in Britain was just beginning to be felt.

The Pagies generously shared their food with me — mostly bread and potatoes — but having another mouth to feed in wartime, when rations were scarce, must not have been easy. Worse still was the danger in which I was placing the whole family. One day Jane reported that the Germans had put up posters offering a reward for information leading to the arrest of any Allied airmen that might be hidden in the area. The Pagies and I were amused by the fact that the reward was 500 guilders for an officer and 300 for an NCO, but the danger that we all faced was no laughing matter. The Pagies were sheltering me at immense risk to themselves. And this was not an isolated act of courage for this kind, brave family.

The previous summer, they told me, they had taken in another airman, a wounded RAF aircrew member. Unfortunately, a tracking dog had led a German search party to the houseboat. The Germans had taken the airman prisoner and had arrested Mr. Pagie. During three days of questioning, he stoutly maintained that he had thought the airman was German. "He did not have a khaki uniform," he told the Germans. "He had a blue-grey uniform, so he must have been a German. His uniform was almost the same colour as yours." Finally, the German Intelligence officer gave up. "*Dummkopf*," he snorted, and let Mr. Pagie go. I hoped that officer was not still in the area. If so, he might think of the Pagie houseboat as a place to look for me.

One morning, just as dawn was breaking, I awakened with a start to the sound of gunshots. Then, to my horror, I heard five more single shots at short intervals. An awful thought crossed my mind. Six shots — six people in the Pagie family. Had the Pagies been betrayed for hiding me and were they now being executed on the bank beside their houseboat, as was the practice with the Gestapo? Then I heard a burst of machine-gun fire. I lifted the bottom of the blackout curtain on the window and peeked out. On the bank, about 10 feet from my window, three German army officers were examining a map in the first light of dawn. Partly concealed in the grass were other German soldiers, with bunches of grass stuck in their helmets for camouflage. After the family got up, Jane explained that the Germans had a large training base nearby where army units were given final training before being sent to the Russian Front. This kind of activity took place several times while I lived with the Pagies. Once, an infantry unit marched by singing a song with a pleasant melody. A couple of years later I heard that song again and learned it was called "Lily Marlene."

Naturally, I had to stay in the houseboat at all times, except for a couple of calm nights when I climbed into a small boat that was tied to the houseboat on the river side. That meant I could get some fresh air and while away an hour or two. The time went particularly slowly when visitors arrived on Sundays. They habitually had the run of the houseboat and a closed room might arouse their suspicions. During these visits, I agreed to sit in a dark, locked clothes closet all afternoon. I passed the time trying to recall poems I had learned as a schoolboy. One of my favourites was a poem by Henry Wadsworth Longfellow, entitled "The Day is Done."

The day is done and the darkness
Falls from the wings of night
As a feather is wafted downward
From an eagle in its flight ...

My hosts and I knew that our living arrangement could not go on forever. We had to find a way for me to move on. Mr. Pagie went to Rotterdam and Amsterdam to try to make contact with the Dutch underground, but had no luck. Jane finally found a solution at the garment factory where she worked. She cultivated a friendship with a young man there who had been an officer in the Dutch Army. After a couple of weeks, she trusted him enough to tell him about me. He came to visit me, and after I convinced him that I was not a Nazi plant, he asked me for one of my identity tags, took a snapshot of me and left. Two weeks later, we got word that the Pagies should take me to the Zaltbommel railway station on July 18 for a 9:00 a.m. train. The station was about six miles away. That did not seem to be a problem until the Pagies learned — to their utter amazement — that I had never learned to ride a bicycle. I explained that I had been raised in rolling farm country where people often rode horseback but where almost nobody owned a bicycle. Unfortunately, there was no time or place for me to learn now, and riding a bicycle clumsily in Holland was like shouting loud and clear that you were not Dutch.

In the end, Mr. Pagie rode his bicycle on the direct route to Zaltbommel. Jane pedalled hers on the back roads, with me as a passenger on the frame. To create the illusion we were a couple of locals going fishing, we carried a fishing pole. At one point, about 20 German soldiers on bicycles overtook us, but they did not pay any attention to us, as they apparently had just come off night duty and were intent on breakfast.

At the station, a man in his late 40s (whom I later learned was Adriaan Ferdinand van Goelst Meijer, head of a secret organization that supplied military information to the Allies) spoke briefly to Mr. Pagie and then slipped me a train ticket to Weert, near the Belgian border. He pointed to a young priest in the crowd. "He is your guide," he said. "Follow him at a distance." Then he asked who my next-of-kin was. He said he expected to go to Switzerland in September and might get word to my father that I had still been alive in July.

Sometime after we boarded the train, my priest-guide (whom I knew later as Father Reinier Kloeg) sidled up to me and surreptitiously showed me my identity tag. At about 11 o'clock, the train stopped at a small town. About 30 young priests crowded onto the train, all dressed exactly like my guide. When the train pulled into Eindhoven, everyone quickly left the train. I could not tell my guide from all the other priests, and I soon lost track of him. I had no choice but to sit on a bench on the platform and wait. An hour passed. Then another. I was getting more anxious all the time.

Suddenly, I saw my guide emerge from the station. I followed him onto another train, which was going to Weert. At Weert, my guide said good-bye and pointed out to me a young man with two bicycles. Once again, I had to break the incredible news that I could not ride a bicycle. The young man, Matthieu Beelen, hid the spare bicycle in a hedge, and I rode on his as an uncomfortable passenger. It was now evening, and I was ending the long day as I had started it, on the frame of a bicycle.

At one point, we hid ourselves and our bicycle in a grain field while my guide watched a nearby house intently. Finally, a woman came out of the back door and hung a large metal washtub on a nail beside the door. That was our signal: the border patrol was out of sight. My guide slapped me on the back, and we both took off running across the border into Belgium. When we reached a small village, Matthieu told me we were going to a pub, where we would join three young men. When two of them got up to leave, I was to go with them.

We reached the pub just after dark, and everything went according to plan — almost. Outside the pub, my two new friends produced three bicycles. Again, I had to explain my incredible disability. Again, I had to ride on the bicycle frame. One of the men was Albert Peeters. We were heading for his family's farm, about six miles away, near the eastern border of Belgium. When we arrived, his mother served me a bowl of thick gruel, made mostly of barley. It tasted delicious, as I had not eaten since early morning. Soon after, I went to bed for a welcome rest. It had been a momentous day.

Before I went to sleep, I thought about the day, and about the six weeks that had passed since my aircraft had crashed in the cow pasture in Holland. During that time, many strangers had helped me, at great risk to their own lives — the young girls in the strawberry patch, the elderly man who had given me his suit and his best boots, his wife who had given me a drink of milk. And the Pagies. Especially the Pagies. To paraphrase the Scriptures, I was a stranger and they took me in; I was without clothes and they gave me theirs; I was hungry and they fed me. I was grateful beyond words for those acts of kindness. And in the days to come, I was to experience the kindness of strangers in even more dramatic fashion.

The Belgian Underground

The Peeters family lived on a peaceful little mixed farm near the eastern border of Belgium, arranged in the typical Belgian style, with the barn and house joined in one building. The family kept a few cows and grew their own vegetables, so their meals were nourishing and hearty — lots of vegetable stews and chowders — and I enjoyed my stay there. But I knew I had to move on soon.

Young Albert Peeters belonged to an underground cell of saboteurs who damaged German communication systems and other vital installations. He knew a network of people who could be trusted. One was a doctor who came to the farm and examined my back, which he said was recovering from muscle damage. He gave me a small bottle of medicine. "Take this to relieve the pain before you go anywhere in public," he instructed. "Then nobody will notice that you have an injury."

Albert also knew two engineers who worked at the mines in nearby Eisden and supplied his underground organization with dynamite. Both were probably in their early 40s. One, whom I knew only as Mondo, was a tall, slender man; the other, introduced as Schalenborg, was shorter and stouter, and spoke some English. He brought me a copy of *Silas Marner* by George Eliot. "I have been reading this to perfect my English," he told me. "I thought perhaps you would enjoy it." I certainly did. I had not read it before, and it was the only printed English I had seen since leaving England.

Mondo had an engineer friend in Brussels named Neve, who apparently knew something about an escape organization. Eight or nine days after I arrived at the farm, it was decided that I would travel by train to Brussels with Albert Peeters and Mondo. Near the end of July, Albert took me on his bicycle to Mondo's home in Eisden, and my guides gave me a third-class train ticket to Brussels. Peeters and Mondo were to be on the same train but in a different car, so that they would not be compromised if I was arrested. They were running a far greater risk than I. If I was arrested, I stood a good chance of establishing who I was and becoming a prisoner of war. If they were arrested, the Gestapo would probably send them to a concentration camp or execute them immediately.

I found a compartment on the train occupied by two nuns and two elderly ladies. I took one of the four remaining seats and pretended to read a French newspaper. I was looking forward to a safe, quiet journey. After we had gone four or five peaceful miles, however, the train slowed to a stop and the women in my compartment prepared to get off. I looked out of the window. The platform was swarming with German soldiers. As soon as the women left, eight of the soldiers piled into my compartment. I pretended to be preoccupied with my newspaper, as I had no idea what would be expected of me. Would they expect me to give my seat to the soldier who was standing? Fortunately, the Germans ignored me. One of them stood all the way to Louvain. Most of the group got off the train at Louvain, and I pretended to doze most of the way to Brussels. I was deeply worried that the German officers might be fluent in Flemish and French and would try to engage me in conversation — or even just ask me for a light.

When we arrived in Brussels, Peeters and Mondo were waiting for me outside the station. "Good-bye, Albert," I said, shaking his hand. "Thank you for all your help." Mondo and I walked on to the Neves' home. I intentionally did not read the street name or the building number, so that I could not give this information if I was captured. By the time we reached the Neve house, I was violently ill. Obviously, the constant strain was getting to me. In the midst of perilous situations, like the one on the train, I found that I could act quite nonchalant. But later, when the danger had passed, a reaction would set in, and I would sometimes even throw up.

I began to feel better at the Neve home. Mr. and Mrs. Neve received us warmly, and after Mondo left to catch a train back home, Mrs. Neve phoned an official of the Swedish Red Cross, who also happened to be active in an escape organization. She spoke in code, pretending to be offering some food to the Red Cross. "I've just received two pounds of peas," she said in French. When she got off the phone, she told me that I was the "two pounds of peas."

The Neves told me that they would be away all the next day, but I would have a visitor, who had a key to the apartment. The next day, a well-dressed, distinguished-looking man arrived at the door. He gave his name as Nemo. He managed the Belgian unit of an escape organization that was about to take me under its wing. He explained that he wanted to satisfy himself that I was who I claimed to be and not a Gestapo plant. He sat down, cradled his briefcase in his lap and started asking me questions. I got off to a bad start. "What is an RAF leave pass usually called?" he asked. I did not know. "I wasn't in England long enough to go on leave," I explained. He gave me a long, hard look. Then he asked about the red lines on top-secret RAF maps that were quite new and had to do with radio navigation. Now I was suspicious. Had I been lured into an elaborate trap to have me reveal everything I knew to German Intelligence?

We spent a tense couple of hours. Gradually, we began to trust each other. Finally, Nemo said, "I suppose you wonder what I have in my briefcase." He opened the briefcase. It contained only a revolver. "I am pleased that it has not been necessary for me to use this," he said. "So am I," I said. Nemo asked whether I was carrying anything that would incriminate me if I was caught. I pulled my Masonic ring out of my pants' pocket. He took it from me. "You must entrust me with your ring," he said. Then he told me that a guide would come the next day and take me to a hiding place.

My new guide was Peggy van Lier, an attractive, auburn-haired woman about 22 years old. She explained how we were to get to my next hiding place, in another section of Brussels. We would travel by streetcar. To give the impression that I was a regular passenger, I would use a ticket that was good for 20 or 30 trips and had already been punched a dozen times.

I said good-bye to the Neves, and Peggy and I caught a streetcar for downtown Brussels. We got off near the city centre and walked for a few blocks. Peggy noticed a man behind us who seemed to be taking the same route as we were. "Is he following us?" she wondered. When we reached the square next to the Bon Marché department store, we turned a corner. Before the man could spot us, she hustled me down the stairs to the underground toilets and pushed me into a stall. "Lock the door," she whispered. "I'll be back." After a long 20 minutes or so, she tapped on the door and we caught another streetcar.

When we came to an apartment building, she led me quickly to a storage room in the basement — my new hiding place. It was furnished with a table, three or four chairs and a bed. Peggy introduced me to "the two Bettys" — Betty Warnon and Elisabeth Liegeois, two young women who lived in one of the upstairs apartments. They warned me that I was to be as quiet as a mouse, because they did not know whether everyone in the building could be trusted. Every morning on their way to work, Betty and Elisabeth brought me breakfast, and every evening after work, they arrived with my supper. The days were long and monotonous; there was nothing to read and no radio. My room had no bathroom, but there was a toilet a few steps from the back of the storage room. The door of the toilet opened onto the back yard. People in the flat above me used that toilet, so I had to be careful to go in there only when nobody was around.

One morning at dawn, I peeked through a crack in the door to see whether the coast was clear. It was not. A man was butchering rabbits in the back yard. After he left, I slipped into the toilet. I was just about to leave when I heard steps coming down the outside stairs. Through a crack in the door, I could see a woman starting to wash clothes in a washtub in the yard. I was trapped. It would only be a matter of time before she either would notice that the toilet was occupied or would try to come in. What was I to do? I noticed that the top half of a long, narrow window in the toilet room was open. Standing on the toilet seat, I looked out. Just above the window there was another window, presumably in the kitchen of the flat above me. Two tin pie plates were sitting on the windowsill. There happened to be a long stick in the room I was in. I found that it would just reach the pie plates. I pushed them off the sill, and they fell to the kitchen floor with a clatter. The woman in the yard looked up and ran up the stairs to investigate. I scurried back into my own room.

I rarely left my little room. One Saturday, however, Elisabeth took me to a passport photographer in the Bon Marché, so that an identity card could be prepared for my trip to Paris. To ensure that he would not ask me any questions in French that I could not answer, she told him that I was her deaf-mute brother. "He's been totally deaf since birth," she said. "Our mother had German measles before he was born, so perhaps that had something to do with it." The photographer was suitably sympathetic. "What a shame," he said. "And he appears quite intelligent, too." I did not know whether the photographer had swallowed Elisabeth's story whole, or whether he suspected something but went along with the game. Either way, it served the purpose.

One evening, the women did not return on schedule. Three or four hours went by and I became worried. It was almost nine o'clock, curfew time, and they would have to be home soon. Then I saw three pairs of men's feet go by on the sidewalk at the bottom of my blackout curtain. One pair of shoes was two-tone brown and white. I heard the men enter the hallway. A doorbell rang upstairs. Then I heard footsteps coming towards my door and a key turning the lock. Three men came in — a tall, well-dressed man, a man of average height in very ordinary clothes, and a small man in sporty looking clothes, including the two-tone shoes. The tall man looked surprised to see me. "*Bonsoir*," he said. "*Bonsoir*," I replied in my best French. The other two said nothing. All three sat down in silence.

My stomach knotted. Had my hostesses been arrested? Were these Gestapo agents waiting to see who would turn up at their apartment building? The three men seemed tense, too. Suddenly, the little one blurted, in an unmistakable Australian accent, "Damn it, I wish we could find someone who could talk English!" "You just found one," I said. "I speak English." We all broke into huge grins. The small man was an Australian pilot, Jeff Silva, and his companion was Jim Whicher, an RAF member of

Silva's crew. They had been shot up by night fighters a few nights before after a bombing raid on Düsseldorf and had parachuted from their burning aircraft near Brussels. Part of Jeff's face was still bright red from where it had been overheated in the fire. The well-dressed man was Albert, their guide from the escape organization. He had not been told that I was in the hideout. At first, of course, he had also wondered whether the women had been arrested — and whether I was the one who was a Gestapo agent. Betty and Elisabeth finally did return, putting everybody's mind at ease, and told us that we would be taking the train to Paris the next day with two guides, Eric and Georges.

My new identity card gave me a Flemish name and indicated that I was an agricultural worker who spoke only Flemish. Betty and Elisabeth gave us all overnight satchels; mine contained only an old pair of socks and the safety razor that the Pagies had given me in Holland. At the station, Eric and Georges gave us train tickets. It was decided that Jeff and Jim, who were shown as French-speaking on their identity cards, should travel together. I would stay by myself, as I supposedly spoke only Flemish — a language in which I could say barely a word.

The train was so crowded we all had to stand in the aisle. I could see German army officers sitting in the last compartment. I was in the direct line of sight of the officer next to the door of the compartment. He was a good-looking fellow about my age. Any time I glanced in that direction, it seemed to me that he was looking me over. About an hour out of Brussels, he got up and headed for the washroom at the opposite end of the car. As he squeezed by me, he put his hand on the wall to steady himself, and as he was passing he said what sounded like "Excuse me, please," in perfect English. I tried not to react, and he continued on his way. Did I imagine he was speaking English? I tried to think of something in German or French that sounded like "Excuse me, please." Nothing came to mind. Before we reached the French border, the officer went to the washroom a second time. Again, as he was passing me, he seemed to say, practically in my ear, "Excuse me, please." It was hard for me not to believe that he was trying to trap me into responding in English.

Before I had time to worry much about this, we arrived at the French border and everybody got off the train. A French official checked out my identity card, and, thank goodness, did not say a word to me in any language. Going through customs, I opened my pathetic little case with its pair of socks and the razor and placed it on the table. The customs officer was busy arguing with the man in front of me. He just glanced at my satchel, put the required chalk mark on it and kept talking to the other man. It was almost too wonderful to believe. We were finally in France. There was a change of trains and a two-hour stopover in Lille. Our guides took us to a restaurant for lunch before catching our next train.

We arrived in Paris an hour or two before dark. I followed Georges from a distance. As he walked through the station, two gendarmes stepped out from behind a large column, stopped him and ushered him into an office. I saw him turning pale. I had no choice but to keep walking out of the station. In a small, open square near the station, I sat down on a park bench and watched the station door. After a few minutes, which seemed like an eternity, I saw Georges emerge from the station. He told me later that the gendarmes had noticed him arriving in Paris several times carrying a case, and they were checking to make sure that he was not a black marketeer.

My instructions were that I was to follow Georges for a while; he would eventually pass a grey-haired man wearing a black beret and carrying a newspaper under his left arm who would be window-shopping. I was to leave Georges and follow the grey-haired man from a distance, which I did. He led me to an apartment, where I spent the night. The next day, I was taken to a suburb of Paris, to the second-floor apartment of René and Raymonde Coache, a friendly couple in their 40s. In the few days I spent in their home, I formed a great admiration for the Coaches. René was a newspaperman who had opened his home to the Resistance movement as a hiding place. Raymonde sometimes acted as a guide in the escape organization.

One day, another guide arrived at the door with a wonderful surprise — Sergeant Ronald Pearce of the Royal Australian Air Force. He had been the tail gunner of another crew of 405 Squadron. Like Silva and Whicher, he had been shot down in the early morning of August 1 while returning from an air attack on Düsseldorf, an operation in which 32 aircraft were lost and 121 crew were killed. I had not known Ronald Pearce well when we were both at Pocklington, but at that moment, I felt like hugging him. I can hardly describe how heart-warming it was to meet him again. In the two months since I had been shot down, he was the one and only person I met that I had ever seen before in my entire life.

Of all the stress of evading capture in enemy-occupied territory, the thing I found hardest to bear was something I had never anticipated: the loneliness of being cut off completely from every person I had ever met. I knew that after this time of travelling alone, I still might come to a messy end, and my friends and family would never know anything about these weeks of life that were so precious to me.

I had an almost overwhelming desire to let my family know that I was still alive. The only way I could do that would be to give myself up and become a prisoner of war. This was out of the question. First, I might have great difficulty proving that I was who I claimed to be and therefore a legitimate prisoner of war, with rights under the Geneva Convention, including the right not to give any information except name, rank and serial number. More important, if I were not treated as a prisoner of war, the

Gestapo would go to any lengths to force me to reveal who had helped me. By design, I knew little about any of the links in the escape chain, not even people's real names in many cases. But I knew just enough to be dangerous if I broke down under torture. The results for all my helpers would be catastrophic. I had no choice but to continue placing my life in the hands of my new friends, and to hope and pray that they could bring me to a safe harbour.

I was not aware of it then, but the most arduous part of that journey was just around the corner. And the most remarkable of all my guides had just entered my life. It was she who had brought Sergeant Pearce to the Coaches' apartment, and now she was taking over the dangerous job of trying to get me safely out of France. Her name was Dédée.

From Paris
to Gibraltar

Dédée brought me to my next hiding place, a villa on the outskirts of Paris. It had a large garden surrounded by a stone wall, which screened it from the street. When we arrived, Silva and Whicher were there, as well as Elvere Morelle, a young nurse who ran the house and prepared our meals. A day or two later we were joined by James Goldie, a Scottish soldier who had escaped from a German prison camp.

As the days passed, I discovered that Dédée was not just another guide, as I had first assumed. She was the person who ran the Comet Line, one of the most complex and daring of the escape organizations that had been formed to get Allied servicemen safely out of enemy-occupied Europe. The Comet Line consisted of hundreds of helpers and stretched from the borders of Holland and Germany to San Sebastien in Spain. Dédée, whose real name was Andrée de Jongh, had formed the Comet Line a year earlier with her father, Frédéric de Jongh, a school principal.

Dédée did not look the part. She was a vivacious, cheerful and slender woman who looked even younger than her 22 years, having started to dress like a schoolgirl to escape the attention of the Gestapo. Earlier in the war, she had worked as a nurse's aide in a Brussels hospital, where she had met many wounded soldiers. Every day on her way home from the hospital, she would read the notices the Germans had posted along the street: "Anyone found aiding the Allies will be shot."

Dédée's sister was a member of the Resistance movement and many of her compatriots were, in fact, arrested and shot. But Dédée was determined to do something to help the Allied cause. In July 1941, Dédée and a friend set off for Spain with 11 Belgian soldiers, travelling in small groups with false identity cards. At Bayonne, Dédée hired Spanish smugglers to guide the party over the Pyrenees. In the second escape she organized, she made the difficult, dangerous crossing into Spain with her party of escaping military personnel. It was the first of 34 trips she made across those mountains with the men she called "my children." When she returned to Paris, her father warned her not to go home to Brussels because the Gestapo had arrested her mother and sister, and they were being held as hostages.

Now Dédée was planning an escape to Spain for her sister's 17-year-old stepson, Frédéric Wittick. He was to accompany Silva, Whicher, Goldie and me across the mountains. First, though, we all had to acquire new aliases and new identity papers. This time, I was a French citizen, born in France. Strangely enough, I do not recall what my new alias was, although I do remember some of the more lighthearted day-to-day moments at the villa.

One afternoon, Elvere took me sightseeing in Paris. Like a regular tourist, I visited the Eiffel Tower, the Louvre, Notre Dame. I felt uneasy venturing outside our relatively safe haven, but I was awestruck by some of the sights of this glorious city, and I knew I was in good hands. Another day, Dédée and Elvere watched in amusement as we gathered plums from a tree in the back yard. The landlord had told Dédée that we could use any plums that fell off the tree. We misunderstood that offer and innocently proceeded to speed up the natural process by shaking the tree. I caught a bug during my stay at the villa, and one morning I awoke with severe abdominal pains. I tried to explain to Elvere in my fractured French that I felt too ill to eat but that a cup of tea might help. I, of course, had in mind the strong black tea with milk that we used to drink with every meal on the farm at home. At last she said, "Ah, tea, *bon*," and disappeared. In about an hour she returned with a couple of pints of some vile-tasting herbal tea. She insisted that I drink every horrible drop. Fortunately, it did cure me — and almost instantly.

After about a week and a half of this relatively pleasant respite from my tension-filled weeks on the run, it was time to move on. As we left the villa, we split up into several small groups, each with a guide. I was to follow "Paul" (in actual fact, Dédée's father, Frédéric) to the subway station. Paul bought tickets at the station while I followed from a distance. After a few minutes, he sidled up to me and slipped me a ticket from his vest pocket, then joined the lineup at the turnstile and headed for the platform. In the lineup, I was feeling quite at ease — until I reached the ticket-taker. When I presented my ticket, he burst into a flood of angry French, which I could not follow. I had no idea what was wrong. "I'm afraid the jig is up," I said to myself. At that moment, Dédée appeared from farther back in the line and began scolding the ticket-taker. "How dare you hold up the line because this poor bum has no ticket!" she exclaimed. "You stand there and argue while the rest of us miss our connection!" Then she flung down the change for a new ticket for me. The ticket-taker punched it, and I walked meekly past his booth. I later learned that Paul had mistakenly given me a used ticket that had happened to be in his pocket.

At the train station, we found that Dédée had reserved a compartment for us all, free from the prying eyes of other passengers. All we had to fear was the inevitable German police control on virtually every train, which required all passengers to produce identity cards for scrutiny. Our cards had been skilfully forged and properly stamped — they had been procured by a member of the underground who worked in a German office in the south of France. A couple of times, the police officer examined our cards without comment.

The train, a fast one by Canadian standards, rushed through the night with its lights blacked out. About midnight, I ventured sleepily out of our compartment to go to the toilet. In the dark, I opened what I took to be the toilet door. A blast of cold air struck me. I had opened the exit door. With a jolt, I was wide awake. I was shaken by the stupidity of this near-accident. Had I taken one more step, I would have fallen into the night, bringing the extraordinary effort and devotion of so many patriots to nought.

When dawn broke, we were speeding along the Atlantic coast of southern France. As the countryside flashed by, I saw German gun installations heavily concealed with camouflage netting. It appeared to me that they were heavy coastal defence guns. Later that morning, the train arrived at St. Jean de Luz in the southwest corner of France, where we got off. A woman known as Tante Go — Elvire de Greef, head of the Basque end of the Comet Line — met Dédée at the station, and we all were taken to different Basque homes in the area and outfitted with rope sandals and berets, typical Basque attire.

My host had served in the French Army during the First World War, but he spoke only a little French and no English, except for a song he had learned from British soldiers in the last war — "It's a Long Way to Tipperary." That evening he sang it for me, with great gusto. Later we were able to converse with the help of one of his neighbours, who spoke English. Through the interpreter, my host said it was a good thing the Germans were stupid and assumed that everyone who wore a beret was a Basque. He said all the villagers knew that the other members of my group were not Basques. "However," he said, "everyone thinks that you are a Basque and that the others are travelling with you." I suppose that my black hair and brown eyes made me look a bit like people in this village, but I took this statement with a shovelful of salt. I assumed that my tension was showing, and that he was trying to reassure me and calm my nerves.

The next afternoon, we started out for the foothills of the Pyrenees with Dédée leading the way and the five of us straggling behind. We eventually arrived at a house occupied by a widow named Francia and her two daughters, aged about nine and 11. As darkness fell she fed us a substantial meal, including fried eggs, an unheard of luxury in those times. While we were finishing our meal, Florentino arrived. He was to be our guide across the Pyrenees. He was a powerfully built Basque, about six feet tall, and he had made many trips over this route with escaping military men. We were told he knew the mountains like the back of his hand.

At about nine o'clock that evening, we set out. It had become very dark, and there were patches of fog and showers of rain. This was considered to be excellent weather for our journey, because it meant that the tracking dogs of the border patrols would be unable to follow our scent. Our instructions were that if a patrol did intercept us, we were to scatter in hopes that at least some would escape. Florentino led the way, followed by Dédée. We five were then arranged with the one deemed to be the fittest in the back. Jim Whicher, who was wounded, followed Dédée. Then came Jeff Silva, Frédéric and I. James Goldie took up the rear. There was no trail, as far as I could tell — just rocks and thorny shrubs and endless climbs up mountain gorges. For part of the journey, it was so dark we had to hold onto the coattails of the person in front. About midnight, we started climbing a dried-out watercourse lined with boulders. It took us about an hour and a half to reach the top. It was so steep, much of the time we crawled on all fours.

About two o'clock in the morning, we paused for a short break. Then we pressed on to the Bidassoa River, near the Spanish border. Florentino did a short reconnaissance in the darkness. When he came back, he put his heavy backpack on my back and took Jim Whicher on his back. Then we started to ford the river. As we reached the deepest part, my feet were barely touching bottom. The current was so strong, I felt that I was on the verge of being swept downstream. Finally I felt a small boulder on the river bottom, which gave me enough footing to lean against the current. From then on, the river became more shallow, and we all struggled up the bank, gasping for breath and sopping wet. Florentino reclaimed his pack and led us quickly across a road and a railroad. We were in Spain — but we were not out of danger. There was still the possibility that we would be stopped by the Spanish border patrol and imprisoned in Miranda de Ebro, the Spanish camp where illegal travellers to Spain were detained. We pressed on through the mountains as fast as we could. The going was hard. In the darkness, some of us stumbled and fell from time to time into thorn bushes.

Dédée strode on ahead of us, apparently not finding the journey nearly as difficult as the rest of us did. The four military men in the group were not in the best of shape, having spent weeks or months in hiding with little or no exercise. About 4:30 a.m., James Goldie collapsed from exhaustion. He was a robust fellow, but he had been a prisoner of war for almost two years and had been in hiding for months. I could feel that he was losing his grip on my coattail. Every time this happened, I would jerk on the coattail of the person in front of me to stop the procession, help Goldie to his feet, get him walking again and give the signal for the line to move on. This happened three or four times in the next hour and a half. I was becoming exhausted, too — so much so that I thought I might pass out. Finally, at about 6:00 a.m., after walking, climbing and crawling for nine hours over terrible terrain, we arrived at a shepherd's cabin in the foothills on the Spanish side of the Pyrenees. I have never felt so exhausted in my life.

Two men and two women lived in the cabin, along with several big dogs. Everybody in our group collapsed on the wooden floor and promptly fell asleep. At one point, one of the dogs woke me up by walking across my body to get closer to the open fireplace. One of the women had hung a shallow iron pot on a chain from the crane in the fireplace. As I watched in fascination, the dog hit the pot with one of his front paws, sending it swinging on its chain. Every time the pot came back towards him, he hit it again. Eventually the swing became so wide, a splash of warm milk landed on the floor in front of him. He quickly lapped up the milk, walked back over me and went back to sleep. So did I.

We awoke about noon. Dédée gave us her final instructions. We were to walk singly towards the nearest town, a suburb of San Sebastien. When we reached a certain restaurant, we were to go in a door beside the restaurant and up a flight of stairs to a sitting room. We did so, and after we had gathered there, Dédée appeared with a Spanish gentleman, who took us to his home in San Sebastien. We had a meal there and spent the night. Early the next morning, we walked to an intersection on the outskirts of San Sebastien. Dédée gave each of us a parting gift, a silver ring bearing the coat of arms of the Basque provinces. At nine o'clock, a limousine flying a small Union Jack on the fender pulled up to the intersection. Dédée kissed us good-bye.

We were out of the clutches of the Gestapo, but as we drove off, my thoughts were with Dédée. Silva, Whicher, Goldie and I were the 37th, 38th, 39th and 40th of the Allied military men she had sheltered and shepherded to safety so far. Now she was going back to enemy-occupied territory to continue risking her life in this perilous work. I wondered what lay ahead for her and whether we would ever see her again.

Shortly after we left San Sebastien, the Spanish limousine driver asked us to get down on the floor. We were about to drive past Miranda de Ebro, the detention camp for illicit travellers. After that, we were able to look at the countryside on our day-long drive to Madrid. I was struck by how arid the landscape was, and by how difficult the farming must have been. We even passed a farm where farmers were threshing grain by the primitive method of driving oxen around on a threshing floor and separating the chaff from the grain in the breeze. Eventually, we reached Madrid. I felt a profound sense of relief as we drove into the walled compound of the British embassy. It was August 20, 1942. I had been on the run for 72 days. Finally, I felt, I could stop wondering whether this was to be my last day — or last moment — on earth.

We were housed in a temporary wooden building that contained sleeping quarters, a dining room and a kitchen. A Spanish woman cooked our food, which was tasty and plentiful, as Spain did not experience the wartime shortages of occupied Europe. And wonder of wonders, the Spanish actually had soap — a commodity that was almost non-existent in the countries I had just travelled through. One of my first pleasant tasks was to take my first bath with soap since I had left England. It was a wonderful respite from the nerve-racking ordeal we had all just been through, but I kept asking myself, as I had many times after narrowly escaping death in the past 10 weeks, why I had been spared. Why me, when so many other young men were being slaughtered in the air and on the battlefields?

The news from the Front was unusually disturbing. An embassy staffer told us that a force consisting mainly of Canadians had made a raid on occupied France the day before we arrived in Madrid. They had landed at a place called Dieppe. He said there were heavy casualties before the force withdrew. (Later, we learned that more than 900 Canadians died in that assault and close to 2,000 were captured by the Germans.) I learned much later that one of the RCAF officers killed while giving air support to the ground forces was Flying Officer Edwin Gardiner, son of James Gardiner, the then-minister of Agriculture for Canada.

I was finally able to send some news of my own to my family. The embassy staff warned us that we could not indicate where we had been or why we were in Spain, but I was thankful to be able to let my family know I was alive and well. I wrote several letters, including this cryptic one to my brother, Murdoch, who was an RCMP constable stationed at Minto, New Brunswick:

Spain, 21-8-42

Dear Mac:

You will probably be surprised to hear from me here. I just came here to build some castles you see and I've had a very interesting trip.

I'll be back at my old address before very long I think and I'll be expecting to hear from you then. Write to my old address and tell me all the news. I'll be expecting some vacation when I get back. I expect I'll go up north if I get a reasonable holiday. Spain is very much like Nevada, but it is more difficult to get about as my Spanish is very weak.

Have you been home this summer? I am anxious to know if they are all well there. Write or cable to my old address when you get this.

Sincerely,

Angus

One evening, an embassy staffer invited us to be his clandestine guests at a small garden party for some of the diplomatic corps. He planned to show a moving picture in the garden. Before the party started, he drove us to his residence, gave us some refreshments and installed us in an upstairs room where we could watch the movie from the window. The movie, as it turned out, had special significance for me and my military friends. I do not remember much about the movie except its title: *One of Our Aircraft Is Missing.*

After a few days at the embassy, I was asked to report to the air attaché, an older man with the rank of wing commander. He told me that the British had an arrangement with the Spanish government whereby members of the British garrison in Gibraltar could go to Spain on leave, provided they carried proper identity cards and were in civilian clothes. Then he said: "Now a very unfortunate thing has happened. A couple of days ago, Captain Collie from the Staffordshire Regiment came to Spain on a 48-hour pass. His leave ended yesterday and he has not reported back to Gibraltar. He is therefore absent without leave somewhere in Spain, so we had to report him to the Spanish authorities and ask them to arrest him. Do you get the picture?" I said, "Would you mind going over that again?" "Of course," he said. "You are now Captain Collie. The nearest police station is just two blocks away. If you turn left when you go out the gate, you will come to it. Take everything you have with you because you won't be back. Good-bye and good luck."

I was pretty sure I knew what was going on, although nobody spelled it out at the time. When we had arrived in Spain, secret agents representing four members of the garrison at Gibraltar had been sent to Spain with proper leave passes and then had secretly slipped back to Gibraltar by speedboat, perhaps the same night. When the leave passes expired, we four assumed the identities of the "absent without leave" soldiers. So, on this late afternoon in Madrid, I acquired my third alias in about as many weeks. I gathered up my few belongings in my little case and headed for the police station.

"I'm Captain Collie," I told the police officer at the desk. "I expect you are looking for me." I was immediately placed under arrest with a police escort. Then a police officer who spoke good English asked me whether I had eaten recently. I said no. He escorted me to a hotel dining room for supper. My three fellow military evaders, to my surprise and their amusement, were already halfway through their supper.

That evening, two state policemen took us to a railway station, and we all boarded a train with hard wooden seats. After travelling all night and part of the next day, we arrived at La Linea, just across the border from Gibraltar. The British consul from Gibraltar and a Spanish government official met us at the station. The Spanish official was a man of about 35 who spoke perfect English. The police handed me over to him, and my friends to other Spanish officials.

My man took me into a small office and handed me a long form to fill out. It contained a host of questions regarding my new personality, "Captain Collie" — the names of my parents, their places of birth, my mother's maiden name and so on. I had to invent plausible answers to these questions while the Spanish official looked gravely on. When I was finished, I looked it over, signed it and handed it back. He scrutinized it carefully. I began to wonder what would happen to me if some error let him know that it was all fraudulent. "So near and yet so far," I thought to myself. "You made a good job of this," he said finally. "I think it is okay." Then he asked abruptly, "What did you say your mother's maiden name was?" Fortunately I had used my real mother's maiden name. "Sarah MacLean," I said promptly. He flashed a mischievous smile. "We know what is going on," he said, "but it's important that we get these forms right, as our government has given the German consul permission to examine them." I was greatly relieved. Then the official had the British consul sign a receipt for me, and he handed me over to him.

When all four of us were in the custody of the British consul, we were driven through the gate to Gibraltar. None of us had ever been there before, but it was a feeling of unimaginable delight, even for an Australian and a Canadian, to be back on British soil. I can only imagine what this moment meant to Jim Whicher and James Goldie. Goldie must have been ecstatic after an absence of more than two years, mostly spent in a German prisoner-of-war camp. In Gibraltar, we were driven directly to a British Army Intelligence office. I was ushered into the office of Major Donald Darling of MI9 (Military Intelligence, Section 9, which was responsible for aiding escape organizations in any possible way). This now-famous MI9 agent, whose code name was "Sunday," interrogated me at length. I first had to satisfy him that I was who I claimed to be and not a German agent posing as Angus MacLean.

Darling asked me many questions about where I had been stationed. "With what squadron?" he asked. "Who was the squadron commander?" "J. E. Fauquier," I replied. "Can you tell me anything unusual about Fauquier?" "Yes," I said, "he has a pet German shepherd dog on the station. That is rather unusual." "Would you happen to know its name?" I told him the dog's name. I presume that he checked with England to make sure I was not lying.

The next thing I had to do was to give him a convincing summary of how and where I had spent my time since June 9. I realized later that Darling was suspicious of me because at that time there was no escape organization in Holland. For this and other reasons, he had to satisfy himself that I had not been arrested by the Gestapo and given my freedom on condition that I work as a double agent and expose what I knew about escape organizations. Such a suspicion seemed to me pretty outrageous.

What I did not know at the time, but learned later, was that a British soldier named Cole, who was absent without leave from his unit at the time of Dunkirk, had become a double agent. Darling undoubtedly realized that traitors were the greatest menace to the escape organizations, and he wanted to make sure I was not another Cole.

When Darling was satisfied that I was genuine, he told me I could send the wartime type of numbered cable to my next of kin. These cables consisted of three numbers, each representing a phrase. The three numbers I sent off to several members of my family, including my sister Catherine in Saint John, meant "Rumour unfounded. Safe, happy and well. Love." After finishing this pleasant task, I was driven to the officers' quarters at RAF Station New Camp and allotted a room. Jeff Silva and D. J. Perdue joined me there. Perdue was an RAF pilot who had been shot down in the northwest part of France and had escaped with the help of an underground organization set up by Dr. Albert Guérisse, who was known as Pat O'Leary. Perdue had travelled to the southeast of France and had been picked up by boat near Perpignan and taken to Gibraltar. He had been evading for five months, much longer than the rest of our small group. We joked about his having the only name that was perfectly fitting to our situation, *perdue* being the French for "lost" or "stray."

The station medical officer examined us and pronounced us fit for travel. I discovered I had lost 35 pounds, down to 130 pounds since June. We were all issued RAF summer kit — shoes, long socks, shorts and a shirt — and we enjoyed a few days of rest and good food. The time off also gave us a chance to remove some thorns that we had acquired in the Pyrenees and now were beginning to fester.

CHAPTER EIGHT

Back in Britain

On a fine day in late August, we boarded the troopship *Llanstephan Castle*, bound for Gourock, Scotland. I was looking forward to a restful trip, a prospect that was short-lived.

I was on the ship about an hour when the officer commanding troops sent for me. He was a "retread" — a permanent force major who had been recalled from retirement when war broke out. His job involved making sure that all troops on his ship behaved as they should, kept their quarters clean and so on. Being a career military man, he was accustomed to certain standards of order and discipline. "As the senior air force officer on the ship," he told me, "you are to accompany me on my daily inspection, and you must ensure that all air force personnel meet our standards."

I could not beg off this assignment. I had to pretend I was on a normal posting, so nobody on the ship, including the senior officers, had any idea what the facts were. In any case, this did not seem like an onerous task. After all, there were only a couple of dozen air force personnel on board and most of them were officers. They would surely co-operate in keeping their quarters up to par, even if my immediate superior seemed to think that air force personnel were a lower form of life than army personnel. Then I discovered the awful truth. My responsibilities also included about 50 women and children on the ship. They were the wives and children of RAF members who had been stationed in the Middle East and were still there when war broke out. They had had no military training, and they saw no reason why they should obey a young officer in shorts.

On our first ship's inspection, everything was shipshape until we got to the RAF dependent women's section. Then everything was a disaster. To say the washrooms were a mess would be a great understatement. There were dirty towels and clothes strewn about; some members of the party had been using the floor as a toilet. The portholes were all open, which was a serious offence. If the ship was torpedoed and began to list, water would rush in through the open portholes. The major told me he expected me to have all this rectified before the next day's inspection. I tried to explain to my charges what was expected of them, and they pretended to understand, but the next day things were not much better.

Day after day, I tried to cajole my charges into meeting the standards set by my stern and demanding superior. Invariably, I ended up trying to mollify him when his demands were not met. The daily discussion following the inspection usually ended with him saying, "You see what you can do. I'm going to pour myself a gin." Things gradually improved towards the end of the trip. The weather became markedly cooler and at least the temptation to open portholes diminished.

One sunny afternoon, I went for a walk around the deck. A civilian passenger, who looked to be in his 50s, was making the rounds in the opposite direction. Every time we met on the deck, he appeared to be looking me over carefully. I thought I must be imagining this, as I had become supersensitive to the gaze of strangers. Finally, he stopped to chat. "You are a Canadian," he said. I nodded. "A Scottish-Canadian." "Yes," I said, thinking he must be an expert on accents. I was wearing my RAF summer kit with nothing to indicate my nationality. "And your people came from the Hebrides, did they not?" "That's true," I said, "but how did you know that?" "You may have noticed that I was looking at you very carefully each time we met. I'm sorry if I appeared rude, but I found you an interesting specimen. I concluded by the colour of your eyes and the texture of your hair, and the shape of your head and so on, that you had to belong to a gene pool which resulted from a prehistoric migration of people up the west coast of Europe from Portugal or even from North Africa. There are traces of them up the west coast of Europe as far as the Hebrides."

He told me that he was a professor of anthropology at Cambridge University and that his specialty was prehistoric migrations. This discussion reminded me of my Basque host's contention that his neighbours thought that I was Basque, but that Silva and Whicher and Goldie were not. I knew, too, that when the Spanish Armada had sailed against England in 1588, they had pressed into service experienced Basque fishermen, some of whom had probably fished on the Grand Banks of Newfoundland. When the Spanish Armada had sailed around the north of Scotland to get back to the Atlantic, some ships had been wrecked around the islands off Scotland. No doubt in some cases survivors had been absorbed into the Scottish population that later travelled to the New World. I also knew that at an early date, the Basques had fished and hunted walrus, then called seacows, from Prince Edward Island. Seacow Pond gets its name from the walrus, which were once plentiful in the Gulf of St. Lawrence. I did not know at that time that the Basques had made any continuing contribution to the Island culture; I learned later that the surname Cheverie is an anglicization of a Basque name and that all the Cheveries on the Island are descended from a Basque fisherman named Antoine Detcheverry, who settled in North Lake near the eastern tip of the Island before 1749. So there were a number of possible explanations why those Basque villagers might have thought I was one of them.

About 10 days out of Gibraltar, we docked in Gourock, Scotland. A Military Intelligence officer met us on the ship, and an officer from the RAF Embarkation Office informed me that I was nominally in charge of Silva and Perdue; however, the three of us would have an armed military police escort all the way to London. Under no circumstances were we to speak to civilians, and we were ordered to say as little as possible to military personnel. There were two reasons for placing us under armed guard. One was that the military authorities wanted to make sure that we were not double agents posing as escaped air force officers. The other was that, if we were who we said we were, we should be prevented from revealing anything about our experiences in enemy territory to the wrong people.

It had become much too cool for our RAF shorts and shirts, so a day or two out of Gourock, we had to change into the nondescript civilian clothing we had acquired while in hiding. I put on the well-worn brown suit the old Dutch farmer had given me months before. When our train arrived in Glasgow, our armed service police escorted us to a hotel for supper and sat behind us while we ate. At the next table, three middle-aged couples began discussing us, at a volume that indicated they wanted us to overhear them. "What a crying shame that the service police have to waste their valuable time rounding up these damned deserters," one said. "They are worse than useless and a disgrace to the country." The couples also wondered aloud why the escorting officers would feed such scum in a good hotel, instead of serving them what they deserved, bread and water. Silva, Perdue and I glanced at each other with amused grins.

When we arrived in London, we reported to the commanding officer at the London Transit Camp. I was told that my trunk and other personal effects could be retrieved from the storage warehouse where the property of missing personnel was kept. Then I was driven to an MI9 office. On the way, I was surprised to see a large billboard, soliciting support for the YMCA, with a more-than-life-size photo of a YMCA tea wagon serving tea to my aircrew. The photograph was the one that had been taken in Pocklington about a week before we were shot down and published on the front page of the *Daily Telegraph*. It made me wonder once again what had happened to the rest of my crew after we had bailed out of the "H" for Harry that night over Holland.

At the MI9 office, I was questioned at length. I was also told to report to the office of the British minister for Air, Sir Archibald Sinclair. He asked me about the adequacy of the escape kits with which aircrew were supplied. The kits contained a file, a rubber bag for drinking water, some currency of countries over which we were flying, a few malted milk tablets, water-purifying tablets and a silk map and compass. I suggested that the kits should also include razors so that aircrew could remain clean-shaven until they reached organized help. (After that, razors were included in the kits.)

On September 12, I sent my father a coded cable of three numbers. My father would be celebrating his 62nd birthday on October 4, and I wanted it to be a happy occasion for both my parents.

> *Love to Daddy. Birthday greetings. I'm well and fit.*
> *Angus MacLean.*

Before his birthday my father also received a letter from the RCAF casualties officer.

Dear Mr. MacLean:

It is a pleasure to confirm my recent telegram which informed you that your son, Flight Lieutenant John Angus MacLean, has arrived safely in the United Kingdom.

Since my letter of June 11th, reporting your son missing, we were able to confirm from the Air Ministry in London, England, that your son had arrived safely in Gibraltar on August 24th. Subsequently, information was received that your son had arrived safely in the United Kingdom on September 10th.

May I join with you and Mrs. MacLean in your happiness over your son's safe return.

Yours sincerely,

W. R. Gunn
Flying Officer
RCAF Casualties Officer
for Chief of the Air Staff

I spent some time on leave in Scotland, some of it in the Isle of Skye, which my paternal grandmother had left in 1858. After I returned to London I learned that I had been awarded a Distinguished Flying Cross for my role in the operation in which I had been shot down. Usually it was a senior officer who pinned such decorations on military men, but this time King George VI himself was going to do the honours at Buckingham Palace.

When that day arrived, Air Commodore Hugh Campbell, a permanent force officer from New Brunswick, rode with me in a staff car — which, incidentally, was driven by an airman named Ross from the Belfast area of Prince Edward Island, not far from my home. Campbell told me he had been visiting Pocklington on the fateful night of June 8 and had waited with rising anxiety as three aircraft from our squadron had failed to return. Then the squadron had received a message from "H" for Harry that we were abandoning the aircraft. Altogether, 37 aircraft, including three from our squadron, had been shot down that night. Our crew was the only one of the three that survived. I learned that the rest of my crew were still prisoners of war in the Stalag Luft III camp in Germany.

When we arrived at the palace, about 50 of us, including James Goldie, who received a Distinguished Conduct Medal, assembled in a waiting room. Then we were ushered into a grand room. King George VI entered and mounted a dais. As our names were called, we marched up to the King and saluted. He pinned our decorations on us, congratulated us on what we had achieved and shook our hands. We saluted and walked back to our seats. It was a formal and somewhat solemn occasion. Still, I could not help but look back in amusement at the scene in the hotel dining room when we had been mistaken for deserters. I wondered what those couples would think if they saw us now.

After my visit to Buckingham Palace, I was sent on a brief tour to speak to aircrew of Canadian squadrons in Yorkshire. I could not tell them any details about my experiences in Europe. Most of what had happened was still top-secret. All I could say was that civilians had helped me evade capture and return to Britain, and that a high percentage of people in occupied Europe were willing to risk their lives to help Allied soldiers. The main purpose of these visits, I was sure, was to exhibit me as living proof that it was possible to be missing for months and still return. My speaking tour included my old base in Pocklington. Sadly, I found few of my old friends there. Since I had been shot down, 405 Squadron had lost 21 crews, a total of about 150 men. The squadron's normal strength was 18 crews.

About the same time, I was told to report to a certain Major Neave at an address on Horseferry Road in London. Airey Neave was a good-looking young officer of MI9, dressed in artillery uniform. He wore decorations, including the Military Cross. He had been wounded and captured by the Germans in 1940, when the British were retreating from Dunkirk. Neave seemed to have an intense interest in my sojourn in Holland. I later learned that earlier that year, he had been one of the first to escape Colditz Castle, the German prisoner-of-war establishment that the Germans fondly believed was escape-proof. In fact, in the First World War it had been used for the same purpose, and as far as I know, nobody did escape from it then. But as the Second World War progressed, the Germans got the brilliant idea of sending to Colditz Castle people who had escaped from other prison camps and had been recaptured. It apparently never occurred to the Germans that they were creating a postgraduate school of escaping, where prisoners pooled their knowledge from previous escapes. The result was that several prisoners did manage to leave Colditz, including Neave.

Now Neave wanted to know all about my stay in Holland — what the Pagie houseboat was like, its exact location and so on. I had no idea what the purpose of these questions was and, of course, I was not told. (The mystery was solved nine years later, when I received a letter from Trix Terwindt, a KLM flight attendant. She had read an item in *Time* magazine noting my election to Parliament, along with three other Second World War veterans, and my name had rung a bell with her. During the war, she had been dropped into Holland by parachute to assist in setting up an escape organization for MI9. She had been instructed to report to an address in Amsterdam; if for some reason she was unable to do this, she was to go to the Pagies' houseboat, where "Angus MacLean" was the password. In her letter, she told me she had always thought that this was a fictitious name. When I wrote back, I was able to assure her that it was not.)

That fall, I found out that I would not be going back to the continent for some time. When I had first arrived in London, an

RAF medical unit had given me a complete examination, including x-rays of my back, to determine whether I should be medically discharged. I was pronounced fit enough to continue as aircrew. This was not surprising, because experienced pilots were not released for minor disabilities. In fact, there was more than one case of pilots on active service with artificial legs, the most famous being Douglas Bader, an RAF airman who had been shot down and captured by the Germans. Although I had been pronounced fit, air force headquarters in London told me that I would never be allowed to fly over enemy territory again. It was decided that, since my entire crew were prisoners of war, German Intelligence probably knew me as an individual, and if I were ever to fall into the clutches of the Gestapo, they would no doubt resort to torture to try to learn who had helped me escape.

Air force headquarters gave me two choices: either become officer commanding the conversion flight at Pocklington, which trained pilots to fly the Halifax aircraft, or return to Canada in about a year. I chose to return home. I was now 28 years old, and I thought perhaps it was time I settled down and got married. Now that my operations against the enemy were over, it looked as though I might have a future to look forward to.

In the meantime, I was posted to 41 Group Andover and attached to No. 20 Maintenance Unit, Aston Down, where I was to learn to fly Hurricane aircraft. After a happy month there, I was attached to No. 8 Maintenance Unit, Little Rissington, to practise flying Wellingtons for a few days. The Air Ministry also sent me on a crash course in chemical warfare, conducted by a civilian expert. The British military considered me a suitable candidate since I had a bachelor of science degree in industrial chemistry. The Allies feared that the Germans might resort to chemical warfare, and the British had built up a capacity for chemical warfare as a deterrent. My introduction to the field included tours of a couple of mustard gas manufacturing plants in northwest England, near Chester. Fortunately, the deterrent worked, and gas was not used during the Second World War, so my newly acquired knowledge never had to be put to use.

In November 1942 I was posted to No. 39 Maintenance Unit at RAF Station Colerne, not far from the city of Bath. This unit rebuilt damaged aircraft and modified other aircraft. Most of the mechanics were women, and they worked under difficult conditions, often in the open. It was the pilots' job to test-fly these repaired aircraft to ensure that they were airworthy and that everything was functioning as it should. We flew a wide variety of aircraft, mostly the various versions of Spitfires, but also Lancasters, Albermerles, Oxfords, Beaufighters and Manchesters. It was an interesting and challenging job.

Despite these distractions, the events of the summer haunted me, and I still had the occasional nightmare. Sometimes I dreamed that I was back in Holland or Belgium or France. I often worried about my special friends who had risked their lives for me. Were they still alive? I received some news — mostly bad — when I went to London in February 1943 on a 48-hour pass. I was walking on the Strand, when, to my astonishment, I met Georges, who had been my guide from Brussels to Paris. He was just about as surprised to see me. "*Restez ici,*" he said. "I come back." In a few minutes he returned with a bilingual friend. He told me his full name — Count Georges d'Oultremont — and he told me what he knew of the Comet Line. Its members had been betrayed to the Gestapo.

In November, two German agents posing as Americans and claiming to have been shot down near Namur, Belgium, had infiltrated the Comet Line. Almost 100 Comet Line workers, including Peggy van Lier, one of my guides in Brussels, and Elvere Morelle, the nurse who had managed our hiding place in Paris, had been arrested. Peggy spoke excellent German and carried pictures in her purse of pre-war friends in Germany. Because of this, she had managed to convince her captors that she knew nothing about escape organizations. When they released her, she entered the first church she came to, burst into tears and knelt to pray. Peggy, along with Georges and Albert, the man who had escorted Silva and Whicher to my hiding place in Brussels (his real name was Prince Albert de Ligne), later escaped to Gibraltar, crossing the Pyrenees in much the same way that I had. Elvere Morelle spent the rest of the war in concentration camps, but survived.

In January 1943, two key members of the Comet Line were caught. Dédée and Francia Usandizanga, the Basque woman who had fed us our last meal before we crossed the Pyrenees, were arrested in Francia's home. A Spanish smuggler had betrayed them to the Gestapo. Three airmen, one British and two Americans, were also in Francia's home, planning to cross the mountains. Dédée was now in prison. When Prince Albert de Ligne learned from Count d'Oultremont that I was in England, he contacted me in London and we had a long talk over dinner. He told me Nemo, the man who had questioned me so carefully when I arrived in Brussels to make sure that I was not a German agent posing as an RCAF airman, had been arrested, along with two friends.

Back in Colerne, I received happier news from the home front. There were letters from many friends and acquaintances in Canada who had read in the newspapers that I was no longer missing. One of the most pleasant surprises in the mail was a package from a Ross woman in Quebec who had gone to Mount Allison with me. She had sent me a pound of maple butter — a priceless treat in wartime England. The next morning, I decided that I should share my bounty with the five officers who sat at my table at breakfast. The maple butter created such a sensation, everybody at breakfast — about 50 in all — begged for a taste. I watched as my maple butter faded away in front of my eyes.

Of course, I also wrote letters back home. One of them was to the Red Cross to thank them for some socks I had received months earlier. The label on the socks read "Moncton branch of the Red Cross," so I guessed that a woman in the Moncton area had knit them. My letter made the local newspapers, under the heading "Praises Red Cross Socks." I said that the socks had served me well, especially when I lost my flying boot when my aircraft had crashed, and I had had to trudge through the fields in Holland with a boot on one foot and only a sock on the other. "They have proved extremely serviceable," I concluded, "and are apparently indestructible. I am still wearing them."

In May 1943 I found out I was going home. I was being posted to the Repatriation Centre in Rockcliffe, Ontario. I flew my last aircraft in England — a Swordfish — on May 7. Shortly afterwards, I sailed to New York on the *Queen Elizabeth*, which had been converted into a troopship. Since this was a fast ship, it travelled without escort, since the likelihood of a U-boat being able to intercept it was not very great. Each state room had six to eight bunks, so there were perhaps five or six times as many passengers as the ship would carry in peace time. The meals were served continuously, and it took 10 to 12 hours to feed everyone on board. The results were that each person got two meals a day. There were lifeboat drills, so that everyone knew where to go if torpedoed. Everyone wore a life perserver at all times. They were called Mae Wests — the reason for this name was obvious when the life jackets were inflated. The passengers were mostly airmen from Britain going to Canada for training, but there were also a few English war brides. The latter were astonished, as we came into New York harbour, to see all the bright lights, and the brightly coloured cars and taxis, something one never saw in England. We were, of course, thankful to have made it safely across the Atlantic.

On arriving at Rockcliffe, I was given leave to visit my parents. It was a joyous reunion. During the visit, my parents told me a bit about the emotional roller-coaster ride they had endured the previous summer. First, they had received the dreaded news that I had been shot down. Then their hopes for my survival had soared when they had found out that the crew had been captured and taken to a prisoner-of-war camp. Later, my parents obtained the addresses of the families of some of my crew members and had their hopes dashed again: they discovered that my crew believed that I had been killed when our plane went down in flames. Finally, in August, my parents learned that I was alive and well. The message came in a somewhat roundabout way, because telephones had not yet been installed throughout all of rural Prince Edward Island, and my parents did not have a phone. When I sent my coded cable from Gibraltar to my sister Catherine in Saint John, she phoned John Alec Ross, who lived in Ocean View, four miles from our farm. He was a special friend of my father's and our neighbour with the nearest telephone. Catherine told him I was alive and well and asked him to relay the good news to my parents. John Alec was having lunch when the phone rang. He immediately jumped in his car, rushed to my parents' place and told them that their prayers had been answered. He was so excited about this news that it was only then that he noticed that he was still holding a half-eaten sandwich in his hand.

Making it home was a crowning satisfaction — here I was among family, friends and scenes of my childhood. I had sometimes thought that I would never see home again — I had a new lease on life. I spent a happy three weeks on the farm, along with my brother and sisters, who had come to welcome me home. They were all in a festive mood, prepared to kill the fatted calf. Strangely, I did not feel in a mood to celebrate, although I did my best to join in. What I really wanted was peace and quiet, a chance to absorb the scenes of my childhood and to relive my earliest memories. I think it was during this time that I began to form the almost subconscious wish to live my life on the land on which my grandparents had pioneered and where they had built their log cabin home. The summer months of the previous year seemed like a bad dream, but my thoughts were often with my friends in the Comet Line, and I longed to know how the surviving members were doing.

Duty in Canada

In June 1943, while we were on the farm in Lewis celebrating my brother Murdoch's 31st birthday, a Belgian traitor betrayed the remnants of the Comet Line. The traitor was working for the Comet Line under the name of Jean Masson, but his real name was Jacques Desourbrie. He turned five Resistance workers over to the Gestapo, including Dédée's father, Frédéric de Jongh, and Raymonde Coache, whom I remembered with such fondness from the days when she and her husband, René, had sheltered me in their Paris apartment. The party of airmen the Comet Line had entrusted to "Jean Masson" were also arrested, but they were only made prisoners of war. A much worse fate awaited their civilian helpers.

In September of that year, the man I knew as Nemo was killed. Nemo, whose real name was Baron Jean Greindl, ran the Belgium part of the Comet Line. Nemo had been arrested in February, and in May he had been moved to the Caserne d'artillerie at Etterbeek. This was an act contrary to international law; the installation at Etterbeek was a target of significance to

Allied bombers. On September 7, a single Allied bomb fell on the barracks at Etterbeek and Nemo was killed.

Six weeks later, the order came from Berlin for the execution of one of our guides, Eric de Menton de Horne, as well as seven of Nemo's friends from the Cantine suédoise, the food-distribution agency Nemo had run. At 6:00 a.m. on October 20, the Austrian chaplain of their prison brought them two hunks of bread and cheese. Then they were taken to a rifle range in Brussels. As the wind howled and the rain beat down on the condemned men, they lined up, eyes uncovered, and said their last prayers. The rifle squad opened fire. The day before, Eric de Menton de Horne had written to his family: "Tomorrow I shall make the great journey ... and you can be proud of me. I regret nothing. I die for the ideal we have all shared. Keep smiling."

While these ghastly horrors of the Nazi occupation were taking place in Belgium and France, life went on relatively normally in Canada, except for vastly expanded armed forces, full war production in factories, Victory bond drives, no new passenger cars and food rationing. On my return in June 1943 to Rockcliffe, just east of Ottawa on the Ottawa River, I had been posted to a unit on that station. Rockcliffe was a peacetime station, located on some high ground overlooking the river and Gatineau on the Quebec side. Although it was greatly expanded during the war, with many temporary buildings added, the officers' mess was based on an old country home and in some ways retained the air of a country club.

Since I was the senior unmarried officer at Rockcliffe, I fell heir to a comfortable and convenient room in an annex adjoining the officers' mess. Like other military bases in Canada, Rockcliffe offered a high standard of food and accommodation compared with wartime English bases. I considered myself to be living in luxury. One Sunday afternoon, I was station senior duty officer. It happened that an afternoon tea was being held in the officers' mess for some special guests. I found myself chatting with a woman who complained about how terrible the war was becoming. "In what way do you think the situation is getting worse?" I asked. "Oh, those awful meatless Tuesdays," she replied, "when the government expects us to eat only fish or fowl." I did not bring to her attention the fact that the war had more gruesome aspects than meatless Tuesdays.

In July 1943, I was promoted to commanding officer of the Test and Development Establishment at Rockcliffe. The main purpose of the unit, located in a hangar across the airfield from the main station, was to do prototype installations of new equipment in various types of aircraft, test the equipment thoroughly and write up blueprints and directions for the installation. The unit had a wide variety of aircraft, but usually just one of each kind. This situation required pilots with a lot of experience and mechanics who knew how to deal with different kinds of aircraft, including flying boats and amphibious planes. I found my new responsibilities interesting and challenging, and the people under my command were generally capable and dedicated to the war effort. Morale in the unit was high. The women members of the Test and Development Squadron, who normally paraded as a separate squadron with all the other women on the station, asked for special permission to parade with us.

I had a chance to socialize with other officers and their wives at the dances held from time to time in the officers' mess; the entire station went on parade, by squadron, every Friday morning; and the central band of the RCAF, also stationed at Rockcliffe, played stirring music for the parades — for me, one of the high points of the week.

Shortly after I arrived in Rockcliffe, I received an invitation to a dinner party at Rideau Hall, the residence of the Governor General. The hosts were the Governor General, the Right Honourable Earl of Athlone, and his wife, Princess Alice. This was a new experience for me. I was provided with a car and driver from the station for the evening. The driver was a young airman of about 19 who was new to Ottawa. The evening was a new experience for him, too. He had never even heard of Rideau Hall. Fortunately, I remembered going past the grounds a few years previously to visit my brother, Murdoch, at the RCMP barracks in Rockcliffe. I also flew over Rideau Hall nearly every day. I had expected there would be at least 20 or 30 guests. I was astonished to find that the party consisted of only seven guests, including a cabinet minister and his wife and two other couples I had never heard of before. It turned out to be a pleasant and completely informal evening. We even played parlour games such as Twenty Questions for a while.

Life in the military suited me well. I enjoyed flying, and I had a secure job with opportunity for advancement and good pay; I was making $12 a day plus living expenses. If I had had two lives to live, I would have spent one in the service; however, since I was limited to one lifetime, I wanted to make the most of it. My wartime experiences had changed my outlook greatly. I had lost all interest in pursuing a career as an industrial chemist, and I wanted to do something more constructive than hold down a secure job in the air force. I thought that it was extraordinary that I was still alive and that as so many people had risked their lives to keep me that way, I owed a lot to the selfless acts of others. I felt if I could do something to improve other people's lot in life, I was deeply obligated to do so.

A door opened in that direction in the summer of 1943. A federal election was expected the next year, and the Conservative Party was getting ready to hold a nominating convention in Charlottetown for the dual riding of Queens. A number of prominent Conservatives in the riding, including Robert Cotton, a prominent businessperson, thought that a serving member of the armed forces should be among those on the nomination ballot. A considerable number of people in the armed services were being nominated to run in the next election. They included such people as Davie Fulton, René Jutras, James Sinclair, Douglas Harkness, and many more. Newspaper reports that I was missing in action, and the much more unusual news that I was safely back in England, had brought my existence to the attention of many Islanders. The fact that I was from a prominent Conservative family and that my father had run in several provincial elections also spoke in my favour. The consensus was that I should be asked to stand for nomination.

In Prince Edward Island, there were two single federal ridings and the dual riding of Queens, in which I lived. All these ridings had elected nothing but Liberals since 1935, and since Confederation, Liberal candidates had won 53 times, while Conservative candidates had won only 20 times. So Conservative candidates were always considered to be the underdogs in federal elections on the Island. Dick Bell, who was in charge of the Progressive Conservative national office, phoned me one day and said he wanted to talk to me. "Would you consider standing for nomination?" he asked. I said I would take a couple of days to think it over. The idea of serving in public life at some point was an appealing one. It seemed to me an avenue by which I could contribute something to humanity. It would also give me a chance to go back to my Island home, renew friendships there and make new ones.

I still longed to be close to the land, preferably where my grandparents had settled. Besides, my parents were getting old, my mother was not well and I wanted to be able to help my parents on the farm. I was the only member of my family in a position to do that. The rest were married and settled elsewhere. I realized that running for political office would have its drawbacks. For one thing, it was expensive. I would have to spend a lot of my own money on the campaign, and if I were elected, I would be taking a cut in pay. At that time, members of Parliament were paid only $4,000 a session, which usually lasted four months. If it went on longer than that, there was no extra pay. MPs received no retirement pension. They did get $2,000 a year in tax-free expenses, plus a free pass for travel by coach on the train. It did not add up to what I was making in the military. I decided, on balance, that it was worth taking the risk as I did not think there was much chance I would be nominated this time, much less sent to Parliament. Although my father had run for the Conservatives in five provincial elections, I was a virtual unknown and not yet 30 years of age. All I really had to do, I told myself, was arrange a few days' leave, appear at the convention and make a five-minute speech. I told Dick Bell I would do it.

The convention was held in November 1943 in the old Empire Theatre in Charlottetown, above the market on Queen's Square. Delegates from every polling division in Queens County were there. Major T. B. Rogers, president of the provincial Conservative association, was the chair, and Hon. Gordon Graydon, leader of the Opposition in the House of Commons and president of the Progressive Conservative Association of Canada, was the guest speaker. The riding was one of two in Canada at that time that elected two members to the House of Commons; the other was Halifax. Five nominations were placed before the convention: Walter S. Grant, W. Chester S. McLure, Matthew W. Wood, John H. Myers and my own. When the ballots were counted, I was astonished to learn that I led the poll with 391 votes. McLure was next with 284. That meant that we would be running as a team in the next election.

In the meantime, I had to return to my RCAF duties in Rockcliffe. As 1944 arrived, more and more of my friends, acquaintances and relatives lost their lives. In late March 1944, I received sad news about James Wernham, the navigator on my crew when we were shot down. He and the other four members of my crew had spent the past two years as prisoners of war in Stalag Luft III. On the night of March 24, he took part in the Great Escape from the prison camp, in which 79 officers crawled through a tunnel they had dug. Unfortunately, all but three were recaptured, and 50 were shot on orders from Hitler. James Wernham was among those who were murdered. A little later I learned that Flight Lieutenant Langford, who had been a student of mine in Camp Borden in August 1940, was also among those murdered. A couple of days later, Dédée's father, Frédéric de Jongh, along with two French friends, died at the hands of a Gestapo firing squad. The Germans were becoming ever more desperate and vindictive. This was no doubt a factor in Hitler's decision to execute prisoners of war and civilian prisoners of the Gestapo.

When I had landed in Holland in June of 1942, the Nazi power was at its zenith. The German armies on the Eastern Front were at their greatest point of advance. The Africa Corps was at El Alamein. Although the United States had entered the war the previous December, its massive power was just beginning to be felt in Europe. At that point it was not at all certain to the people of occupied Europe that they would ever be liberated from Nazi oppression. So it was only a firm faith that right would eventually triumph over the powerful evil that was Hitler that motivated such wonderful people as Dédée, Frédéric, Nemo, Eric, Father Kloeg, the Pagie family and many others to do everything they could to help downed airmen — with a dedication that approached religious zeal.

As time passed, things began to change. The German surrender at Stalingrad on February 2, 1943, was the first major indication to those in occupied Europe that Germany was not invincible. Resistance workers in occupied Europe were buoyed by Allied success in North Africa, the greatly increased bombing of Germany by the Commonwealth air forces at night and the American air force by day, the Allied invasion of Italy and the general trend of the war. By early 1944, it looked as though liberation was not far off. Occupied peoples became even more anxious to help the Allied cause; Nazi retribution became even more brutal. In spite of betrayals, and the murder of many Resistance workers, the Comet Line continued to function. On June 4, 1944, two days before the Allies invaded occupied Europe, it sent three Americans and two RAF airmen to Spain.

On June 6, an officer down the hall from me, an early riser, awakened me. D-Day had arrived. The radio was broadcasting reports on the invasion. Everybody listened intently to the news during those crucial days in June. People in Prince Edward Island were especially interested in information about the North Nova Scotia Highlanders and other units in which many of their friends and neighbours were serving.

In Europe, the spirit of the Comet Line continued. The inimitable Tante Go, the woman in charge of the Basque end of the Comet Line, carried on. By this time, Florentino had led more than 200 airmen over the mountains to safety. About a month after D-Day, he crossed once more with messages for Allied Intelligence. On the return trip, just as he was descending to Urrugne at three o'clock in the morning, he was ambushed and had one leg badly smashed by machine-gun fire. He was taken to police headquarters and questioned in French, Spanish and Basque, but he refused to talk. He was then sent to a civilian hospital in Bayonne.

Within 24 hours, Tante Go, through her information network, knew exactly what had happened, where Florentino was and even the name of the young man in the next bed. One day she visited the young man with a gift of some fruit. As she was about to leave, she dropped her purse between the two beds and, stooping to pick it up, whispered, "Two o'clock." At two o'clock, three men in German Army uniforms came to the hospital to move Florentino by ambulance to another place. The three men — in reality, Tante Go's husband and two of his friends — took Florentino to a safe place on the outskirts of Anglet. It was here, a few weeks later, that he was liberated by the Allies he had served so well.

In early March of 1944, I had been promoted to the rank of wing commander. Had I chosen to remain in England, I would have reached that rank more than a year sooner; dozens of officers were being killed or taken prisoner virtually every night and survivors had to be promoted to fill the vacancies. However, the rate of promotion was of secondary importance to me. The big plus was my continued enjoyment of the gift of life. Barring an accident, it looked as if I was going to survive the war, and even live a normal life span — a prospect that on many occasions in the past few years had seemed highly improbable.

Life for me continued in fairly routine fashion in the summer of 1944. Mark 10 Lancaster aircraft were being manufactured in Malton, Ontario, and in July they were being equipped with a Martin mid-upper turret fitted with .5-inch machine guns. I was the only available experienced Lancaster pilot, so in addition to my regular duties, I had to do about 40 hours of flying Lancaster 10 aircraft with the Martin turret, including flights to the Martin factory in Baltimore, Maryland. The tests and the flying in connection with them took up all the month of August, but when September arrived, I reverted full-time to administering the Test and Development Establishment.

That September I received a card from Bill Kerr, one of my old aircrew, from Stalag Luft III. I was trying to keep as close contact as possible with my aircrew. I had arranged for my sister Catherine in Saint John to send parcels to the prison camp on my behalf, and I visited the parents of the Canadian men whenever possible.

Kriegsgefangenenlager
Sept. 3, 1944

Dear Angus:

Received your parcel last week Angus and will be able to tell you why it was appreciated so much at this new camp when we meet again. Jock Shields has been repatriated so you should be hearing from him shortly. We all hope the world is treating you well and hope some day we may be able to repay you for your kindly visit to our people. Mother certainly was surprised. Goodbye for now and best of luck.

Bill Kerr

In April of 1945, Canadian prime minister William Lyon Mackenzie King called a federal election for June 11. All military personnel running in the election were given a few weeks' leave without pay, so I took my leave and went home to Prince Edward Island. In my last flight before leaving Rockcliffe, we tested survival suits. I thought this was a fitting prelude to an election campaign.

Queens, the riding in which Chester McLure and I were running, was one of two dual ridings remaining in Canada. It was a terrible system. All the candidates were listed on the ballot in alphabetical order, and the voter could choose any two — or just one, for that matter. The candidates who came in first and second were elected. The party expected its two candidates to co-operate closely and win together as a team, but the voting system had the effect of putting us in competition with each other.

My running mate, Chester McLure, was a portly Charlotte-town businessperson who had been a Conservative member of Parliament in the early 1930s. We were running against two sitting members — Cyrus MacMillan, a native of Wood Islands who was dean of the faculty of Arts and Science at McGill; and

Lester Douglas, a Charlottetown businessperson who had run the Strathcona Hotel on Water Street. Both were highly regarded, strong candidates, and Queens had generally elected Liberals since about 1921. McLure had the notion — an accurate one, as it turned out — that one of the Liberals would be sure to come first, which meant that he and I would both be aiming for second place. I was surprised to find that McLure, who had such a fine public image, was something less than a team player. In fact, to put it mildly, he was desperately committed to his own political survival. That came to light early in the campaign.

The previous fall, Flight Lieutenant William Bracken, a pilot in the Test and Development Establishment, had asked me to be an usher at his wedding in Summerside in May. He was marrying Miriam Nicholson, with whom I had gone to high school in Summerside. I had gladly agreed. As soon as the election was called, I told McLure about this commitment, which meant I had to be away the Saturday of the wedding, in the middle of the campaign. He was free, of course, to work without me that day. One of our poll workers from the Southport area told me later that McLure had canvassed in his area that Saturday. When the poll worker asked McLure why I was not there, the reply was, "Oh, he's up in Summerside seeing some girl." When I told the poll worker the real reason for my absence, he was outraged. Two or three other similar incidents took place during the campaign. I ignored them, although they probably damaged my reputation to some extent. I felt that these unbecoming tactics stemmed from McLure's desperate need to be elected. It convinced me that people who gave up their normal careers to serve in Parliament should get a pension at retirement age to compensate them for their loss of private income.

In the meantime, there were more momentous events taking place in the world. On May 8, 1945, V-E Day arrived, signalling the end of the war in Europe and resulting in great jubilation in

Canada and other Allied countries. Now people began to think more about the war with Japan. A number of Islanders had been captured at Hong Kong and were prisoners of the Japanese. It was expected that military personnel would soon be transferred from Europe to the Far East. On May 12, a heading in the Charlottetown *Guardian* announced: "Victory Bond Drive Over the Top." I do not know what effect, if any, the end of the war in Europe had on the outcome of the election. Our campaign committee carried on with an active advertising campaign, with full-page advertisements nearly every day in the newspapers. The Liberals, under Prime Minister Mackenzie King, had been in power continuously for 10 years. Our slogan was, "It's time for a change."

Just before voting day, I received a letter from an overseas friend and benefactor — Jane Pagie, whose family had sheltered me in their houseboat in Holland. The letter was addressed to "Angus MacLean, RCAF, Canada," and had been forwarded to me by RCAF headquarters in Ottawa. Jane wrote that her father had been arrested by Dutch authorities as a suspected Nazi collaborator. Well-meaning Dutch people had reported him, having observed him appearing to fraternize with the Germans during the war. When I was on the houseboat, the neighbourhood was frequently teeming with German troops from a nearby training base. They would be out on training exercises, which often took the form of mock battles between two German forces. To allay any suspicions they might have about his sheltering Allied servicemen, Mr. Pagie pretended to be friendly with the Germans. I was distressed about Mr. Pagie's misfortune, especially after the terrible risks his family had taken to help me and other airmen. I wrote immediately to the Department of External Affairs in Ottawa. Some contents of this letter had to be rather vague because the details of my escape, and the activities of escape organizations, were still classified as top-secret.

162 Dorchester Street,
Charlottetown, P.E.I.
June 4th, 1945

SECRET
Department of External Affairs,
Ottawa, Ontario

Dear Sirs:

Yesterday I received a letter in broken English from Jane Pagie of Ryksweg 188 E, Orthen ('s Bosch) Holland (N.B.). The gist of this letter was that this girl's father is under suspicion by the Dutch Police as having been collaborating with the Germans during the occupation of Holland. This girl asks that I should come to her father's rescue as a witness to his innocence in this regard.

I wish to state that I know Mr. Pagie intimately and that I spent several weeks in his company in Holland in 1942, and further that Mr. Pagie has on many occasions risked his life for the Allied cause. Any suggestion of him having collaborated with the Germans I feel is completely without foundation. If he has appeared to have been friendly with the Germans during the occupation of Holland, this was only for the purpose of deceiving them into believing that he was their friend.

I would be deeply grateful for any action you might be able to take which would help to establish with the Dutch government Mr. Pagie's innocence of collaborating with the Germans. The most expedient action possible would be appreciated, as the situation is probably causing grave anxiety to Mr. Pagie and his family, if not actual danger.

I would further take the liberty of recommending that Mr. Pagie's work for his country and the Allied cause should be recognized by his Government or by the British Government by the granting of some suitable honour or award.

Mr. Pagie has, at great personal risk and under the most difficult conditions, frequently worked in the interests of those who were fighting against the Germans.

If any further information is required from me I would be only too glad to furnish it. My address until June 12th will be 162 Dorchester Street, Charlottetown, P.E.I. My address after that date will be RCAF Officer's Mess, Rockcliffe, Ontario.

Yours sincerely,

J. Angus MacLean,
Wing Commander
O/C Test and Development Establishment
RCAF Station, Rockcliffe, Ontario

Two days later, the acting under secretary of State for External Affairs replied.

Department of External Affairs
Canada
Ottawa, June 6th, 1945

Dear Sir:

I have your letter of June 4th concerning the case of Mr. Pagie who is believed to be under suspicion by the Nether-lands Police. This matter is being brought to the attention of the Netherlands authorities and if any further informa-tion is desired, I note that you will be glad to supply it.

Yours very truly,

Acting Under Secretary of State for External Affairs

Wing Commander J. Angus MacLean
162 Dorchester Street
Charlottetown, P.E.I.

As a result of this intervention, Mr. Pagie was cleared of all suspicion. Being able to help this man who had risked so much for me was one of the more satisfying moments of my life.

Most of my attention in that period, however, had to be focused on the election campaign. In early June, a provincial election in Ontario gave us a morale boost. The Conservatives under George Drew, who had been premier for two years, were returned to power with a large majority. McLure and I kept busy calling on electors, visiting poll committees and speaking at rallies a couple of nights a week. As election day approached, our provincial organization stepped up its advertising: "It's Time for a Change" and "Elect McLure, MacLean, McPhee and Strong." Colonel Ernest Strong was the Conservative candidate in Prince and a leading Charlottetown lawyer; Frank McPhee, who had been a Conservative MLA, was running in Kings.

The election results on the Island were close. The day after the election, Lester Douglas led the polls with 8,997 votes; Chester McLure came second with 8,698; and Cyrus MacMillan and I were tied with 8,626 votes each. When the votes of men and women in the armed services were counted, Douglas still led, McLure was second and I came third, 40 votes behind McLure. Although the national prospects of the Conservative Party had seemed to be much improved, the final results were disappointing. The Conservatives, led by John Bracken, gained 28 seats, all but five in Ontario, but the Liberals still had a slim majority. In Queens the Liberal majorities were reduced by more than 1,000 votes, which was an excellent improvement from a Conservative standpoint, considering that voting patterns were far less fluid or fickle than they later became.

Like many of our supporters, I was disappointed that I had not been elected when I came so close, but I was pleased that I had done so well. After all, I had not even expected to be nominated. For me, the defeat was in no way crushing. The war was still on in the Pacific, and I had plenty of responsibilities as long as I was still in the air force. Anyhow, my way of thinking was that I would never enter any contest in which I could not gracefully accept defeat. The voters of Queens had spoken and that was that. The day after the election, three of my officers were on duty in the Maritimes in a Hudson aircraft. I joined them in Summerside and flew back to Rockcliffe with them in time to report for duty at the end of my leave.

England no longer needed more bomber aircraft, but radio location equipment installed by the Canadian National Research Council was now being tested. In July and August, I had to do some Lancaster flying. Then suddenly V-J Day arrived. Atom bombs were dropped on Hiroshima and Nagasaki, and on August 15, 1945, Japan surrendered. The Second World War was over.

Demobilization began. Prisoners of war held by the Japanese were being released; most Canadians serving in Europe were returning home. Almost everybody in the service was looking forward to civilian life. Ex-servicemen and women were receiving grants to go to university. The government was selling surplus jeeps to farmers for $370. One day in late September, my telephone rang. It was a friend of mine, an officer in the Postings and Careers Branch at air force headquarters. "Angus, you know that posting overseas that you've been expecting for the past two years?" he began. "It's just come through. You are being posted to Europe, to a non-flying administrative post."

My assignment, it turned out, in some respects was an ideal one. In the last year of the war, as Europe began to be liberated, the RAF had set up small units in Europe to try to determine what had become of the more than 40,000 aircrew who had never been accounted for. It was important to find out, so that estates could be settled, widows could know they were legally widows and families could find out where their sons were buried. As the war ended, and all of Europe became available for this research, these units were expanded into much larger Commonwealth units. I was to become officer commanding the No. 2 Missing Research and Enquiry Unit, with temporary headquarters in Brussels. All personnel in these units either had to be bilingual in English and another European language, or had to be evaders who had themselves been posted as missing but had escaped to Allied territory.

I was eager to take on this job. My new posting would give me a chance to help in the search for missing aircrew — many of whom were friends or former students of mine — and that was an important job in itself. A bonus for me was that I could also try to track down some other people who had been in my thoughts and prayers for the past three years — the brave civilians who had risked their lives to keep me alive.

CHAPTER TEN

Missing Persons

Before I left for Europe in late October 1945, I spent a couple of weeks on the farm in Lewis with my parents. My father drove me to the train station in Charlottetown when my leave was over. On the way to town, we passed a neighbour, Louis McKenna, who was delivering the mail with a horse and road cart. I remembered that, six years before, when my father had driven me to Charlottetown to report for duty with the RCAF, we had passed the same mailman, driving the same horse and cart. "I would have thought Louis would have been in one of the services," I remarked. "What do you mean?" my father asked. "He was overseas in the army for nearly five years." I realized then that our neighbour had quickly reverted to his place in civilian life — and seemed to be savouring it.

Life in Prince Edward Island, as in the rest of Canada, was gradually getting back to normal. As demobilization took place, men and women in uniform were becoming a common sight in the train stations and on the streets of Charlottetown. Exceptionally large numbers of Islanders had enlisted in the services; the

Island, in fact, had the highest percentage of volunteers from any province except British Columbia. Many, of course, did not return. From my own church congregation, eight men had made the supreme sacrifice. Many Islanders were also among the tens of thousands of servicemen who were still unaccounted for in Europe. Now I was on my way to help track down these missing Allied servicemen, a task that I knew would be a formidable challenge.

In Halifax, I boarded a troopship loaded with British servicemen who had been prisoners of war in the Far East. They had sailed to Vancouver, crossed Canada by train and were now heading home across the Atlantic. On the ship, I was among a small group of Canadians who were being posted to various places in Europe for the Missing Research and Enquiry Unit. As we pulled out of Halifax, a voice on the loudspeaker informed us that all troops aboard the ship had to line up for vitamin shots. This was because the former prisoners of war were getting vitamin shots to help counteract the effects of their deficient diet in the Japanese prison camps. No exceptions were being made for us; we were all getting our shots, whether we needed them or not. A similar bureaucratic blind spot showed up at the dinner table. One day, the messing staff had the insensitivity to serve rice. This, of course, disgusted the former prisoners of war, who never wanted to see rice again in their lives. In most cases, the former prisoners of war were very thin and suffering from malnutrition. They had been prisoners for varying lengths of time. Any I spoke to had only one thing on their minds — getting home to England. They were loath to talk about their experiences in the camps, and the subject was rarely discussed.

When we arrived in Britain, the new personnel who were to serve with the No. 2 Missing Research and Enquiry Unit took another ship from Tilbury to Zeebrugge and then on to Brussels by train, where we absorbed a small unit that was already operating from Brussels. Shortly after we arrived, the town major, a British official, arranged for us to set up our headquarters in an apartment building at 23 avenue de la toison d'or (the Avenue of the Golden Fleece). It was part of the avenue that surrounds the original city, where the medieval city wall had been. The first floor contained our kitchen and messes, the second was reserved for offices and the remaining seven upper floors were our living quarters. We also had a detachment in The Hague, in Holland.

Our area of responsibility was to be Belgium, Holland, Luxembourg, Czechoslovakia and the area that was then the French-occupied zone of Germany, in the southwest section of that country. The unit was composed of officers from the British, Australian, New Zealand and Canadian air forces, and non-commissioned ranks from the British and Canadian air forces. I found it strange — but exhilarating — to walk the streets of Brussels as a free man. Previously, Brussels to me had been associated with my time as a fugitive — hiding in a basement flat from the Nazis and their sadistic propensities. Now the city was a place where I could take care of some unfinished business.

The work of the Missing Research and Enquiry Unit was a great challenge. There was no rule book and a limited amount of experience on the subject, so we had to be inventive and persistent in our search for the missing airmen. Many, of course, had gone down in the North Sea; the bodies of some had washed up on the coasts of Holland and Belgium. In Holland, one of our teams learned of a crash that had happened in a flooded area. After the water receded, there was no sign of the wreck. We discovered that the soil was so muddy and fluid, the aircraft had sunk out of sight. It had to be excavated to remove the bodies in it.

There were also many unmarked graves to be found. From captured German documents, we detected that the Germans had generally buried identifiable bodies in civilian graveyards. Quite often, the local people could tell us many details, such as the date of the crash, but they could rarely answer the key question of where the victims were buried. They knew only that the Germans had left the area with the bodies, so matching crashes with graves was a huge problem. Flight Lieutenant George Nadeau, one of our excellent officers, discussed this problem with me one day. We decided to make a graph from the data on the German documents. By this process, we discovered that, at any given time, the Germans were using only two civilian cemeteries in all of Belgium to bury aircrew. After using two cemeteries for about a month, they moved on to two others and so on. From that point on, once we knew the date that an aircraft had crashed, we could narrow our search down to two cemeteries.

In some cases, an aircraft had crashed with bombs aboard or had exploded in mid-air. Then the crew had been blown to bits, and the Germans had buried the remains they could find in a mass grave. In these cases, the first problem was to match the mass grave to an aircraft. For example, a crew of seven might be buried in a common grave as only four or five. The army grave service would then have to exhume the remains, and one of the unit officers would have to examine the remains in detail to determine how many crew they represented. Sometimes, this could be established through identity disks or laundry marks — we learned that laundry services in England assigned a unique number for every customer — but sometimes our unit had to resort to the grim task of counting particular bones. Mass graves were usually in civilian graveyards. The Germans tended to bury unidentified intact bodies on German bases. For example, there were more than 500 graves of unknown airmen on the German Night Fighter Base at St. Trond. We had them all exhumed and were able to identify all but one.

We had one case over which the British Air Ministry was being pressured by a local member of Parliament. A crew of seven had parachuted over the Ardennes in the south of Belgium. Six of the crew became prisoners of war; the seventh never reappeared. I put George Nadeau on the case. Researching reports of the RAF interrogation of the surviving six crew members, he pinpointed as accurately as possible where they had landed. Then he applied the parachuting sequence of the aircraft and found that there was a gap in his diagram where the missing airman would have landed. George then enlisted the help of a local forester. After a couple of days' search, they found notes that the airman had written, saying that he had broken both legs on landing in this remote area and was unable to move. Then they found his bones. They had been scattered over the area by wild boars.

During my off-duty hours, I devoted much of my energy to a search of a different kind. In the past couple of years, I had lost all contact with any of the Resistance workers who had helped me. I still did not know the real names of most of them, and I had intentionally not taken note of any addresses of places where I had been sheltered. I had wanted to ensure that I would be unable to divulge this information to the Gestapo if I were captured and tortured. But now I was determined to track down my helpers. I felt that it was important to let these people know how eternally grateful I was for what they had done for me and for other Allied servicemen. In many cases, of all the people they had helped and sheltered, I would be the first who had the opportunity to come back and thank them, and let them know that the escape attempt had been a success.

I had a chance to express my gratitude in a formal way during the first few months I was in Brussels. The Allied authorities had organized a ceremony to pay tribute to the many people who had worked in the underground for the cause of freedom. I was asked to make a statement, which I did in my inadequate French: "Ladies and gentleman, it is a very great pleasure for me to take part in this ceremony today. I am one of the 1,800 British Commonwealth service personnel which you helped to escape under the German occupation. I am sure that if it had been possible, all the personnel would have come to Brussels today to see you officially recognized. Because they can't be here today, I would like to thank you, on their behalf and mine, for all that you have done for us. Ladies and gentlemen, with all my heart, thank you."

I also wanted to express my gratitude in person to the helpers who had saved my life. My first stroke of luck came when I discovered that a British Intelligence officer was stationed in Brussels. To my great delight, he told me that Dédée had survived and was now living in Brussels. Dédée looked like her old self, in spite of two nightmarish years in the Ravensbruk and Mathausen concentration camps, including months in solitary confinement. She still retained her lighthearted spirit, as well. She could find humour in almost any situation, even in the horrors of Ravensbruk. She told me that the camp was so crowded, the women had to sleep two to a cot. Because the beds were so narrow, each occupant had to lie on her side all night. One night, she said, she was amused to hear the women in the bunk above her in the midst of a disagreement. "Look at her," one of them said of her bunkmate. "She's lying on her back, like a queen."

Dédée gave me the address of the Neves, the couple who had sheltered me in their apartment, at 144 avenue Lambertmont. When I visited them, they told me that they had fled to the south of France and worked as farm labourers with false identity cards until France was liberated. I also visited Mondo, the Belgian engineer who had taken me to the Neves' home. He was one of the few helpers I knew who had avoided the clutches of the Gestapo. Sadly, he told me that Schalenborg, the other engineer from Eisden, who had lent me his copy of *Silas Marner*, had not been so fortunate. He had died in a concentration camp. His widow, a dentist by profession, had gone into a deep depression as a result of her husband's death. I tried to visit her, but she was not seeing anyone; however, I was able to make a statement on her behalf to MI9, telling them how her husband had helped me. As a result, she received some financial assistance from the British government.

I visited the Peeters family, who had sheltered me on their farm, and the following summer I had the pleasure of being a guest at Albert Peeters' wedding.

I also went to Paris to visit René and Raymonde Coache at 71 rue de Nanterre, where they had sheltered me for several days. Raymonde had been one of the Comet Line workers arrested when the Belgian traitor known as Jean Masson had betrayed them. She was imprisoned in Belgium for a time. Then the Germans put her and other prisoners on a train bound for Germany. While she was on the train, the Allies liberated Brussels. Belgian crews managed to delay her train until the Allies were able to overtake it and liberate it. René had escaped to England. Later he parachuted into France to work with the Resistance as a radio operator. René and Raymonde both arrived back at their flat on the same day. Until that day, neither had known that the other was alive. I rejoiced in the survival of these wonderful people. (Twenty years later, I had the pleasure of visiting the Coaches again in their flat. Their adopted daughter, then 18 years old, was amazed to see her parents — and the stranger from Canada — burst into tears when I walked in the door. The perils of Nazi-occupied Europe forged lifelong bonds among the helpers and the helped.)

Matthieu Beelen, who had guided me across the border from Holland into Belgium, visited me in Brussels. He told me that he and some others had been arrested, imprisoned and given the *Nacht und Nebel* (Night and Fog) treatment — in which the Gestapo prevented anyone from knowing what had become of them.

Reinier Kloeg, the young student priest who had been my guide in Holland from Zaltbommel to Weert, had been arrested at his parents' home in Rotterdam in February 1943, six weeks before he was to be ordained. He spent nine months in a prison in Scheveningen and three more months in a prison in Utrecht. A German military court condemned him to death in February of 1944. At 5:00 a.m. on March 15, he wrote his farewell letter to his parents and brothers and sisters and went bravely to his execution at dawn.

Of course, I also went to Holland to see the Pagies, the Dutch family who had hidden me in their houseboat. They were now living in Orthen, as shellfire had destroyed their houseboat during the fighting that resulted in the liberation of Holland. Of all the wonderful people who were my helpers, the Pagies sheltered me and put their lives at risk on my behalf for a far longer period than anyone else. They had had to hide me and feed me from their own meagre resources without help from anyone outside the family. They did this simply because they believed it was the right thing to do, and that "right" would triumph in the end. This was an attitude shared by the many people who had helped me, but it may have been reinforced in the Pagie family because their ancestors were refugees from the Reign of Terror in France during the French Revolution.

During my stay in Brussels, our unit had a detachment in The Hague, which I visited on duty from time to time. But in spite of my many trips to Holland, I failed to find out the identity of the mystery man who had slipped me a train ticket to Weert and pointed out my next guide. This man had promised to try to get word to my parents that I was alive, and he had kept his promise. In September of 1942, my father received this cable from Switzerland: "In July your son was alive and well." I did not know whether the name of the sender on the cable was genuine. (It was not until much later that I learned that he was Adriaan Ferdinand van Goelst Meijer, and that he was a former major in the Dutch cavalry.)

I did have a reunion with a couple of other friends, Count Georges d'Oultremont and Prince Albert de Ligne. And, through Dédée, I met Franco (Jean-François Nothomb DSO), the dedicated young man who carried on the Comet Line after Dédée was arrested. We met in Brussels. Franco later became a priest and moved to America. (Several decades later, in 1970, he was a special guest at an annual meeting of the Canadian Branch of the Royal Air Force Escaping Society, in Kingston, Ontario.)

I also found out where Eric de Menton de Horne's home was, and I went there to visit his parents. Eric had been one of two guides who took me and James Whicher and Jeff Silva from Brussels to Paris in the summer of 1942. He was later captured by the Germans and executed. The family home was a lovely country mansion not far from St. Trond. The family had consisted of Eric, a sturdily built young man with fair hair and a ready smile, and an older brother and younger sister. His brother had joined the RAF in England and was killed in a flying accident. When his father arranged a memorial service for his dead son, the Gestapo arrested him, and he spent the rest of the war in concentration camps.

The Germans had taken over the de Menton de Horne home as an officers' mess, and the family deplored some of the damage that had been done to the house; however, they took satisfaction in saving the family car from the Germans. At the time of the German Blitzkrieg in 1940, they had hidden the car in a concrete pit used for storing turnips and had covered it with oats. Then they had disguised the pit by building a wall around it to form a grain bin. In all the years the Germans were around, they never suspected that a very desirable car was in their midst.

I was afraid that my visits to the estate were bringing back sad memories of Eric and his barbaric execution. However, the family seemed to enjoy seeing me, and I sensed that Eric's father, Ritter de Menton de Horne, took pleasure in showing me the farming part of their property, which he knew that I, as a farmer, appreciated. In the orchard, he showed me a huge cherry tree, the largest I had ever seen. When I asked what variety it was, he said it was so old, he thought it was a chance sport — an accidental hybrid — that may have grown from seed. It was so superior, people travelled from far afield to get cuttings to graft onto their own trees. Ritter de Menton de Horne was in poor health from his years in the concentration camps, and he died while I was still in Brussels.

My months in Brussels were bittersweet. I had the pleasure of again seeing Gwen, who was in the RCAF women's division and was stationed in England. She came to visit me with another friend in Brussels. I also found it gratifying to reaffirm bonds of friendship with people who had helped during the war, and to see that my friends were getting some recognition for their sacrifices. In the summer of 1946, for example, the British government invited Dédée to London in recognition for her role in returning more than 200 Allied airmen to Britain. I drove her to Calais, and from there she boarded a boat for London. At Buckingham Palace, King George VI decorated her with the George Medal. As a further token of appreciation, the undersecretary of State for Air presented her with a specially mounted clock from an RAF bomber. I also had the honour of contributing to the citation for the Distinguished Service Order that Britain conferred on Florentino, our Basque guide across the Pyrenees.

That summer, we were also reminded of personal tragedies. Two years earlier, Dédée's father, Frédéric, whom I had known as Paul, had been executed by a German firing squad. In July, his family had his body returned from Paris to Brussels. I had the sad honour of attending his funeral service. Another day, I represented the RCAF at a memorial mass in a village east of Brussels in memory of a Canadian airman who had been sheltered there. I drove to the village with a wreath of flowers. When I arrived, I learned that his name was Edward Blenkinsop. I knew at once who he was. He had been a student of mine when I was a flying instructor at No. 4 Service Flying Training School at Saskatoon in the fall of 1940. I remembered him as a bright, attractive young man from Victoria, British Columbia, with dark hair and an engaging personality. In fact, he was one of my favourite students.

From what I could learn from the local people in their limited English, the Germans had rounded up 70 young men from the village to work as forced labour in Hamburg. Blenkinsop posed as a local Belgian and went off to the labour camp rather than betray the people who had sheltered him. He thus saved them from being shot on the spot, which was the fate of many civilians caught helping Allied airmen. He died of tuberculosis in Belsen Concentration Camp. As I sat through the memorial service on a beautiful sunny day in an unfamiliar Flemish village, I recognized across the language barrier a quotation from the Gospel of St. John: "Greater love hath no man than this, that a man lay down his life for his friends." I could not hold back the tears.

In the fall of 1946, our headquarters moved to the French-occupied zone in the southwest of Germany. Our new offices were on the top floor of Schloss Schaumburg, an old castle about 50 miles southeast of Bonn. Beside the castle were our living quarters, in an old country hotel, the Walldecker Hof. The castle, which dated back to 900, had been the home of several notable people through the centuries, including Archduke Stephan Victor, Palatine of Hungary. It included a bear pit and a quadrangle inside the main gate paved in 64 squares of black and white cobblestones that formed a chessboard. On two sides of the quadrangle there was a balcony, presumably built so that spectators could watch games played with living chess pieces.

We did not have occasion to use either the bear pit or the cobblestone chessboard, but we did take advantage of the fact that the castle contained a chapel with an old hand-pumped pipe organ. For Christmas Eve, we organized a midnight mass in the chapel. Chris Barre, our warrant officer, was an amateur musician, and he experimented with the organ long enough to master "Silent Night," which, of course, is a German carol. We were in an area where most of the people living north of us were Protestants and those to the south were mostly Catholics. Our unit was probably evenly divided. Paul Adams, one of our officers who spoke fluent German, went looking for a priest who would conduct the mass. In short order, he found a personable middle-aged priest who was flattered to be asked. And so we ushered in Christmas 1946 — in most cases with feelings of homesickness and thoughts of far-away family and friends.

That winter we were feeling somewhat isolated. We were the only non-French unit in the French-occupied zone and had to acquire all our supplies from the British zone, so maintaining the supplies we needed was sometimes difficult. We had no medical officer, no padre and no mechanics. For these specialized services, we depended on the British zone or on our own improvisations.

Our unit had about 90 serviceable vehicles, none of them equipped with antifreeze. When our steel barrels of antifreeze arrived, the drivers noticed a hole in one barrel, but assumed it was okay since the barrel was still full and its contents were the right colour. When the first cold snap arrived, it left us with several burst cylinder heads and damaged radiators. Some enterprising black marketeers had drawn off the antifreeze from one barrel and filled it up with coloured water. We had similar bad luck with our winter fuel supply. When our truck drivers drove to Cologne to pick up our coal, they learned that it was being delivered on a flatcar. By the time it reached Cologne, not much of it was left. We found out later that local people had piled onto the flatcar and shovelled off most of our coal as the train was pulling out of the station at a nearby city. As a result, we ran out of fuel during a cold spell and some of the lead pipes in the old hotel froze and burst.

We were not allowed to play a role in the German economy. We could not eat in German restaurants or stay in civilian hotels. We were paid in "BAFO bucks" (British Armed Forces of Occupation) — vouchers good only on military bases; however, we did employ quite a few Germans, mostly as domestic workers, and for a while a former German army major worked in our office. The local people that I did meet were friendly, in spite of the fact that we had been officially enemies just a year or two before.

During the war, I knew that Jewish people in occupied Europe were required to wear a Star of David to identify themselves, and that often they were arrested on the streets of Holland and Belgium, and I had heard about the existence of concentration camps. It was not until after the war that I became aware, along with the rest of the world, of the full extent of the horrors of the Holocaust. That knowledge did not embitter me against all German people. It seemed to me that most Germans had been conned by Hitler, and by the time they realized what a monster he and his followers were, they were helpless to do anything about it. Living in Germany brought home forcibly the stupidity of war, and the importance of ensuring that a society does not fall into the clutches of a power-hungry maniac, but maintains the ability to choose whether to keep or get rid of the government in power. In the words of Lord Acton, "Power tends to corrupt and absolute power corrupts absolutely." It was obvious to me that many of our so-called enemies were just ordinary people like us, with similar ambitions in life.

One day, I went to check in at an officers' transit hotel in Bayreuth, in the American zone. The desk clerk was a young

German. I arrived just in time to hear him tell an American major, who was just ahead of me, that the place was full. The only accommodations left were bunks at the YMCA. I was about to ask the desk clerk where I could find the YMCA when he said, "I have your reservation, sir. Come this way." When we were out of earshot of the disappointed major, I said, "There's some mistake. I have no reservation." "Oh, yes, you have," he said. "The general is in London for a few days, and I'm giving you his suite for the night." "Why do I rate this special treatment?" I asked. "You are the first Canadian officer that has come here and I owe a great deal to Canadians," he said. "I was in the German Army in Holland and was badly wounded. My right leg was shattered. I was in a German field hospital and they were just about to amputate my leg when the place was captured by the Canadian Army. I was immediately taken to a Canadian army hospital, where a medical team operated on my leg. See, my leg is as good as ever. I'm deeply grateful to Canadians for that. Good night, sir, and sleep well."

I am a country boy, and one trait of the German people that I appreciated was their regard for the natural environment. Near our headquarters there was a forest plantation. During the war, an American bomber had crashed with bombs on board and flattened about a half-acre of trees. One morning when I was driving past the forest I saw a group of Germans carefully planting new trees where the forest had been wiped out.

I was also fascinated by the ingenuity people showed in using every available scrap of land. I used to watch shepherds herding huge flocks of sheep along the Autobahn, the national high-speed highway. The sheep would graze calmly on strips of green grass on the median and on the shoulders of the road. In those days, the traffic was not heavy, but when a car or truck did come along as the sheep were crossing the road, the sheep dogs would hold up their charges long enough to let the vehicle go by.

Once in my travels through Germany, I stumbled across an old friend. One day when I was driving back from Bremen through the British-occupied zone, I was looking for signs of a British unit where I might have lunch. Well past lunch time, I spotted a suitable place, a British army unit headquarters. At the officers' mess, I asked the duty officer whether I could have a snack of some sort. Politely but firmly, he said no, the kitchen staff were fully occupied preparing for a special tea that was to take place at three-thirty, but I could join in the tea. When I asked what the special tea was about, he said that it was in honour of a Belgian brigadier who was coming to inspect the Belgian army unit that was part of that formation.

When the guests arrived for tea, I stayed well in the background while a number of senior British army officers were presented to the Belgian brigadier, a tall, lean, distinguished-looking gentleman. As soon as this formality was over, the brigadier strode over to me, shook my hand and said, "My old friend Angus, what in the world are you doing here?" It was Prince Albert de Ligne, the Resistance worker who had brought Jeff Silva and Jim Whicher to my hiding place in Brussels in the summer of 1942. As we chatted, we received some surprised looks. The British officers seemed to be asking themselves what this Canadian air force type and a Belgian brigadier could possibly have in common. But from then on, my welcome at the officers' mess was much warmer, and I was given every hospitality. It was a pleasant interlude in my long drive back to the French zone.

I had a somewhat different chance encounter with an old acquaintance in London later that year. Occasionally I had to report to RAF headquarters in London in connection with the work of my unit. One evening, I was walking to my hotel, the Regent Palace, when I passed the usual line-up of "ladies of the night." I did not pay much attention to them. Suddenly one of them left the line and rushed up to me. "Squadron Leader

MacLean," she said, "how lovely to see you! And you have been promoted. I see you are now a wing commander." I was so astonished, it took me a few seconds to collect my wits and recognize her. During the war she had been a motor transport driver in the Women's Auxiliary Air Force on one of the RAF stations on which I had served. One of her chores had been to pick me up at the officers' mess every morning and drive me a couple of miles to the hangar from which I was flying. As we spoke, she reverted to the demeanour of an NCO speaking to an officer. She asked where I was stationed and whether I expected to be going back to Canada soon. As I was leaving, she said, "It's wonderful to see you, sir. You made my day." I wished her well.

I had another memorable conversation with a woman one day when I was driving through the French zone on my way back to our headquarters. A ferocious thunderstorm broke out and the rain spilled down in torrents. Near a small village, I saw a woman walking along the road without an umbrella. She was carrying sacks of groceries and she was soaking wet. I stopped and offered her a lift home. She spoke fluent English. She gladly accepted the ride and then insisted that I come in for coffee. As I sat in the living room drinking my coffee, she set up a small folding screen in front of me and went behind it to remove all her wet clothes, chatting nonchalantly all the while. I had not previously encountered this form of courtesy, so I was a bit surprised, to say the least. As she flung her wet clothes on the top of the screen, I noticed a photograph on the table of a large Moroccan officer in uniform, brandishing a scimitar. "Who is this gentleman in uniform?" I asked her. "Oh, that's my husband," she replied cheerfully. "He'll be home very shortly." As soon as she finished dressing, I remembered some urgent business I had to attend to in my office.

From time to time, I had to drive to RAF headquarters in Bremen to be briefed, along with other air force unit commanders, on the difficulties of dealing with our supposed Allies, the

Russians. Berlin was then under Allied control, but the city was surrounded by the Russian zone, and the Russians were making it difficult for the Allies to cross their zone. That, of course, made it awkward to transport supplies to Berlin and eventually led to the Berlin Airlift, the Anglo-U.S. operation that kept Berlin supplied by air in 1948 - 49 when the Russians and East Germans cut off ground access to Berlin from the West. There were also ominous signs of things to come in neighbouring Czechoslovakia. Once I had to drive to Prague to set up the work of our new Czechoslovakian detachment. The Communists had not yet taken over that country, but everywhere I went in the city, I was followed by someone — presumably a Communist agent.

In the spring of 1947, our headquarters moved again, this time to the Hotel Lamm in the small town of Schramberg in the Black Forest area of Germany. About that time, I received a letter from Robert Clements, who lived in Montague, about 10 miles from my old home in Prince Edward Island. Robert Clements was well and favourably known, and I had met him briefly at a Masonic lodge meeting. He asked for any information I could give him about the circumstances of the death of his son Robert, an RCAF pilot who had been reported missing and presumed dead after a bombing operation in Germany in October 1943.

I had a search of RAF and German documents done, and wrote to Mr. Clements to tell him that his son had been the pilot and captain of a Mark III Lancaster, and that the other six men in the crew were members of the RAF. They were reported missing on operations on the night of October 2 - 3, 1943. Their target was Munich. The aircraft had exploded in the air over Otlingen, in what was now the American zone, and all the crew had been killed instantly. I told Mr. Clements that since our unit did not work in the American zone, I had contacted the commanding officer of the No. 3 Unit, who was giving the case first priority. I also assured Mr. Clements that whenever additional information was available, it was to be passed directly to me, so that I could send it to him as quickly as possible.

The Clements family later erected a memorial plaque to Robert in Hillcrest United Church in Montague, based on the information I was able to supply. It reads:

> In loving memory of P/O Robert K. Clements,
> Pilot and captain of a Lancaster bomber
> killed 32 miles northwest of Ulm, Germany,
> while on a bombing mission to Munich
> Oct. 3rd 1943, age 23

In its report, the No. 3 Unit said the bodies of Robert Clements and the rest of the crew had been buried in four coffins in a single mass grave. "No ceremony was held, the Friedhofmeister and a number of civilian workers who assisted him being the only people present ... The bodies were later exhumed; Robert's was identified by his pilot officer's uniform. They were later re-buried in the War Cemetery at Durnbach, Germany."

The elder Robert Clements had a younger son, Gilbert, who was 15 when his brother was killed. Gilbert went on to have a distinguished career: he was elected seven times to the Prince Edward Island Legislature, served in the provincial cabinet and was later appointed lieutenant governor. Gilbert and his wife, Wilma, visited Robert's grave in 1984. I believe that had Robert lived, he would have been equally outstanding. Perhaps the leaders that Canada so sorely lacked in the 1970s and 1980s are all buried in foreign lands as a result of the Second World War. After all, the many airmen who died in the war were all healthy, intelligent and well-educated men. They had to be to qualify as aircrew.

In one sense, we found it gratifying to be able to help families like the Clementses end months or years of uncertainty about their missing relatives, but our task was ultimately a sad one. Occasionally members of my unit recovered the remains of airmen who at one time had been their close friends. Sometimes we found the graves of men I had taught to fly certain types of aircraft. To examine the shattered bones of a former friend gives a far more vivid and lasting meaning to the phrase "supreme sacrifice" than all the speeches and bugle calls and minutes of silence can ever do. Of the 3,500 cases our unit solved while I was in Europe, none had a happy ending. We found not a single instance in which a missing airman was still alive.

My tour of duty with the Missing Research and Enquiry Unit ended in the late summer of 1947. Canada had committed itself to providing personnel for the project for two years, and that term was now up. The work of the service would continue for several more years on a smaller scale and under the administration of the RAF.

A year before my term ended, I had been asked to report to a senior officer of the RCAF in London, England. He told me that 20 permanent wing commander commissions in the air force were to be filled. Acting group captains would fill 18 positions, and I was on the shortlist for the remaining two. I mulled this offer over for a while. In one way, the offer was extremely good. Almost all wartime officers being granted permanent commissions were expected to drop at least one rank, and here I was being offered a permanent commission at my present rank. However, I had been a wing commander for almost three years; a number of survivors of my class of 1939 were now a rank above me, acting group captains, and at least one of my early students of 1940 was a group captain. The offer was not as generous as it looked. I had forfeited the chance of rapid advancement by opting for repatriation to Canada in 1943 instead of staying in England.

I considered my parents, and the fact that I was the only member of the family able to take over the farm and give support and assistance to them in their declining years. Murdoch, my only surviving brother, who had served in the navy and in the

RCMP, was now set up in business in Moncton, New Brunswick. I decided to take my chances on civie street. When I told the senior officer I had decided not to accept a permanent commission, he seemed surprised. I suppose he thought I was a little crazy. Perhaps he was somewhat relieved that I had demonstrated this mental instability *before* I had a chance to sign up on a permanent basis.

Federal Politics

CHAPTER ELEVEN

Political Debut

When I came back to Canada in September 1947, the RCAF sent me on a speaking tour through Western Canada to alert the public to the new developments in Europe — the drawing of the Iron Curtain by the Communist bloc. Our former Allies, the Russians, were looking more and more like enemies, raising the possibility of another war, even more terrible than the one we had just been through.

In November 1947, I was demobilized. Gwen was still living in Western Canada. Her father, a medical doctor, died that year, and she returned home to Saskatoon to help her mother adjust to life as a widow. Gwen and I continued to be friends, although we were not courting at the time.

That winter, I settled down on the old home place in Lewis. I revelled in the peace and quiet, and in the joy of being with my parents again — and of simply being alive and being home. I could see changes starting to happen in my home community. For one thing, there were fewer farms operating than before the war. Across the Island, people were heading for the cities, under the assumption that you either had to farm on a large scale — hundreds of acres of land compared with the traditional 75 to 100 acres — or get out. Rural electrification programs were making it feasible to modernize homes and install indoor plumbing. The government was accelerating road paving. That eventually made it easier for people to do their shopping, banking and other business in Charlottetown and the larger towns, bypassing the villages. And many farmers were switching to a more mechanized form of agriculture.

Before I returned home to the Island, I had bought my first car, a secondhand Ford with the driving controls on the right side. It had belonged to an embassy in Ottawa; on the Island, it created quite a stir everywhere I went. Once I was settled, I started modernizing the house and barns. In the summer of 1948, I had the hand-hewn Island sandstone foundation of the house replaced with a concrete foundation, and I installed indoor plumbing in the house and running water in the barns.

I was attached to our farm, the home of three generations of MacLeans. I decided that if I was going to make a living there, I would have to specialize in some crop. Until I decided on the crop, I carried on the work of our mixed farm, with its dairy cattle and Cheviot sheep, the descendants of the ewe that a relative had led to my great-grandfather's farm a century before. I was not at all sure that I wanted to engage in large-scale farming — I did not want to spend the rest of my life working to pay for expensive machinery — however, I did buy a tractor and a couple more parcels of land.

I had learned from my observations of the older and more mature society in Europe to value land highly. After all, in the basic biological relationship of people to their environment, land and sea are things that have fundamental value, and of these two, only land can be privately owned. In the late 1940s, land in Prince Edward Island was badly undervalued — if it could be sold at all.

A cousin of mine, a widow, fell heir to 125 acres of land that our grandfather had owned in the late 1800s. She offered this land to me, and I bought it, as well as 225 acres adjoining it. In total, I bought 500 acres — land that had not been cultivated was cheap. I considered it a suitable investment into which to put my savings.

Our old homestead contained about 100 acres of woods. One day in the fall of 1948 I went for a stroll to see the hemlocks by the brook, which is one of the headwaters of the Montague River. In the slope, I spotted an excavation. I figured that it had to be old, because in it was a spruce tree that I guessed had been growing there for at least a century. When I got home, I asked my father about the excavation. "Oh," he said, "you've found one of the little dams. There are two of them on our property. My father was aware of them when he settled here in 1863."

My father explained that the dams had been built so white pine masts could be floated downstream to Georgetown. During the Napoleonic wars, the Baltic source of white pine masts for the Royal Navy was cut off, so another source had to be developed in the colonies. The navy had to replace its masts every two years, otherwise they would become brittle and break during storms. Suitable white pine trees on the Island were reserved for the Crown, regardless of whose land they were on. Contractors cut the trees and hauled the logs by oxen to the nearest brook, which was dammed at various points to make it deep enough to float the masts until they reached a bigger stream. From Georgetown, they were shipped to England. The largest masts required by the navy were 34 inches in diameter at the butt and 102 feet long. I doubt whether any of the Island trees were quite that large, although they were pretty impressive. When I was a boy, you could still find some of the huge stumps in open fields.

The woodlot always delighted me, not only for its aesthetic and practical value, but also because of the history it represented. There was, and still is, a wide variety of species in the woods, including red spruce, fir, red maple, sugar maple and hemlock. Some of the hemlocks are 500 years old, which means they were growing when Columbus was a boy. (In 1972, the International Biological Program Survey selected a patch of our woods as one of their sites because of the quality of the red spruce growing there.) My father and grandfather had always carefully managed the woods, and I planned to follow their example. In the next couple of years, though, I became caught up in other matters. Now that I was again a resident of Queens County, I had to decide whether I would run in another election, assuming that people wanted me to. At that time, the federal Liberals were still enjoying a reign of power that had not been interrupted since 1935.

When the 1949 federal election was called, I was nominated again, once again with Chester McLure as my running mate. Chester had been a member of the previous Parliament, as had one of the Liberal candidates, Lester Douglas. That meant that if I were to be elected, I would have to do better than one or both of the sitting members. When the votes were counted, I came in a fairly close third. It appeared that I was following in my father's footsteps. Although he always made a good showing in a difficult riding for a Conservative, he never quite won.

It has always struck me as rather sad that my mother's total political experience consisted of watching her husband and son never quite win elections. By the time I moved back home to the farm, she had almost completely recovered from the stroke she had suffered, although she still had not regained her ability to sing. But in 1950, she contracted pneumonia and died quite suddenly, at the age of 75. My father, left without his companion of 48 years, devoted himself to work on the farm to ease his loneliness.

I took another run at politics that year when the death of Lester Douglas created a vacancy in the dual riding of Queens. I was nominated that fall, and I spent most of the winter meeting poll workers in Charlottetown and all the towns and villages of Queens County. I used to stay in these centres for two or three days, either in a local hotel or in someone's home. I would meet the local poll committee in the evening and then spend the next couple of days going door-to-door, meeting everyone I could. At that time, the electorate was not very fluid. People generally stayed with the political party into which they were born, so there was not much point in arguing about politics; however, I found people in the constituency were always friendly, regardless of their political persuasion, and I insisted on calling on both Liberals and Conservatives, often against the advice of the local poll workers.

When I was campaigning in Mount Stewart, the poll workers warned me against calling on a certain woman. "She's a terrible Liberal," they told me. "She'll put the run on you for sure." I planned to visit her anyway. When I rang the bell at her house, a rather severe-looking woman came to the door. I introduced myself. "You needn't have bothered calling here," she said. I told her I just wanted to meet her; if she did not want to vote for me, that was her business. "Oh, I didn't mean that, at all," she said. "I meant I'd be voting for you whether you called here or not. Now, I just put the coffee pot on. Come on in and have a cup of coffee." It turned out that she had a grudge against the Liberal candidate because of a personal matter. "Wild horses wouldn't drag me to the poll to vote for him," she said. But she swore me to secrecy. I was never to reveal her defection. I never did, but her confession confirmed my belief that Islanders sometimes voted quite differently than their neighbours suspected.

One of the advantages of stopping over in a village or town was that I got to know every district pretty well. Those visits also seemed to raise the morale of the poll workers. By the end of the campaign, I had a good grasp of what people were thinking and of their problems. At that time, the Cold War was in its early stages, and the awful possibility of a nuclear conflict was one of the worries that weighed on people's minds. And of course, there were the chronic issues of high unemployment and low farm prices. The most recent war had not boosted the economy of the Maritimes nearly as much as that of Central Canada, where the production of aircraft and war machinery of all kinds had been concentrated.

In the spring of 1951, four byelections, including one in Queens, were called to take place on June 25. George Drew, the national Conservative leader, spoke in Charlottetown at a Conservative rally, and there were hopeful signs that the Conservatives would make a breakthrough. When the results came in, the Conservatives had won all four seats. I won in Queens by a margin of 453 votes. Two of the other new MPs were Gordon Churchill in Winnipeg South Centre and Walter Dinsdale in Brandon-Souris (Manitoba). The third was the former National Hockey League player Howard Meeker, who won in Waterloo South. All four of us were veterans of the Second World War.

The win was a great morale boost for the party. It appeared that voters were in the mood for a change. I think that all those days and nights in the towns and villages had helped, as well; my opponent had spent most of his time in Charlottetown. And I discovered that, in some cases, my father's good reputation had rubbed off on me. One day after the election, I stopped at a country store to buy some milk. A man who had just paid for his groceries congratulated me on how well I had done in that poll. I said I was sorry, but I did not recognize him. "You wouldn't know me," he said. "I'm the Liberal poll chairman." Then he told me that his poll committee had done a postmortem of the election the previous night in his home. "We gave you all the Conservative votes, of course, and then we gave you every vote that was the slightest bit doubtful, and you still had two more than that. Minnie made tea and sandwiches for the committee, and while they were eating, they were discussing who the traitors could possibly be. It never occurred to any of them that it was Minnie and I." He said he and his wife had voted for me because they knew and admired my father.

When the fall session of Parliament opened, I packed my bags and rented a room in Ottawa. There were only 44 of us in the Conservative caucus, so we all had plenty of work to do. We did not have formal shadow cabinets in those days, but we were all given responsibilities in certain areas; mine included fisheries and Atlantic Canadian issues. I also devoted a lot of time to helping war veterans unsnarl red tape concerning pensions and other kinds of assistance. I had a good relationship with the people at the Department of Veterans Affairs, so I was able to intervene successfully quite often, and this was very satisfying.

I also did a lot of work on behalf of older constituents. In those days, people aged 65 and older had been born before the Island government had started registration of births and deaths. To qualify for the old-age pension, people without birth certificates had to produce two other documents indicating their date of birth — usually, church baptismal records and family Bibles. I routinely led dozens of 65-year-olds through the bureaucratic maze to get their old-age pensions.

In my first two years in Ottawa, I shared an office in the Centre Block with Howie Meeker. Our secretarial help came from a typing pool in the basement. I made my maiden speech in the House of Commons on October 18, 1951. Among other things, I argued for the dispersal of industry to the outlying sections of the country, rather than keeping it concentrated in Central Canada. This would help relieve the congestion in the large cities and make them a less tempting target for atomic bombs. Moving some industries away from the cities would also improve the economy and social life of rural communities — places that I felt were well worth strengthening.

I felt that life in the country had more to offer coming generations than growing up in the city. "I would say, too," I continued, "that children brought up in small towns and villages and in the country have an advantage over those brought up in the largest cities, who must live among the flashing lights and the ringing bells. The child of the modern city must feel something like a ball in a pinball machine. On the other hand, a child living in the country either consciously or unconsciously comes to recognize that he is part of God's creation, a fact that stands him in good stead in later years."

I pointed out that since Confederation, there had been a constant flow of the cream of the Island's population to the United States. I felt that this was because the needs of Islanders had been largely ignored by the central government. "We in Prince Edward Island, and indeed the people from the Maritime provinces generally, have been accused of complaining constantly and of wanting something for nothing. I think we have been justified. In my constituency, even in such small matters as public works, we seem not to have been given fair treatment. For two elections now we have been promised public works. We were told we were going to have a new federal building in Charlottetown, that we would have naval barracks and possibly a new drill hall, and that contracts were going to be let in the area for the repair of small naval vessels. None of these things has materialized."

I continued with a farming analogy, "A few weeks ago, a litter of pigs was born on our farm, and as is usually the case, there was one runt. In the crucial few days of their lives when the struggle for survival is very keen, it was easy to observe that the runt was getting pushed around badly. My hired man was looking at the litter and he said, 'I notice every time the underdeveloped pig attempts to improve his position he is pushed around and ends up trying to gain nourishment from a mammary gland which is not functioning.' Those were not his exact words but that was the general meaning. Every time I think of that, I think of Prince Edward Island. We are the little fellow at the far end of the Canadian table and little meat, let alone gravy, ever reaches us. That condition should not be allowed to continue. The government of this nation should be above petty provincialism and should treat all sections of the country the same way."

Because of my background, our caucus often called on me to speak on defence issues and on matters affecting the Maritime provinces, including farming and fishing. I have always been especially interested in conservation in all its forms, so I often spoke of the need to protect farmland from erosion and other forms of degradation, and of the need to protect fish stocks. In the early 1950s, of course, the fishing industry was in excellent shape compared with today, but even then, there were portents of things to come. The Fisheries minister, James Sinclair, had noted in the House that there had been signs of depletion of fish stocks in parts of the Grand Banks off the coast of Newfoundland. I considered this an understatement.

I pointed out in the House that marine life in the northwest Atlantic fishery had been tremendously depleted in the previous 450 years. Indiscriminate hunting and fishing had exterminated walrus and various types of birds in the Gulf of St. Lawrence, and had greatly diminished the numbers of whales. "The number of fish has been reduced tremendously and the whole balance of nature has been upset." Then, as now, some people were blaming seals for the depletion of fish stocks. I argued that, two or three centuries in the past, when North American waters were teeming with fish, there were also far more harbour and grey seals in existence. I suggested that the depletion might be traced partly, at least, to runoff that had polluted the shore waters.

Outside the House, I socialized mainly with the "new boys" in Parliament, especially the MPs who had recently been elected in byelections. We went bowling together, and we got together to celebrate important occasions, such as another Conservative byelection victory. Some of us liked to amuse ourselves at these parties by performing satirical political songs in the style of Gilbert and Sullivan. (I had developed a weakness for comic opera in my university days, when I sang in the chorus of productions of *HMS Pinafore* and *The Mikado*.)

In May 1952, there were two byelections — one in Victoria Carleton, New Brunswick; the other in the riding of Ontario, in Ontario. The latter included the city of Oshawa. Mike Starr, the mayor of Oshawa, was the Conservative candidate. The local party association thought it would help Mike if we held a canvassing blitz the Saturday before the election. Walter Dinsdale and I volunteered to go knocking on doors in Pickering.

At one house, an elderly man came to the door. When we introduced ourselves, he asked whether we knew Donald Fleming. Of course, we did. He was the Conservative member of Parliament from the Toronto riding of Eglinton. "I know him well," the man said. "In that case," Walter said, "can we assume that you will be voting for Mike Starr?" The man replied, "You haven't got it quite right. I'll be voting for Mike Starr even though I know Donald Fleming well." We thanked him and left, wondering what grudge he held against Fleming. We did not find out, but Mike Starr did well in the byelection in any case. He changed a Liberal majority of more than 3,000 votes into a Conservative majority of more than 3,000. In the New Brunswick riding, Gage Montgomery, the Conservative candidate, retained a Conservative majority.

We were winning far more byelections than we had expected and the future of the party looked bright. Our leader at that time was George Drew, the handsome, distinguished-looking former premier of Ontario. I found him to be a decent, friendly sort of person, but he had a public-image problem. For some reason, many people thought that he was a bit of a stuffed shirt. Despite this perception, Drew led the party again in the 1953 election.

My home life had undergone some dramatic changes. Although Gwen and I had kept in touch, as friends, during the war, we had not really contemplated anything more than friendship for the longest time. Life during and after the war was so turbulent that people often did not marry until much later than our parents' generation had. Such was the case for Gwen and me. One day, we were both ready to settle down and have a family, and so, in October 1952, Gwen and I got married. We had rented a small apartment in Ottawa South until the session ended that winter. When the election was called, we boarded with friends in Charlottetown during the campaign.

Shortly after we were married, we were given a concrete example of some of the changes I had started to see in my home province after the war. One Sunday, Gwen and I went to the Presbyterian church in Belfast, a few miles from our farm. I wanted her to see this lovely, historic church, built by settlers from the Hebrides who had been brought to the Island in the early 1800s by Lord Selkirk. After the service, Gwen asked me, "How is it that there are so many old people in church?" I replied, "They are cramming for their finals." In fact, of course, the church, like the rest of the community, was suffering from the results of yet another out-migration of young people seeking employment in the States or elsewhere in Canada.

In the 1953 federal election, Chester McLure and I were both nominated to run in Queens. Since we were both sitting members, I felt that with teamwork we both should be able to win again. But McLure was convinced that one of the Liberals would come in first and therefore the only real contest was for second place — in effect, between the two of us. As in our previous two campaigns together, Chester, who was now 78, saw me as his nemesis.

One day when we were canvassing in northeastern Queens, we ran out of time before we could visit a certain poll. We told the poll chair we would come back another day, but he insisted that there was one family we had to see that day. It was a young couple living with the wife's parents. The poll chair said her husband was a great admirer of Chester's, and the young couple probably would vote for him. Chester decided it was crucial that we visit this family. When we drove into the yard, I let Chester out at the door and turned the car. As I got out of the car, an old gentleman answered the door and said to Chester, "Is that MacLean with you?" The man came straight to where I was. "Aren't you from somewhere near Iona?" he asked. "Yes," I said. Then he asked whether I had any connection to Big Duncan MacLean. I told him he had died before I was born, but that he was my grandfather. "That's all I wanted to know," the old gentleman said. "We will all be voting for you." On the way back to Charlottetown, Chester muttered something about the poll chair's lack of competence.

After the election, I called in to see this family to find out why they had voted for me. The old gentleman told me he had been born in Valley, a school district of Iona parish. "In October 1888, when I was 10 years old, your grandfather called at our house and asked me how it was that I was not in school. We were very poor, and I told him that I had no shoes, and it was too cold to go to school barefoot. Your grandfather said, 'I'll make you a pair of boots,' and he measured my feet right then and there, and delivered an excellent pair of boots a few days later. As I guess you know, your grandfather learned to be a shoemaker when he was young and could make excellent boots." The old gentleman was returning the favour to me, his benefactor's grandson, 65 years later.

In the midst of the campaign, Prime Minister Louis St. Laurent happened to be in Charlottetown during the July 1 Dominion Day celebrations. He was flying in from Newfoundland that day, and a non-partisan ceremony was planned in front of the Provincial Building, the cradle of Confederation. I happened to be in Charlottetown, too, and I strolled over to Great George Street to join the crowd of about 200 who were waiting for St. Laurent to arrive. My two Liberal opponents had gone to the airport to meet the prime minister. On the way back downtown, their car was held up in the traffic, and St. Laurent's limousine arrived at the Provincial Building ahead of them. His driver opened the car door for him, and he climbed out, looked around at the crowd and saw nobody he knew. Then he spotted me. For him, mine was a familiar face as I sat opposite him in the House of Commons. He smiled and quickly walked across the roped-off area to shake hands with me. "I'm so glad to see you," he said. At that point, the two Liberal candidates arrived to find their leader consorting with the enemy. I think the crowd rather enjoyed that vignette, even if the Liberals did not.

On election day, Chester McLure's worst fears were realized. A Liberal, Neil Matheson, led the poll, I came in second and Chester came in third. We had expected the Conservatives to make substantial gains across Canada in the election; we were sadly disappointed. The Liberals were back in power again, with another majority government, and we had only 51 seats, about the same number we had had before the election. A few seats did change, however. Tom Bell, a Saint John lawyer who had served in the merchant navy in the war, won the riding of Saint John - Albert. Tom and I shared an office, and it was a very congenial arrangement. He was an excellent MP.

Our caucus met every Wednesday and sometimes we had special meetings if there was an issue before Parliament that we needed to discuss. We often decided who should lead off in debates, and the leader sought our suggestions as to what he should say on certain matters.

Gwen by now had settled into farm life and remained on the farm until Christmas. Our first child, Jeannie, was born five days after the election and spent her first few months of life on the farm. When I returned to Ottawa after Christmas, Gwen came with me and then went on to Regina with the baby to visit her sister. For most sessions of that Parliament, we were able to rent small apartments for all or part of the winter months. Our eldest son, Allan, was born in December 1954.

Unfortunately, when the House was sitting, I did not see nearly as much of my children as I would have liked. The House sat from 2:00 p.m. to 6:00 p.m., and from 8:00 p.m. to 10:00 p.m. most days. The early hours of my day were filled with meetings and office work. Consequently, the children would be fast asleep before I got home at night and were rarely up before I went to the office in the morning, and I saw them only on weekends. I found this quite stressful. I was torn between my duties at work and my desire to be at home with my family, and although we hired a young woman to help Gwen in the house, I felt badly about leaving so much of the home responsibilities on Gwen's shoulders. As well, during my first six years in Parliament, another demand on my time was a request from the RCAF to continue in the air force reserve. Although I agreed, it meant that I had to be on active service for three weeks every year, as an understudy of a station chief administrative officer. I usually put in my three weeks at Summerside, Prince Edward Island, or Uplands, Ontario. Gwen now joined me at social events and when possible attended political meetings. I found her a great asset. People seemed more supportive of a family man and his wife than of a bachelor.

Usually I ate supper in the parliamentary restaurant. Tom Bell, my office mate, had set up a dart board on the wall of our office. After supper, we often played a game or two before going back to the House for the evening session. Our next-door neighbours were Roland Michener (who later became Governor General) and Bob Mitchell, both newly elected members. Michener liked to relax on the chesterfield in his office after supper. While he was doing so, he began hearing the sound of a drip in the wall, as if a pipe were leaking. He reported this to a House of Commons official, who notified Public Works officials. They examined the blueprints of the building, found no sign of pipes in that wall, but concluded that a pipe must have been installed at some later date. The Public Works people then went to Rollie's office to listen to the drip. They decided that they would have to tear the wall down to get at the leak. One of them suggested that it might be easier to reach the pipe from the other side of the wall. Tom Bell and I heard a knock at our office door. We opened it to find a delegation from the Public Works department. Their problem was solved instantly when they saw what was happening in our office: Tom and I were in the middle of a game of darts. Every time a dart landed on the dart board, it made the sound that had perplexed Michener and the Public Works staff.

In the mid-1950s, the United States government invited two parliamentarians from each member country of the North Atlantic Treaty Organization to visit four state governments, four universities and the U.S. State Department. I was chosen from the Canadian Opposition, and René Jutras, also an RCAF veteran, represented the government side. A member of the U.S. State Department accompanied us on the tour. He was a small man, of Portuguese descent. He spoke several languages fluently, but he in no way looked like a U.S. government official. Three or four times, when we arrived at an airport, a local official would look us over, ignore the State Department official, and then say to me, "I assume you are from the State Department."

One of the two French representatives was a man named Walker, pronounced "Walkeer." When I asked him the origin of his name, I learned a bit of history I had never heard of before. He told me that after the French Revolution the government of France had set up a colony of about 1,000 Scots to establish a linen industry in France. They learned to speak French but continued speaking Gaelic for about a century. Walker spoke good English and also knew a few words in Gaelic. He was a Presbyterian.

In January 1955, I was appointed deputy Opposition whip, which increased my workload and the number of speaking engagements I was invited to take in Ottawa. I had never believed in knee-jerk, partisan reactions in political life. If a government member said or did something I liked, I had often said so. I think that I had a reputation among both the Liberals and the Cooperative Commonwealth Federation (CCF) as being fair and reasonable, and I had frequently been appointed to represent the Opposition on all-party committees. But by the mid-1950s, I was finding it increasingly difficult to find something positive to say about the government in power. The Liberals were becoming more and more autocratic and the debates in the House were becoming more rancorous. By then, the Liberals had been in power continuously for two decades, and they acted as though they had a divine right to rule and should not even be questioned.

A prime example was C. D. Howe, then the minister of Defence Production and Trade and Commerce. Howe had a well-deserved reputation for arrogance. To my mind, he had the makings of a dictator. He had been born and educated in the United States, and he did not seem to understand or even care about the parliamentary system. During the Second World War, he had held an important position as minister of Munitions and Supply. The federal government had assumed considerable powers during the war, and in the name of patriotism, Parliament had generally approved whatever the government proposed in aid of the war effort. Howe seemed to think that should be the normal state of affairs. He acted as though it was absurd that a project that he supported could be held up by mere members of Parliament.

My maternal grandparents, Murdoch MacLean
and Catherine Munroe. (*circa* 1905)

My paternal grandparents, Duncan MacLean and
Margaret MacLean. (*circa* 1900)

My paternal grandmother with my parents, George and Sarah MacLean, and my older siblings, before I was born. (1909)

With my siblings Murdoch, Mary and Effie and our friend Euphemia McGowan (middle). I'm on the far right. (1927)

With my friend Harry Smith,
at West Kent High School. (1930)

At militia summer camp,
in Petawawa. (1935)

With two friends from Mount Allison
University. I'm on the right. (1937)

Graduation with a science
degree in industrial chemistry
from Mount Allison
University. (1939)

On the farm in Lewis the summer before
the Second World War. (1939)

Visiting Gwen Burwash
while on leave in Saskatoon. (1940)

My parents, George and Sarah MacLean, during the war.

The Peeters family hid me for over a week in their house.
I'm second from right. (1942)

Father Kloeg, who guided me from
Zaltbommel to Weert in 1942, was
executed by the Gestapo in 1944.

Florentino, the Basque guide who led our group over the Pyrenees in 1942.

The punched Metro
ticket that almost ended
my escape. (1942)

Het Nederlandsche Roode Kruis

No. 165728

g.   a.

➡ Formulier, na invulling, in te zenden aan het *CORRESPONDENTIE-BUREAU* van het Nederlandsche Roode Kruis, Jan Pietersz. Coenstraat 10, Den Haag, Tel. 770517.

VERZOEK
door tusschenkomst van het Duitsche Roode Kruis aan het Internationale Comité van het Roode Kruis te Genève om inlichtingen.

ANTRAG
durch das Deutsche Rote Kreuz an das Internationale Komitee vom Roten Kreuz in Genf auf Nachrichtenvermittlung.

1. **Afzender**   W/ Schutte, Willem,
   Absender   (naam, voornaam en adres)
                       (Name, Taufname und Adresse)

   Enschedeesche straatweg 13 Hengelo (O)

Verzoekt aan
Bittet an

2. **Geadresseerde**   Geo A. Mac Lean, Lewis, Beatons Mill
   Empfänger   (naam, voornaam en adres)   ℞ P.E.Island.
                        (Name, Taufname und Adresse)   CANADA.

het volgende mede te deelen:
folgendes zu übermitteln:

(ten hoogste 25 woorden uitsluitend persoonlijke en familieaangelegenheden betreffende)
(Höchstzahl 25 Worte nur persönliche und Familienangelegenheiten betreffend)

   Your son is all right.

                    Willem.

EXAMINED BY D. B/. 80

                                                   Handteekening
                                                   Unterschrift

3. **Geadresseerde antwoordt aan ommezijde:**
   Empfänger antwortet umseitig   W. Schutte

A.F. van Goelst Meijer sent this message, dated July 25, 1942, to my father from Switzerland. My father didn't receive the message until September, after I had reached safety.

CANADIAN PACIFIC
TELEGRAPHS

DIRECT CONNECTION WITH
POSTAL TELEGRAPH - CABLE CO.
COMMERCIAL CABLES - - IMPERIAL CABLES

CANADIAN
PACIFIC

COMMUNICATIONS

ONEY TRANSFERRED
BY TELEGRAPH

C.O. 1M
This is a full-rate Telegram or Cablegram unless otherwise indicated by signal in the check or in the address.

TELEGRAM		CABLEGRAM	
FULL RATE		FULL RATE	
DAY LETTER	DL	CODE	CDE
NIGHT LETTER	NL	DEFERRED	LC
NIGHT TELEGRAM	NM	NIGHT CABLE LETTER	NLT

W. D. NEIL, GENERAL MANAGER OF COMMUNICATIONS, MONTREAL.

STANDARD TIME

```
2    10    Imperial   Gibraltar Aug. 25th, 1942.

LC
Murdock McLean,
Minto, N. B.

        Safe well Happy.


                McLean.   9.49 AM.
```

First message I sent to my family after reaching Gibraltar.
(August 25, 1942)

Dédée (Andrée de Jongh), leader of the Comet Line, who helped me
escape the Nazis, shows me her George Cross certificate. (1945)

I had the sad honour of attending the funeral of
Frédéric de Jongh, Dédée's father, in Brussels. He had been
executed by a Nazi firing squad in Paris in 1944. (1946)

For a period of time in 1946, my office was located in this castle,
Schloss Schaumburg.

Mr. Pagie and his daughters some years after the war. (*circa* 1948)

My parents and siblings (*back row*: Murdoch, Effie and me;
front row: Mary, my parents, Catherine and Margaret). (1948)

Sworn in by the Clerk of the House of Commons for the first time. (1951)

George Drew, P.C. Leader (*middle*), poses with the four new P.C. MPs
who won byelections the same day (*left*: me and Gordon Churchill;
right: Howie Meeker and Walter Dinsdale). (1951)

On October 29, 1952, I married Gwen Burwash.

With Diefenbaker, right after I was sworn in
as minister of Fisheries. (1957)

My staff at the House of Commons: John Smethurst, Kevin McKenna, Gwen
Davies, me, Muriel Martin, Arleta Heenan, Rosemary Trainor, Lowell Allen
and Florence Field. Absent are Martin Gilmore, Sandra MacLean and Joan
Flemming, who joined my staff at a later date. (1959)

Receiving an honorary LL.D.
from Mount Allison
University. (1958)

In my office in the West Block
Tower. (1958)

I'd go directly from
the House of Commons
to Uplands while I was in
the RCAF reserve. (1959)

I was minister in attendance to the Queen and
Prince Philip during their royal visit to P.E.I. (1959)

Queen Elizabeth and Prince Philip watch
a horse race while I study the program. (1959)

I often met with fishermen and visited wharves like this one in Rustico, P.E.I. (1960)

Enjoying oysters with my fellow Island MPs: Orville Philip, John A. Macdonald, me and Heath Macquarrie. (1959)

Adele MacEachern, a dietician from my department's Test Kitchen, serving Diefenbaker and me a nutritious fish meal. (1960)

Our children: Jean and Allan standing, Rob and Mary riding, in Ottawa. (1960)

With my family in front of the Peace Tower. (1965)

Campaigning with party leader Bob Stanfield in Malpeque. (1968)

Campaign manager Wylie Barrett and campaign worker Dianne Taylor
show me the schedule. (1968)

Attending a Parliamentary Conference at the British House of Commons. (1969)

I was part of the Canadian delegation to the Parliamentary Conference on European Co-operation and Security in Belgrade. (1974)

Governor General Roland Michener and Norah Michener,
Gwen and I and Prime Minister Pierre Trudeau and Margaret Trudeau
at Rideau Hall. (1973)

Walter Baker and Joe Clark present me
with a retirement gift from the caucus. (1976)

John Diefenbaker visited P.E.I. three weeks before his death. (1979)

B.C. Premier William R. Bennett visited P.E.I.
shortly after I became premier. (1979)

I always found René Lévesque to be
warm and sympathetic. (1979)

With my Maritime colleagues, N.S. Premier John
Buchanan and N.B. Premier Richard Hatfield,
and Prime Minister Pierre Trudeau. (1980)

At the Constitutional Conference in Ottawa with
my minister of Justice, Horace Carver (*centre*),
and Alberta Premier Peter Lougheed. (1980)

To this day, people still stop me on the street to thank me for cancelling P.E.I.'s five percent involvement in the Point Lepreau nuclear power station. (1979)

Visiting the oil rigs off the eastern shore of P.E.I. (1979)

Terry Fox stopped in Charlottetown during his Marathon of Hope Run. (1980)

Examining old census records with
librarian Eleanor Vass. (1981)

Arriving at CFB Greenwood, N.S.,
to visit 405 Squadron. (1981)

Receiving an honorary LL.D. from U.P.E.I.: Donna Meincke, President Peter Meincke, me, Gwen and Chancellor Gordon Bennett. (1985)

In front of the P.E.I. Pavilion at Expo '86 in B.C. with the staff and a P.E.I. government delegation. Recently elected Premier Joe Ghiz is in the back row, third from right. (1986)

Gwen and I with Jane Pagie (*right*), 35 years after she pedalled me on her bicycle to this railway station and helped me escape. (1977)

The City of Rotterdam and the Dutch underground invited me to unveil a street named after Father Kloeg. Matthieu Beelen stands to my left. (1988)

I attended a dinner with A. F. van Goelst Meijer in Waardenburg, 46 years after he helped me escape. (1988)

My Scottish relatives, Alasdair and Sorley MacLean,
whom I visited on the Isle of Skye. (1988)

Hauling wood with my son Rob on our farm in Lewis. (1988)

Count Georges
D'Oultremont,
whom I knew only as
"George" when he
guided me from
Brussels to Paris in
1942. (1991)

Receiving the Order of Canada from
Governor General Ray Hnatyshyn. (1992)

My long-time secretary and friend, Rosemary Trainor. (1995)

Still not forgotten by the pundits. (1995)

Seventeen years after I appointed him
to my provincial cabinet, Pat Binns
is sworn in as premier. (1996)

Gwen and I visiting Gwen's sister Elinore
in Regina. (1993)

With my three grandchildren: Sarah, Sophie (*in my arms*) and Jessica. (1998)

Preserving our family woodlands
is very important to me.

In 1955, Howe proposed an amendment to the Defence Production Act that would have extended indefinitely the powers over the economy that he had held during the Korean War. The Opposition objected strenuously to the bill, on the grounds that it was an undemocratic piece of legislation. I considered it a serious threat to the rights of Parliament. My reading of history — as well as my observations during the war and in post-war Germany — had taught me that unchecked power will almost always be abused, and that the erosion of freedom is an insidious process.

On June 8, I spoke at length — interrupted several times, of course, by a scornful and impatient Howe — against the bill. "It is a fact of history," I said in part, "that most civilizations of the past, setting out to make sure that they would continue into the future, taught that their sole danger was from without and that they could be destroyed only by attack from without. History teaches us, however, that in nearly all cases civilizations have ceased to exist not as the direct result of attack from without but because of rot from within. And the principles upon which they first prospered were whittled away to such an extent that eventually those civilizations collapsed from within.

"That is my fear at the present time. Many people take the shallow view that progress is inevitable and democracy is permanent. I see no reason why our civilization or our way of life should be considered immune from the forces which have existed throughout history. I feel there is a real danger that in our efforts to defeat totalitarian attack from without we will destroy our civilization from within." The upshot of the debate was that the Opposition succeeded in placing a three-year time limit on the powers over the economy that were being proposed.

Outside the House, our personal relationships with many of the government members remained cordial. Prime Minister St. Laurent had always struck me as being a gracious gentleman of the old school. He demonstrated his thoughtfulness to me in the fall of 1956, when he wrote me a letter commenting on a story in *Weekend* magazine about my adventures in Europe during the war. That story had come to light — 14 years after the fact — because of a visit to Canada by a woman who was a former member of the Dutch underground. A guest of the Air Force Association, she had helped a number of Canadian airmen to escape. Journalist Robert McKeown, in trying to track down some of these airmen, came across my name in a list provided by the Royal Air Forces Escaping Society. He discovered that this was the same Angus MacLean who was a member of Parliament, and he decided to interview me. The result was a two-part series in *Weekend.* In his letter, St. Laurent congratulated me "on both your stamina and your ingenuity at that time." He concluded, "It will be a good thing for future generations to have such stories as symbolic of our activities in the last war, which I hope will remain the last one for many generations."

Despite St. Laurent's natural courtesy, the level of animosity in the House reached an all-time high that year. Again, Howe was at the centre of the controversy. He needed Parliament's approval to lend $80 million to Trans-Canada Pipelines Ltd. to start construction on a pipeline that would bring natural gas from Alberta to southern Ontario. The debate that ensued had more to do with the rights of Parliament than with the merits of the project itself. In mid-May 1956, Howe informed MPs that they must pass this legislation by early June, otherwise the government would invoke closure, the rarely used device that limits debate and forces a vote on a bill.

The Opposition was outraged by this dictatorial attitude. In the interests of defending the rights of Parliament, we spoke at length to hold up the vote as long as we could. The government finally imposed closure and the bill passed, but public opinion was on our side. The arrogance of the government was becoming all too evident. As a result of George Drew's leadership in the pipeline debate, the future of the Conservative Party looked much brighter; however, Drew reluctantly resigned as party leader because of ill health. The party held a leadership convention in Ottawa in December 1956. I voted for a man who I felt might be able to lead us out of the political wilderness — John George Diefenbaker, a former lawyer and long-time member from the constituency of Prince Albert, Saskatchewan.

CHAPTER TWELVE

Life in the
Diefenbaker Cabinet

John Diefenbaker was unortho-
dox, and some people felt that we would be taking a chance in
selecting him as leader. I thought we should take the risk. The
only other candidates for the job were two other lawyers, Donald
Fleming from Toronto and Davie Fulton from Kamloops, British
Columbia. I believed that Diefenbaker was our brightest hope.
We had been out of power for 21 years. I worried that time was
running out on our hopes for rebuilding a strong national party.
I was well aware of Diefenbaker's flaws: he was somewhat aloof,
he was not a strong caucus man, he was given to histrionics and
he mistrusted many of the people around him. On the other hand,
he could hold an audience spellbound, he had a great gift for
lampooning his opponents without being offensive and he was
not identified with Bay Street.

The Liberals under Louis St. Laurent seemed to be oriented
towards Central Canada, and the Conservatives, under George

Drew, had a similar image. Diefenbaker was a Prairie boy, with a reputation as a defender of the poor and unfortunate. I felt that under his leadership we could dispel the myth that the Conservative Party catered only to the rich and powerful. Diefenbaker's political philosophy was one with which I could identify. I had always objected to any policy that resulted in the rich getting richer and the poor poorer. I think the majority of our caucus believed strongly in social justice and more opportunity for the poorer end of the economic spectrum. Diefenbaker clearly personified that philosophy. I did not take an active role in supporting any of the three contestants for the leadership, but when delegates asked for my advice, I told them that I was voting for Diefenbaker, because I considered him the best choice.

The leadership convention took place in the Ottawa Coliseum on December 14, 1956. Oddly enough, the seeds for some of the party's future troubles were sown at that early date. Traditionally, leadership candidates were nominated by one francophone delegate and one from English-speaking Canada. Diefenbaker chose two anglophones, George Pearkes from British Columbia and Hugh John Flemming from New Brunswick. The result was that some of the Quebec delegates felt slighted and walked out of the convention. They included Leon Balcer, an MP from Trois Rivières and a past-president of the national Conservative association, a man who was a great asset to the party and who could have greatly enhanced our position in Quebec. Instead, this incident smouldered for years in the minds of both Balcer and Diefenbaker.

In those days, I did not know Diefenbaker well on a personal level. He was not good at attending caucus meetings, and he did not socialize much with the rest of us outside the House. He was something of a loner. Occasionally, though, he asked my opinion about an issue that was on his mind. One day shortly after he became leader, we happened to be walking together in the corridor.

He asked me what I thought were the worst mistakes previous Conservative leaders had made in their public presentations. I told him that one of their worst mistakes had been making promises prematurely. "I don't think you should talk about what you're going to do as prime minister until the time comes when that statement becomes credible," I said, "and people begin to think that maybe you will form the government. If you talk like that too soon, people will just think you're dreaming." Diefenbaker jotted that observation down. I do not know whether he called it to mind when the election campaign started the following spring, but in any case, his campaign caught fire quickly. His skill at swaying crowds soon brought him to the point where people saw him as a potential prime minister.

The election was set for June 10, 1957. I was again nominated in Queens. Chester McLure had passed away, and a political newcomer, Heath Macquarrie, a university professor from Victoria, Prince Edward Island, became my running mate. Two young war veterans were nominated in the other two ridings on the Island, John A. Macdonald in Kings and Orville Phillips in Prince, and we all worked as a team. As the campaign progressed, people seemed to think of us as the wave of the future. Heath Macquarrie was a most congenial teammate, a vast improvement over Chester McLure. We always maintained a high regard for each other, even when we engaged in good-natured sparring for the amusement of our audiences. One night at a party meeting in Charlottetown, Heath, who was several years younger than I but balding and prematurely grey, concluded his remarks by observing that I was longer in the tooth than he was. When it was my turn to speak, I assured the audience that Heath was telling the truth. "But since I am several years older," I continued, "I assume he will not resent some advice from me. I would advise him never again to make a statement in public that is so hard to believe." The crowd loved it.

I noticed an entirely new mood in this campaign. Diefen-baker was attracting huge crowds across the country, and we could sense a definite shift in the political wind. One day a shrewd old Conservative worker asked me how I thought the campaign was going. I told him I noted one change: every few days, someone volunteered that he or she was going to vote for me for the first time. "You'll have a big majority, Angus," the old fellow predicted. "They're just like rats — for every one you see, there are 100 more." I would not have put it quite that way, but he was right. For the first time since Confederation, we won all four seats on the Island.

On election night, June 10, Gwen and I went to the home of friends in Charlottetown, Ed and Helen Tanton, to watch the results on television. The telephone rang constantly as excited poll workers reported the results in their districts. One telephone call had nothing to do with politics, but it pleased us nonetheless: Gwen's sister, Elinore, had just given birth in Regina to a baby boy, whom they named David. When it became apparent that we were sweeping the Island, Gwen and I drove to the CFCY television studio in Bonshaw, where I made a brief television appearance, and then we joined the victory party in the Charlottetown Hotel.

When the votes were all counted, we found out that I had won by a margin of 1,872, more than twice as much as any Conservative candidate on the Island since Confederation. It was also a huge increase over my 95-vote margin in the previous election. Heath won by 926 votes, more than any previous Conservative candidate in the riding; Orville Phillips, with a margin of 234 votes, became the first Conservative elected in Prince since 1904; and John A. Macdonald won by 452 votes, at that time the largest margin of any Conservative candidate in Kings in this century. Across the country, the Conservatives won 112 seats. It was a minority government, but it was the first

Conservative government in Ottawa since 1935. The Liberals, under the leadership of Louis St. Laurent, won 105 seats; the other parties, 48.

Our success in Prince Edward Island was due, I think, to three factors. First, the public was simply in the mood for change. Voters had decided the Liberals were too arrogant and had been too long in power. Then there was the "Diefenbaker factor." Diefenbaker had a great talent for latching onto any grassroots grumpiness towards the Liberals and exploiting it to the hilt. As a campaigner, he was a political treasure. Without him, I doubt that we would have won more than one seat on the Island. The third reason was that all four Island candidates had worked together as a team during the campaign.

A few days after the election, Diefenbaker instructed George Hees, a Toronto MP (later to become minister of Trade and Commerce), to get in touch with me. At that time, we did not have a telephone on the farm in Lewis, as the telephone lines had not yet reached our area. Hees telephoned my sister, Effie Smith, a widow who ran a store in Orwell Cove, and her son George brought the message to me. My instructions were to go to Ottawa immediately. I flew to Ottawa that evening, and when I arrived I was told to report the next morning to the Centre Block, from where I was to go to Rideau Hall with my colleagues. I had had no inkling up to that point that I was being considered for a cabinet post, as Prince Edward Island did not always have a member in the cabinet. It was not until I was sworn in that I discovered precisely what my new job was — minister of Fisheries. All the other members knew in advance what their departments were to be, but because of some slip-up I had not been told. That cabinet post suited me fine, as I was interested in natural resources, and I was already familiar with many of the issues in Fisheries. In selecting his cabinet, Diefenbaker used three factors: geographical representation, his perception of each member's ability, and previous political experience, although the only member of caucus who was an ex-cabinet minister, Earl Rowe, who had served in R. B. Bennett's cabinet, was not appointed to cabinet. I had expected that he would be appointed so that we could draw on his experience.

For the first two months, there were only 16 of us in the cabinet. One of my colleagues was the man I had worked for in a byelection in 1952, Mike Starr from Oshawa. Many people thought Mike and I looked alike — so much so that some people had trouble telling us apart. One busy day, just after the cabinet was sworn in, Gwen and I walked down Sparks Street to sign a lease on a house we were renting. A man stopped us and congratulated me profusely on my elevation to the cabinet. "I've worked for you ever since that first byelection," he said. I was nonplussed. I did not know who he was, but I figured he had to be from somewhere in Queens County. I was just about to confess that I could not place him when he said, "May I speak to you privately for a moment?" He led me to a store entrance, leaving Gwen standing on the sidewalk. "For heaven's sake, Mike," he said, "now that you are a minister of the Crown, you can't go walking down the street hand in hand with a strange woman!"

That was not our only case of mistaken identity. One evening our caucus gave a reception for officers of the national Conservative Party at the Chateau Laurier. I happened to catch the eye of a middle-aged woman who was standing a short distance away. She was staring at me. The next time I looked her way, she seemed to be quite agitated. The third time, she came storming over to me. "I have worked for you ever since you have been in politics," she said, "and if I am not worth speaking to, Mike Starr, you know where you can go!" "I'm sorry," I said, "but my name is Angus MacLean." That made her more agitated than ever. "What has come over you, Mike?" she asked. "Are you off your rocker, pretending to be somebody else?" Fortunately, the real Mike Starr was in the room. I told her I would take her over to him, which I did. He greeted her immediately. She was at a loss for words.

I settled into my new job — in an office in the tower of the West Block that Sir John A. Macdonald had inhabited almost a century before — quite happily. Diefenbaker, and some of the cabinet ministers, mistrusted the civil service, on the assumption that they had been too cosy with the Liberals for too long. I had no such problems. The senior officials in my department were all very co-operative and seemed to appreciate having me as their new minister. I always felt that Diefenbaker's problems with the civil service stemmed, at least in part, from his paranoia. He did not trust them, and they knew it, so his suspicions became a self-fulfilling prophecy.

There were several Islanders on my office staff, including Lowell A. S. Allen, my executive assistant, who came from Summerside; Florence Field, my private secretary, who was a MacPherson from Uigg; and Rosemary Trainor, my confidential secretary, who moved from Charlottetown to work for me in December 1957 and remained with me — except for a three-year period after I left Parliament — until I retired from politics in 1981. She was a tremendous asset to me throughout my political career. She was highly efficient and knew the riding well. She made sure that requests from constituents were dealt with promptly. She always made sure that any Islanders visiting my office were shown every courtesy and often arranged for me to take them for a meal in the parliamentary restaurant. Florence Field had previously worked on James Gardiner's staff when he was minister of Agriculture. When Lowell Allen left to work for a private company, I hired John Smethurst, an RAF veteran who had been on the staff of the wartime RAF station in Charlottetown and who had married an Island woman.

Other secretarial staff included Arleta Heenan, Gwen Davies, Muriel Martin, Kevin McKenna, Sandra MacLean, Martin Gilmore and Joan Flemming. My first deputy minister was George Clark. Unfortunately, he died of a heart attack in Tokyo in 1962. I decided that Dr. A. W. H. Needler, who was then in charge of the station in Nanaimo, British Columbia, would be a good candidate to replace him. I suggested him to the prime minister, who technically was in charge of hiring deputy ministers. "Fine, Angus," he said. "Whatever you want is fine with me." That was typical of Diefenbaker. I always found him to be reasonable and co-operative as long as he was dealt with diplomatically. He did not once interfere with the business of my department. I was never quite sure whether that signified a vote of confidence in my judgement or a Prairie boy's indifference to fish. (Diefenbaker was, however, a big fan of sport fishing.)

I am not sure that all my colleagues enjoyed the same level of trust. Mike Starr and I were the only ministers who held the same portfolios throughout the Diefenbaker government. Some ministers appointed later may have retained their departments also, but others were promoted to more difficult departments while others were moved to less sensitive portfolios.

In those days, of course, we did not face the crises that were to plague the fisheries in later years, although we did deal with conservation issues that foreshadowed events of today. For instance, we were making a strong case internationally for the reduction or elimination of the hunt for certain types of whales. We were concerned about the decline of Atlantic salmon, which was caused by a number of factors, including runoff from the soil, the dams that had been built on salmon streams and perhaps overfishing. On the West Coast, we also worked at restoring salmon stocks to streams that had been blocked by landslides and other debris. On the Great Lakes, our Fisheries Research Board tried to solve the problem of an infestation of lamprey eels. They had apparently attached themselves to ships travelling from the ocean to the Great Lakes, and were now leeching onto lake trout and killing them. Through the Department of External Affairs, the government was also trying to establish a 12-mile territorial zone to protect Canadian fishing interests, although these negotiations did not bear fruit until the 1960s.

It seems odd in these days of depleted fish stocks, but the big worry when I was minister of Fisheries was finding markets for our more-than-abundant supply of most species. In those days, fish was still a cheap food, with a second-class image. Our department contained a research section, known as the test kitchen, whose main function was to develop recipes for tasty fish dishes and to find more uses for fish byproducts. At one point, we were even experimenting with fish flour, made from fish heads and tails. I remember giving at least one interview to reporters citing this product as a high-protein addition to baked goods. One of my roles was selling the idea that people should eat more fish. I attended many luncheons, each with a dozen or so varieties of fish dishes on the menu, promoting fish as a tasty and nutritious food. During one of these occasions, a Fisheries Council of Canada luncheon at the Chateau Laurier in Ottawa, I extolled the virtues of fish as part of a weight-loss diet. Going so far as to quote from Shakespeare's *Julius Caesar* ("Yond' Cassius has a lean and hungry look"), I suggested: "He could well have retained his slim figure yet lost his hungry look if he had eaten more fish."

Cabinet met regularly every week and quite often there were additional cabinet meetings on urgent matters. In addition, there were a number of cabinet committees that also met at least once a week. In addition to my departmental duties, I served on a cabinet committee that had the responsibility of ensuring that draft bills were not flawed in any way before being introduced in the House. I also chaired a cabinet committee that passed most routine orders-in-council, such as transferring pieces of federally owned land to other jurisdictions for roads or other public uses. We had to make sure that we did not pass any orders-in-council that had political implications and should be referred to the whole cabinet. We also attended caucus each week and listened carefully to the advice and warnings of all our backbenchers. The Prime Minister's Office (PMO) had a rather small staff and they were civil servants for the most part and did not do more than advise on technical matters. We all worked hard, and each MP participated fully in our government.

For me, one of our most unsettling tasks as a cabinet was making decisions that were literally a matter of life and death. At that time, capital punishment was still the law, but cabinet had the right to commute a death sentence to life imprisonment, which we did fairly often when there were mitigating circumstances in a case or when there was the slightest doubt of guilt. In one case in which we did not commute the death sentence, the murderer confessed to several other unsolved murders before he was hanged.

In my first year in cabinet, Gwen and I rented a fully furnished house from a physician who was taking a postgraduate course at university. When he returned to Ottawa, we rented a house owned by a CCF MP who had been defeated in the 1958 election. Our next-door neighbour was a retired civil servant. One day, our daughter Jeannie, who was then about six, was with him in his yard, playing with seed pods from a maple tree, tossing them in the air and watching them spin to the ground. Our neighour was fascinated by this phenomenon. "Where did you learn to do that?" he asked. "My daddy showed me," Jeannie replied. "Your daddy must be a smart man," our neighbour said. "Well, I guess he is fairly smart," said Jeannie. "He would hardly be the minister of Fisheries if he wasn't."

Jeannie may have been impressed by my exalted estate, but it did not leave me much time to spend with her or the other children. By the late 1950s, we had four pre-school-age children. Allan was born in December 1954, Mary in June 1956, and our youngest, Robert, in September 1958. I recall that when Robert arrived, I took a box of cigars to the next cabinet meeting, as was the custom of the day. As a cabinet minister, I had to travel often to various parts of Canada and sometimes overseas. Once when I was packing to catch a plane for a conference in Newfoundland, I explained to the children where I was going. I arrived back in Ottawa a couple of days later, but as usual, my workdays began early and ended late. Three weeks after I came back, one of the children asked Gwen, "When is Daddy coming home from Newfoundland?"

My cabinet colleagues and I did not have much time for the social life we had enjoyed in Opposition. There were, of course, some lighthearted moments. Ellen Fairclough, who was the first woman cabinet minister, had been part of our bowling group when we were backbenchers, and we were good friends. She tended to get discouraged when she felt she was being unfairly blamed for some problem, and I sometimes wrote notes to her, usually in the form of limericks, to cheer her up. One day, after she had taken over the Immigration portfolio, Gordon Fairweather, a new Conservative MP from Saint John, made a speech in which he mentioned Immigration in a way that she felt reflected badly on her ability as a minister. She was unhappy about this and said so in the cabinet room before a cabinet meeting. I wrote her a limerick on the spot and passed it to her.

> Said the lady Ellen Fairclough
> I've had just about enough
> What with Fairweather friends
> And equine nether ends
> It's tough, tough and rough

That bit of nonsense cleared the air. Ellen burst out laughing.

Ellen was a popular cabinet minister and was well regarded by the Opposition parties as well. I suspected that some of the older members had some reservations about the wisdom of appointing a woman as a cabinet minister, but I considered her as one of my special friends. Diefenbaker was the first prime minister to appoint a woman to cabinet, and I was impressed that he felt the role of women as cabinet ministers was long overdue.

Less than a year after we formed the government, we headed off on the campaign trail again. Diefenbaker was worried about the possibility of his minority government being defeated at an awkward time, and he was looking for a clear majority to be able to carry out the programs he wanted to implement. In January, the new Liberal leader, Lester Pearson, gave him the excuse he needed to go to the Governor General and ask for the dissolution of Parliament. In his parliamentary debut, Pearson moved a no-confidence vote, demanding that the government resign at once and hand the reins back to the Liberals, without benefit of an election. The motion was defeated, but Diefenbaker maintained that the Liberals were obviously not going to co-operate. The election was called for March 31, 1958.

Already, the government had accomplished a great deal. As I told the audience at my nomination meeting in Charlottetown, we had done more in an eight-month period than any other government since Confederation. Among other things, we had increased old-age pensions, raised disability and blind pensions and veterans' allowances, extended the period of unemployment insurance benefits, made available $300 million for housing projects and provided $25 million in special grants to the Maritime provinces. Those grants had a tremendous effect on the Maritimes. For the first time in years, people in the region felt that the government in Ottawa understood their problems and was prepared to do something about them.

Diefenbaker was in top form in the campaign of 1958, drawing huge crowds wherever he went. On election night, he got his majority government, in spades. When the votes were counted, the Conservatives had the biggest election victory in history — 208 seats. The Liberals were left with 48, and the CCF won eight. The Conservatives again swept all four seats on the Island. All of us had increased vote margins. In Queens, I won by a margin of 6,182, and Heath Macquarrie won by 5,693.

Perhaps the Conservative Party won too many seats across Canada in that election. It was hard to keep a caucus of that size united or to give the backbenchers enough to do. And the election triumph did little to alleviate Diefenbaker's paranoia or his indecisiveness. Perhaps he simply was not callous enough to make the tougher decisions. When a cabinet colleague that he respected disagreed with the rest of us, he would go to almost any lengths to get unanimity. Thus we ended up stewing over some important issues week after week.

One matter on which I felt Diefenbaker should have taken a firmer stand was the conversion loan episode, which came to our attention one fine afternoon in the summer of 1958. I received a message from the PMO: Diefenbaker was holding an emergency cabinet meeting in an hour's time. When I entered the room, I could see that Diefenbaker was worried. We soon found out why. Donald Fleming, the minister of Finance, was proposing that about $6 billion in wartime Victory bonds that had not yet matured and that paid 3 percent interest, should all be converted at once into new bonds paying, in some cases, 4.5 percent interest, the going rate of interest at the time. This scheme had been proposed to Fleming by James Coyne, governor of the Bank of Canada. Fleming argued that, with all these Victory bonds maturing over the next few years, they were "overhanging the market." This argument made no sense to me, and probably not to most of the cabinet.

At the time I could not understand why Fleming, normally so tightfisted over any proposal to spend money, showed no concern that the conversion loan would add millions of dollars a year in carrying charges on the national debt. I wondered whether he had been advised honestly by his financial experts, or whether some political or financial junta had sold him a bill of goods. I felt the bonds should be converted only when they matured. When the Victory bonds had been sold, their maturity dates had been spread out over a number of years, so that they could be replaced by new bonds in an orderly way. Converting five Victory bond loan issues at one time sounded to me about as sensible as a doctor advising a patient to eat five meals at one sitting, so that he would not have to worry about his poor appetite for a couple of days.

But the deed was done. To our horror, we learned that Fleming had already approved the printing of new bonds and had already informed the financial institutions. He indicated that he thought Diefenbaker had given him the green light to do this, but that obviously had not been the prime minister's intention. I think most of us in cabinet felt at first that the plan should be cancelled anyway, and Fleming moved to a less sensitive department. But after hours of discussion, we concluded that it was too late. We had to give our reluctant — and retroactive — approval. The prime minister did not demote Fleming. He was from Toronto, and Diefenbaker presumably feared alienating the heart of Conservative strength in Ontario.

I found out later that 90 percent of the Victory bonds were held by the banks and other financial institutions. Most individuals who had bought the bonds had already cashed them, because as interest rates rose, their cash value declined. But the banks, which now owned the bonds, made a killing on the premature conversion. The value of their bonds rose overnight from about 86 percent of face value in some cases to 100 percent — a total gain of hundreds of millions of dollars. I had expected that we would be slaughtered in the House over the conversion loan. But the Liberals were strangely silent. Only Dr. W. H. McMillan, a Liberal MP from Welland, Ontario, raised a question in the House.

It appeared to me later that the Liberal Party's financial position improved greatly around that time. The party seemed to recover quickly from the costs it had incurred in two recent general elections, and it was able to finance such extravaganzas as their "thinkers' conference" in Kingston, Ontario, in the fall of 1960. This conference was to sound out people's opinions as to what directions the Liberal Party should take on important issues in the future, and to recruit new, chiefly younger, members. John Turner was one of those who joined the party at this time.

From a political standpoint, life looked fairly rosy in the late 1950s. The party was high in the polls and things were going smoothly — the continuous questions about the cancellation of the Arrow aircraft and the arming of Bomarc missiles with atomic warheads had not yet surfaced. I enjoyed some personal moments of gratification, as well. In 1958, I was surprised and honoured when I learned that my alma mater, Mount Allison University, planned to confer on me the honorary degree of doctor of laws and letters. Rev. Ross Flemington, who had been principal of Mount Allison Academy when I graduated from it 25 years previously, performed the ceremony, as president of the university.

During those busy first years in office, I tried to get back to the farm in Lewis, and to visit my constituents, as often as possible. It did not happen very often. We still kept some sheep, so we had to hire somebody to do the farm work. Even during election campaigns, I could not spend all my time on the Island, as I had to keep an eye on my department in Ottawa and, like other cabinet members, I was occasionally asked to campaign in another province on behalf of one of our candidates.

I felt fairly secure in my own riding. Since 1951, I had won bigger voting margins than any other politician on the Island since Confederation. Some of the credit for that belonged to Diefenbaker. He was immensely popular with Islanders and remained so long after his star had plummeted in Central Canada. His visits to the Island, usually during election campaigns, were always a pleasure. He knew he was on friendly territory and among kindred spirits, and his lighter side would often emerge. One day, I rode in the car with Diefenbaker to a political meeting in Montague. As we were driving past the Roman Catholic church in Vernon River, I told him about Father Doyle, a great humorist who had served in the parish a little more than half a century before. One story Diefenbaker liked concerned the time that Father Doyle was trudging up the hill to the parish house one hot day in July, shortly after he arrived in Vernon River. A man with a horse and wagon caught up to him and stopped. "You must be Father Doyle," he said. "Get in. My name is Joe Murphy." "Where do you live, Joe?" the priest asked. "Just a couple of miles up the road," Murphy replied. "How is it I don't ever recall seeing you at mass?" Father Doyle asked. "Well, although my name is Murphy, I happen to be a Presbyterian," he replied. When the two men arrived at the parish house, Father Doyle got out of the wagon and looked up at his new acquaintance. "You know, Joe," he said, "we're both getting along in years, and we haven't much farther to go, so I'm going to give you a little tip." "What would that be, Father?" "Well, when you climb the golden stairs and arrive at the pearly gates, and St. Peter asks who you are, just tell him you're Joe Murphy from Vernon River and let it go at that."

Diefenbaker liked the Father Doyle stories so much, he immediately commissioned me to gather all the little remarks of the priest that I could find. I did that for several years. (Years later, after Diefenbaker died, I learned that Sir John A. Macdonald, another Conservative prime minister, also had a weakness for

Father Doyle's witticisms. He had heard some of them from Joseph Pope, his under secretary of State, who was from the Island, and had asked Pope to collect Father Doyle jokes.) On one occasion in recent years the Institute of Island studies asked me and Sister Christina, a grandniece of Father Doyle's, to do a review of Father Doyle's life at a meeting in Montague. She gave the facts of his life, while I told some famous jokes and witticisms. The program was recorded for radio.

Diefenbaker's popularity no doubt gave the provincial Conservatives a boost. In September 1959, about a year and a half after the Diefenbaker sweep of 1958, the Island elected a Conservative government, led by Walter Shaw, for the first time in 28 years. The provincial Conservatives' campaign included a promise that they would urge Ottawa to build a causeway linking the Island to New Brunswick. They called themselves "the Party of the Causeway." I thought this was a mistake. On one of my trips to the Island, I made a speech in Summerside in which I pointed out some of the technical problems involved in building a causeway, and some of the dangerous stresses to which the structure would be exposed, particularly in the winter months. I also had reservations about the possible effects on the fisheries and on the ocean environment in general. I certainly did not believe that a fixed link to the mainland would be the panacea that its promoters pretended it would be.

Nineteen fifty-nine was a busy and important year for me. From January 16 to January 25 I represented the Canadian government at a Canadian Trade Fair in Kingston, Jamaica. On April 1, I represented the government at a special dinner hosted by Air Marshal Hugh Campbell, the chief of the Air Staff, to celebrate the 35th anniversary of the RCAF. On September 29, I was guest of honour at the official opening of a new million-dollar school at Caraquet, New Brunswick. It was, among other things, to teach the latest fishing techniques. I was accompanied by

Martin Gilmore, my secretary, and Lou Bradbury, director of Fisheries Industrial Development.

On November 18, the Nova Scotia and federal governments gave a special reception for Anastas Ivanovitch Mikoyan, first deputy chairman of the Council of Ministries of the Union of Soviet Socialist Republics. His plane landed at Shearwater Air Base for a refuelling stop on its way to Mexico. The reception was held in Halifax and I represented the federal government. As a memento for the occasion Mikoyan gave me an unusual souvenir — a small music box decorated with a miniature Sputnik.

However, the most memorable event on the Island that summer of 1959 was a visit by Queen Elizabeth and Prince Philip on July 30. As the Island representative on the Privy Council, I was appointed minister in attendance to the Queen for her visit to the Island, taking over from New Brunswick Minister Hugh John Flemming at Shediac, New Brunswick, where I boarded the royal yacht *Britannia* for an overnight stay and a trip across the Northumberland Strait to Charlottetown. We had a formal dinner that evening with the Queen and Prince Philip; the next morning we had an informal breakfast on our own. While I was eating breakfast, the valet assigned to my room packed up all my clothes and sent the suitcases somewhere to be taken off the yacht in Charlottetown. I had never had a valet before, so I was unprepared for this — and somewhat dismayed to find that he had packed the only belt I had brought along. Luckily, I was wearing a suit and tie, because one of my duties was to present the lieutenant governor and other officials to the Queen when we arrived in Charlottetown. When the royal yacht docked in Charlottetown and the Queen disembarked, I followed a few paces behind, beltless, hoping that the swarms of photographers on the dock would not catch a candid shot of a cabinet minister with his pants down.

Later, there was a reception and dinner at Government House in Charlottetown. Among the guests were Premier Alex Matheson and the Bishop of Charlottetown, Malcolm MacEachern. Matheson was a huge man, about six-foot-six; the bishop looked to be about the same size. I was standing in the lobby chatting with them when Prince Philip came along. "I know which one of you is nearer Heaven," he said, "but which is the taller?" After dinner, the Queen asked me to accompany her out to the lawn to look at the stars, since the Island air was so beautifully clear. I knew a bit about the stars; I had taken a course in astro-navigation during the war, but I had forgotten much of what I had learned. The Queen, on the other hand, knew many of the stars by name. It was a side of her that surprised and impressed me. On August 1, the entire cabinet attended a special dinner in Halifax given jointly by the Nova Scotia government and the federal government to bid bon voyage to the Queen and Prince Philip.

In 1960, Gwen and I bought a house on Clemow Avenue in Ottawa. At the time, the children ranged in age from two to seven, and the whole family thought that it was time to get a dog. We decided that the most suitable dog for the city would be a small, short-haired animal. One day, Gwen and a couple of the children went to the local animal shelter in search of such a dog. All the small dogs there that day seemed to be high-strung, yappy and boisterous, but a big, young, long-haired Scotch collie totally enraptured Gwen and the children, and he was invited to join the family. We called him Taffy. He was quiet, with a slightly sad, pleading expression, and he turned out to be a lovely dog, intelligent, obedient and gentle. He loved us all.

One weekend in August, the entire family was away, so we had to send Taffy to a boarding kennel for the weekend. Monday was a hectic day. Gwen needed the car to take the children to the doctor for their shots, so I went to Parliament by bus. In the confusion of that scorching hot day, Taffy was momentarily forgotten. About five o'clock that afternoon, the telephone rang. The people who ran the kennel called to remind us that we had not picked up Taffy, who would now have to be sent home by taxi. Shortly after, as I trudged up our street in the August heat after a three-block walk from my bus stop, a taxi passed me. I could see Taffy in the back seat, sitting up straight, apparently well aware of the fact that for once, he was top dog in the family. The neighbours were quite amused.

Taffy travelled to the Island with us every summer, and when the family moved there in 1969, he stayed on the farm. He seemed especially bonded to Jeannie. When he was very old, Jeannie went to England for a few months, and Taffy seemed to miss her terribly. The day she arrived home, she walked the last couple of miles to the farm. Taffy, who had been in failing health, trotted a couple of hundred yards to meet her. That night he died, and the whole family buried him sadly the next morning in our pet cemetery, in a grove of maples. Taffy joined Prince, Rover and other farm dogs in their final resting places.

My overseas trips included a journey to Tokyo in November 1960 to the 12th Colombo Plan conference. The Colombo Plan was an association of governments of Canada, Japan and other Asian countries that considered matters of trade. The heads of the delegations received an invitation to the royal palace, where we were to be presented to the Emperor. William Frederick Bull, our ambassador to Japan, arranged to pick me up at the doorway of my hotel. About 20 minutes after the appointed time, I finally spotted him walking up the street, coat flying out behind him. He explained that his car was stuck in a traffic jam a few blocks away, and that we would have to take a taxi to get to the palace on time. We grabbed a cab, and Bull, who spoke a little Japanese, told the driver to take us to the palace. The driver stopped instantly, in the middle of the traffic. This request apparently did not make sense to him. I produced my invitation, which was written in Japanese and English. He read it, shrugged and set off for the palace. When we arrived at the gates, he and the palace guards had a discussion in Japanese. I again produced my invitation. We discovered that we were at the service entrance, so we set off for the proper gate. A similar performance took place: discussion between guard and driver; scrutiny of my invitation. The guards eventually let us in, and we managed to get to the reception before the Emperor arrived. Apparently, that was the first time a taxi had ever been allowed into the grounds of the palace.

Back in Ottawa, the government faced one of its toughest challenges so far. In the winter of 1958 - 59, the cabinet had to decide what to do about the Avro Arrow, a Canadian-developed supersonic interceptor aircraft that was being built just outside Toronto. This was a problem we had inherited from the previous Liberal government, which had started the project. More than $300 million had already been spent in development costs, and more than 14,000 people were employed in the aircraft's production. The Arrow was an excellent aircraft, built for Canadian conditions. Unfortunately, it was also expensive, and no other country seemed prepared to buy it. The Americans claimed that manned aircraft were out of date. The St. Laurent government had postponed making a decision on the Arrow until after the 1957 election. Diefenbaker's minority government had not been in a good position to attempt such a controversial move, so the issue hung over our heads until February 1959. The cabinet defence committee, consisting of Diefenbaker, Defence Minister George Pearkes, Donald Fleming, Raymond O'Hurley and one or two others, finally passed sentence: the Arrow development was going to be discontinued. Donald Fleming considered the Arrow a terrible waste of taxpayers' money. When it was cancelled, I got the impression that he was filled with glee, and that he could hardly wait to tell Avro that it was all over.

I thought the decision was premature. The government had not given enough thought to the effects cancelling the project would have on the economy, which had already been feeling the effects of rising unemployment. Much of the cost of developing the Arrow had already been paid for, and we were not going to recoup that cost by cancelling the project. I thought we should explore all possible ways to exploit the technical capabilities that had been built up in developing the Arrow. There was little chance to debate the matter in cabinet, however. The decision had been made by the cabinet defence committee, and that was that. However, I was shocked at the company's reaction to the cancellation. They decided to destroy and scrap all the prototypes that had already been built.

The public's reaction to the cancellation of the project, especially in the Toronto area, was predictably hostile. That marked a turning point in Diefenbaker's relationship with the public and the press. From then on, he became more cautious than ever about making major decisions. His indecisiveness created a climate of unease within the cabinet. And that turned out to be his — and our — undoing.

The Fall of
John George Diefenbaker

These days, it is hard to imagine the climate of fear that existed in Canada in the late 1950s and early 1960s. The world was in the depths of the Cold War. Russia and the United States seemed perpetually on the brink of a high noon showdown, nuclear style. Some Canadians were building new homes with bomb shelters in the basement; the federal government had its own bunker ready in Carp, Ontario. It was no wonder that most Canadians held strong views, pro and con, on nuclear arms. The Diefenbaker cabinet was no exception.

In August 1957, about two months after our government came to power, Russia had fired the first intercontinental ballistic missile (ICBM). Overnight, the whole world's strategic position was upset. Manned aircraft were no defence against ICBMs. Then, in October, Russia launched its first earth satellite. It was clear they were ahead of the Western world in ballistic missile research. It was also clear that Canada and the United States had a common interest in defending themselves from possible bomber or ICBM attacks from the North. In May 1958, the two countries signed an agreement to establish a joint air defence, known as NORAD (North American Air Defence Command). The United States was developing ground-to-air defence missiles, known as Bomarcs, to defend against ICBMs and bomber attacks. We agreed in 1958 that two of the Bomarc bases would be in Canada. The task of dealing with these complex problems, and the resulting negotiations with the Americans, fell to a cabinet defence committee, consisting of the prime minister and the ministers of Defence, Finance, Defence Production and External Affairs. The decisions on these issues were pretty much cut and dried before they came before the entire cabinet for approval.

When the Bomarcs were first discussed in cabinet, I pointed out that, since they were not long-range intercontinental missiles, they would explode on Canadian territory if ever used. I said this should be explained to the public before we made a decision; however, it appeared that the decision to acquire the Bomarcs had already been made by the prime minister, the Defence minister, George Pearkes, and the rest of the cabinet committee on defence. My warning was swept aside that day as being of little consequence, although this factor later became an issue in the debate over nuclear warheads.

Once we made the commitment to install the Bomarcs, I believed that we had to follow through and equip them with nuclear warheads. In my view, the Russians were less likely to attack if the Bomarc bases along the U.S.-Canadian border were effectively armed. My experiences during the Second World War probably influenced my reasoning. When I was in England in 1942, I had been given a crash course in chemical warfare because I happened to have a degree in chemistry. What was not generally known at the time was that the British were manufacturing vast stocks of mustard gas in the northwest of England, purely as a deterrent. It worked, because the Germans never did use chemical warfare in that war, although they had the capacity to do so.

The cabinet, like Canadians in general, was sharply divided on the nuclear arms issue. Howard Green, the External Affairs minister, was working hard internationally for disarmament; Doug Harkness, the Defence minister, was equally adamant that we had to fulfill our NORAD obligations immediately. Meanwhile, voters were flooding Diefenbaker's office with letters opposing nuclear warheads. He always paid close attention to his correspondence, which he considered his pipeline to the grassroots. Month after month, he postponed making a decision and this hung over our heads during the election called for June 1962.

Another incident that militated against our government was the Coyne affair. When we had come to power in 1957, and Donald Fleming was appointed minister of Finance, James Coyne was the governor of the Bank of Canada. He had been appointed by the Liberal government to succeed Graham Towers, the first and only governor of the Bank up to that time. Coyne was considered by many an unsuitable person for this position, which paid $50,000 a year, a huge salary in those days and $13,000 more than the prime minister received. Coyne was opinionated, inflexible and unreceptive, as was Donald Fleming. A clash of personalities was inevitable — they both had an exaggerated sense of their own importance.

In 1959 Coyne gave a series of public speeches in which he criticized government policy, a role completely inappropriate for his position. By March 1961, at the suggestion of the Bank of Canada board of directors, he promised to make no more political speeches. By this time, however, Fleming seemed to have developed an extreme animosity towards Coyne. He was further outraged when the board of the Bank increased Coyne's pension from $11,000 a year to $25,000, a princely sum in those days.

In June 1961, under instructions from Fleming, the board reluctantly demanded Coyne's resignation. Two of them phoned Fleming and suggested that Coyne be allowed to finish his term, which expired six months later on December 31. Fleming told them that cabinet would not allow this, a statement that was completely unjustified. Coyne refused to resign and 10 days later, Fleming introduced a brief bill in Parliament that, when passed, would have said: "The office of the Governor of Bank of Canada shall be deemed to have become vacant." When the Opposition asked Fleming if the bill would be referred to a committee of the House, Fleming said, "No," without seeking advice or asking cabinet's opinion, and thereby walked into the Liberal trap. The Liberals had control of the Senate, and when the bill reached the Senate, a committee there gave Coyne a platform from which to create sympathy for himself and enmity for the governnment, aided and abetted by the Opposition. I felt strongly that Coyne should have been allowed to finish the remaining six months of his terms as unobtrusively as possible, and then be replaced by a more suitable person.

Nothing was settled by the time we headed into another election, in June of 1962. In the midst of the campaign, the dollar was devalued, a move that the Liberals pounced on gleefully, flooding the country with "Diefenbucks" — imitation dollar bills with 92 1/2 cents printed on them — a gimmick that the Liberals used to intimate that the Canadian dollar was not worth its face value. At the beginning of the campaign, everyone assumed that we were going to stay in power, and that the election was little more than a formality. I did not feel that way. I thought that the public would at least try to reduce the government's majority. Since it is as easy for a million people to change their minds as it is for one, we could even end up losing the election.

As it turned out, my worries were well founded. We were reduced to a minority government with 116 seats. The Liberals had 100; Social Credit won 30; and the newly formed New Democratic Party, 19. However, we managed to retain all four seats on the Island. Sadly, we had lost a friend and a fine MP in 1960, when John A. Macdonald died suddenly as a result of a heart attack. John A. had been elected in 1957 and 1958, and had been a member of the provincial legislature for a number of years. He was a war veteran, having served with distinction with the North Nova Scotia Highlanders. John A. was universally liked and would have had a great future if he had lived. His widow, Margaret Macdonald, was elected in a byelection in his riding in 1961 and was re-elected in 1962.

Diefenbaker chose to interpret our poor showing nationally as a mistake on the part of the electorate. He seemed to believe that, given the chance, voters would rectify their error and return the Conservatives to power with a clear majority. I thought we should sit down with the leader of the Social Credit Party to determine what we could do to get that party's support, and perhaps give the government a normal life span of four years. Together, the Conservatives and the Social Credit Party formed a majority; the Socreds' views on national issues were similar to ours, and I could see no reason why they would want an early election. However, Diefenbaker remained totally rigid on this point. He acted as though even minor flexibility was too high a price to pay to save the life of the government. Attempts were made, without success, by some of my fellow cabinet ministers to bring the Social Credit leader, Robert Thompson, on side and thus avoid a defeat in the House, which would require another election to be held.

Two months after the election the prime minister announced that I would be the Canadian representative attending the Trinidad and Tobago Independence Celebrations in Port-of-Spain, Trinidad, from August 30 to September 5. I brought with me a message from the prime minister to Dr. Eric Williams, prime minister of Trinidad and Tobago, conveying the good wishes of the people of Canada to the people of Trinidad and Tobago in their attainment of independence. My wife accompanied me, and it was an interesting and historic week, and a respite from the worries of our government's future.

As the months went by, the issue of nuclear warheads still hung over our heads. The situation was exacerbated by the Cuban missile crisis in October, when the world watched in fear as U.S. president John F. Kennedy and Soviet Union chairman Nikita Khruschev engaged in a potentially disastrous showdown. More than ever, it seemed vital that Canada make up its mind about its role in North American defence. That winter, Robert Thompson, the leader of the Social Credit Party, issued an ultimatum to Diefenbaker. If the government wanted his support, it must make a decision, one way or the other, on the nuclear arms issue. Still Diefenbaker procrastinated. I felt helpless in this situation — as though I were a lemming in the middle of thousands of other lemmings that were about to leap over the cliff. What was happening, I thought, spelled certain doom for the government. As it turned out, I was right.

On February 3, 1962, Doug Harkness resigned from the cabinet over the nuclear weapons issue. Two days later, Pearson moved a no-confidence motion in the House. I sat across the aisle from the prime minister, and as the vote was taking place, he leaned over and asked me to go to the parliamentary library to find out what a previous prime minister, Arthur Meighan, had said when his government lost a no-confidence motion. I sped off to the library and returned with the reference before the vote was counted. Pearson's motion passed by a vote of 142 to 111. I do not remember exactly what that reference said. I think Meighan had simply made the standard statement about going to the Governor General — which is what Diefebenbaker did, the next day. We were launched on another election campaign. As a caucus, we were in terrible shape to go into an election — open division in the cabinet, secret meetings, plots to get rid of Diefenbaker, a few cabinet ministers jockeying for the prime minister's job. The plots to get rid of Diefenbaker were usually initiated out of Toronto. Most of caucus realized that dumping Diefenbaker would be like jumping out of the frying pan into the fire.

I thought it was urgent that we reorganize ourselves as a government and as a caucus to reinforce our strengths. Diefenbaker's strength was in political campaigning. One possibility would be to appoint a deputy prime minister, perhaps Leon Balcer from Quebec, to remove much of the weight of administrative duties from Diefenbaker. The day after our defeat in the House, our caucus met at nine o'clock in the morning. Diefenbaker offered to resign. Senator Alf Brooks, Senator Gratton O'Leary and I all appealed for party solidarity. I had not intended to speak, but as the meeting progressed I became so distressed by the gravity of the situation that I rose on the spur of the moment and spoke with all the persuasiveness I could muster. I felt that I was witnessing political suicide — that we were all heading for political defeat if we continued on the course we had embarked on. The attacks by a miniority of caucus members on Diefenbaker, I felt, were not only unjustified but politically stupid.

That dramatic caucus meeting has been chronicled in several political histories, including *Visions and Indecisions* by Patrick Nicholson. Nicholson described the scene this way: "Senator Alfred Brooks then spoke, and he was followed by the articulate Senator Gratton O'Leary and by Fisheries Minister Angus MacLean, whose usual taciturnity gave place to emotion and eloquence as, in perhaps the most moving speech of the meeting, he appealed for party solidarity." Peter Stursberg, in *Diefenbaker: Leadership Lost*, quoted Alvin Hamilton, the Agriculture minister, on the same meeting: "Then, these great loyalists like Brooks and Angus MacLean spoke. I never heard MacLean so beautifully fluent." In Stursberg's book, Erik Nielsen, MP for Yukon, recalled: "It was a most moving caucus. Senator O'Leary made one of the most moving speeches that I have ever heard in all my life. And Angus MacLean, who is a very quiet, unassuming, self-effacing individual, leaped on a table and spoke, tears streaming down his face. Everyone, after all this huge emotional orgy, was united, and then a couple of days later, everything was split asunder by this cabinet break-up."

As Nielsen observed, by the time the caucus ended, the situation looked upbeat and hopeful. The cabinet ministers had all pledged allegiance to Diefenbaker. George Hees, who had been eyeing Diefenbaker's job, even embraced the prime minister and walked out of the meeting with him, announcing to the waiting press that we were all united behind the leader and ready to take on the Liberals. Three days later, Hees and Pierre Sevigny, the associate minister of Defence, showed up unexpectedly at the prime minister's residence, 24 Sussex Drive, and told him they were resigning.

It now seems likely that Sevigny and Hees had been blackmailed by an enemy of Diefenbaker's who knew about their alleged association with Gerda Munsinger, a German woman suspected of being a security risk. At that time, their involvement with Munsinger was not public knowledge. In fact, it was not until three years later that the "Munsinger affair" surfaced in the House and turned into a well-publicized sex-and-security scandal. Diefenbaker could have dissipated some of the animosity that had been stirred up against him if he had revealed to the public why Hees and Sevigny had resigned. He refused to do this, presumably out of consideration for the ministers' wives and families.

Donald Fleming also decided not to run in the election, for personal reasons (his son Donald had been seriously injured in a car accident). Diefenbaker has been criticized in print — unfairly, I think — for leaving the impression that he would appoint

Fleming to the Supreme Court and then failing to do so. I was a witness to the actual events. Patrick Kerwin, the chief justice of the Supreme Court, had died, and it was expected that a member of the court would be promoted to chief justice and that a new appointment would be made to fill that vacancy. One day as a cabinet meeting ended, Diefenbaker whispered to me, "Stay, Angus, I need a witness." After everyone but Fleming and I had left, Diefenbaker said to Fleming, "I would like to appoint you to the Supreme Court." Fleming's reply was something like this: "Mr. Prime Minister, I have given years of my life in service to our party. If you don't see fit to appoint me chief justice, I cannot accept your offer." So that was that. It was the only time I had ever heard of a lawyer refusing an appointment to the Supreme Court. Fleming must have known it would be almost unheard-of to appoint a lawyer with no experience as a judge as chief justice of Canada. I concluded that he had other plans.

In spite of the chaos in the cabinet, Diefenbaker launched an energetic campaign, with results much better than the Liberals and many Conservatives thought possible. In the 1963 federal election, the Liberals ended up with 129 seats to our 95, another minority government. Nevertheless, they were in and we were back in Opposition.

From where I sat on the Opposition benches, the Liberal government, under Lester Pearson, seemed determined to eliminate some of the country's most cherished symbols. I liked Pearson as a man; he was approachable, modest and friendly, with a whimsical sense of humour. (My judgement of him may have been coloured by the fact that his parents had shown my mother-in-law great kindness when she was a young schoolteacher in Ontario.) On the downside, he seemed ill at ease as a parliamentarian, after having spent 20 years as a diplomat. And he appeared to have irrational hangups about some of the symbols of our heritage.

The Red Ensign was a case in point. Over the years, various people had raised the question of whether the Red Ensign was distinctive enough to be a suitable flag for Canada, but few had considered this a matter of prime importance. Not Pearson. He seemed to think that it was his mission to remove from the flag any symbol remotely connected with Christianity or with any other country — no thistle, shamrock, rose or fleur-de-lis. Pearson chose the annual meeting of the Dominion Command of the Canadian Legion in May 1964 to propose a new flag. Some people felt that broaching this subject in front of this particular audience showed great courage; others felt that it was an act somewhere between undiplomatic and insulting. Sadly, at that point, not much thought was given to representing Aboriginal culture in our national symbols. Personally, I had no objection to seeing a maple leaf used as a national symbol, but I also felt, as many other Canadians did, that we should retain in our national flag some symbols of the European cultures of our country, as all our provincial flags do.

I received letters to this effect, including some from the province of Quebec. In a speech in the House in July, I pleaded with the government to take the wishes of millions of Canadians into account. "After all," I said, "a flag is a thing of the heart. There are millions of Canadians who want the Union Jack retained in the flag in some way. At the present time many of them who would not otherwise do so support the Red Ensign simply as a reaction to the demand of the government that the Union Jack be removed from the flag. But these are reasonable people. They would be willing to compromise. It is true they want the Union Jack, but many of them would not care if it were in lengthwise or sideways or even edgewise, as long as it was there. They put great stock upon the Union Jack. They know it to be a flag of freedom, a flag of Christendom."

I said many Canadians felt that any move by the government, especially a minority government like Pearson's, to deprive them of their flag, would be an infringement of their rights. I continued: "Prime ministers come and go, but the flag should be a permanent thing. Only last Saturday one of my constituents in conversation with me summed up the attitude of many of my constituents by saying, We are approaching a deadlock on this matter, but there is a perfectly simple solution. Leave the flag alone and change the prime minister.'"

Pearson stayed on for another three years, but the Red Ensign went. The new flag with the red maple leaf flew officially for the first time in February 1965. After months of debate, the Liberals had invoked closure and their resolution on the flag passed in the House. I thought the whole thing had been badly handled. The government should have listened to all points of view to try to find a compromise, so that as many Canadians as possible could look on their new flag with pride.

We had another federal election in November 1965. Pearson, of course, was hoping for a majority. We gained two seats, and the Liberals gained two, and they were still a minority government. Heath and I were both re-elected in Queens, with increased margins over the previous two elections. Two new Conservative candidates, Mel McQuaid in Kings and David MacDonald in Prince, defeated the Liberal incumbents, and Conservative support increased throughout the Maritimes.

On the government benches there was a new MP from Montreal who was to rise to national prominence — Pierre Elliott Trudeau. My earliest impression of him was of a spoiled brat who made a show of being contemptuous of anything traditional. His famous remark that MPs were "nobodies" 100 yards from Parliament Hill typified his scorn for his fellow parliamentarians. One convention of the House is that members are expected to wear a tie. Trudeau would show up in sandals and without a tie, but would throw a scarf around his neck and knot it. As part of the ritual for the opening of Parliament, MPs stand at the bar of the

Senate chamber to listen to the Speech from the Throne. I happened to be standing next to Russell MacEwan, the MP from Pictou, Nova Scotia. "Gosh, Angus," he said, "I had no idea this was going to be so formal." I said, "What do you mean, Russ?" "Well," he said, "Trudeau's got shoes on."

I must confess that I was not always prepared to dress appropriately for my varied duties as a member of Parliament. When the Shah of Iran paid an official visit to Ottawa in April 1963, Diefenbaker, as the leader of the Opposition, asked Gwen and me to represent him and his wife, Olive, at a dinner at Rideau Hall, the Governor General's residence, on April 25. We attended the dinner, which took place on a Friday night. The next morning, Gwen sent my tuxedo to the dry cleaner. A few hours later, we were informed that the Shah was giving a dinner that evening at the Chateau Laurier, and the Diefenbakers wanted Gwen and me to take their place again. We phoned the dry cleaner to retrieve my tuxedo. No answer. It was not open on Saturday afternoons. Then we tried to rent a tuxedo. No luck. As a last resort, we borrowed a tuxedo from a neighbour who was about my build, and we made it to the dinner on time.

In the House of Commons, besides wading into headline-grabbing issues such as the flag debate, I kept hammering away on matters that were perhaps less glamorous, but were no less important — veterans' and old-age pensions, the plight of farmers, the decline of rural communities. In May 1966 I cited statistics showing that between 1941 and 1956 the number of farms on Prince Edward Island had decreased to 9,442 from 12,230. (That trend continued; today there are fewer than 2,000 farms.) Some of this, I said, was due to the inability of some farmers to make the transition from small family farms to large commercial operations. Another factor was that many farmers simply became discouraged and gave up hope of making a living on the farm, and "rural blight" set into the community. "Even in a province such as Prince Edward Island where agriculture is of such importance," I said, "there are places where in living memory there were perhaps 30 students going to a one-room school and now there is not a single resident." Perhaps I was thinking of my own community, where the population had fallen to about a dozen people from more than 100 over the previous three decades.

At the time I made that speech, Gwen and I were making plans to move back home to Lewis. Gwen and the children usually spent most of the summer there. Unfortunately, parliamentary recess rarely coincided with school vacations, so I usually spent at least part of the summer in steamy Ottawa. Our house would be shut up all day when I was there alone, and when I got home, at about 10:30 at night, it would be 80 degrees downstairs and about 90 upstairs.

We felt that the children would be better off in Prince Edward Island. We lived in the Glebe in downtown Ottawa, which in a way was a village within the city, and they would miss that. But they did not like the impersonality of the big schools in Ottawa. (They were shocked to find out that their new high school, Montague Regional High, a creation of the provincial Liberals' drives for consolidation, was much bigger than any school they had gone to in Ottawa.) And they considered themselves Islanders. They loved the farm and the outdoor life. Gwen and I thought this was something we should encourage. Besides, the farm kept calling me home, as it had for many years. I had never felt completely at home anywhere else. I certainly could not visualize living in a city for the rest of my life. I have always felt that it is a great advantage to own land, especially a farm. It is a laboratory of life; it makes you realize that, like every other living thing, you are part of the web of life.

I had not lived full-time in Lewis since I was first elected to Parliament in 1951. When I went to Ottawa, my father managed the farm for a few years with the help of a hired man. He enjoyed that; my mother had died in 1950, and his work on the farm eased the loneliness of being a widower. But in the fall of 1956, he had been hurt in an accident. He had driven to Chester Martin's store in Caledonia, and he had taken our son Allan, then two, to help Gwen, who was busy with our third baby. I was in a back field with a couple of hired men, sawing the winter's supply of wood with an engine-driven saw bench. My father parked his car at the store and stood by the open door to pick Allan up. Just then a pickup truck backed into the car door, crushing my father's pelvis.

I followed the ambulance to Charlottetown and spent most of a long, lonely night waiting to see whether my father would survive emergency surgery. (At one point, I remember, I went out to the car to pass the time by listening to the radio and was pleased to hear that the Conservatives, led by Bob Stanfield, were winning a provincial election in Nova Scotia for the first time in 26 years.) My father recovered and lived for 10 more years, but it was clear that our farm operation had to be greatly reduced. We disposed of all the animals except for a flock of sheep, and hired a couple to manage the place on a much smaller scale.

In April 1967, some remarks I made in the House of Commons made headlines across the country. The Halifax Chronicle-Herald played the story on the front page, with a banner headline across the top of the page that said: "Traditions Eroding: MP Considers Leaving." The *Globe and Mail* headline read: "Thinks of Emigrating Over Discard of 'Royal.'" I made that speech, which Canadian Press described as "emotion-packed and moving," at the height of the debate over unification of the Canadian armed forces. I was opposed to unification; on a number of occasions I argued that unification would not produce the economies the Liberal government was claiming and that it would greatly depress morale in the armed forces. I was also opposed to the government's plan to remove the word "royal" from the armed forces under the new unification bill. To me, that represented the last straw. I told the House that because of the erosion of traditions that I and millions of other Canadians held dear, I was seriously thinking of moving to another country "in the best interests of my children and my children's children." To me, this was just another in the series of moves Pearson's Liberals were making to dismantle Canadian institutions. Closer to home, in my own party, another institution, John Diefenbaker was under fire.

Many of the Conservative MPs had never sat in Opposition before. Some of them thought that this situation was intolerable. They were mostly people who had run for the first time in 1957 or 1958 and had no experience of how hard it was to get elected under any of the leaders before Diefenbaker. They could not see that even now the Conservative caucus was stronger than it had been under any other leader since R. B. Bennett. From 1935 to 1963, five of the nine elections had been disastrous for the Conservatives. The four under Diefenbaker had been markedly better. Now, oddly enough, these MPs were labouring under the delusion that they would do better without Diefenbaker. Unfortunately, the malcontents within the party had a leader, too. His name was Dalton Camp.

Camp was an advertising man who ran the 1963 federal election campaign that sent us back to Opposition. The next year, he became national president of the party. The party presidency is an unpaid, part-time, elected post. The president is elected at the party's annual meeting and by tradition usually serves a second term by acclamation. The president is usually an MP or a senator. (The office of national director, on the other hand, is a full-time, paid appointment made by the party leader.) Egan Chambers, a former MP from a Montreal riding, had been elected party president in 1963 and a second term should have been almost automatic. But when he arrived at the 1964 annual meeting, he found that Dalton Camp had been campaigning for the position. Chambers, not willing to create dissension over the issue, withdrew his name, and Camp was elected president.

Camp was a native of New Brunswick who had started out as an active Young Liberal. He had abandoned the Liberals, however, in 1952 to write advertising copy for the Conservatives in the provincial election campaign. He wrote clever, effective copy under the pen name L. C. House, which, apparently, stood for "Let's Clean House." The Conservatives, under Hugh John Flemming, scored a smashing victory, and Camp did his best to spread the notion that it was he and he alone who had finessed this win. The election results propelled Camp into a political advertising career. Many provincial Conservative parties hired him to handle their election advertising. He, of course, reminded would-be customers of his successes, although not of his failures. After Camp became party president, he kept his ears open for murmurs of discontent, and then organized and stimulated it. The strategy was to have the party force a leadership review. Since most of the caucus supported Diefenbaker and believed that the party should be grateful to him for his outstanding service, Camp had to turn to the few malcontents to achieve his purpose.

I was disappointed and amazed to learn that my running mate in Queens, Heath Macquarrie, was involved with Camp's scheme. Heath and I had always had a co-operative relationship, and I was greatly in his debt for his doing much more than his fair share of constituency work while I was tied down by my cabinet responsibilities. I could not understand why he would turn against a man who had contributed so much to his own success. By then, under Diefenbaker's leadership, Macquarrie had been elected four times, with large margins each time. Diefenbaker had even given him an appointment as a parliamentary secretary, even though the Island already had a cabinet minister. Many of our constituents, especially those in rural areas, remained fiercely loyal to Diefenbaker, no doubt recognizing his empathy for the underdog and his undeniable contributions to the welfare of the Maritimes. But unaccountably, Heath apparently leapt into the anti-Diefenbaker campaign. In his book *Red Tory Blues*, he observed: "In the weeks leading up to the annual meeting, I devoted long hours to the Camp cause."

The annual meeting at which the "Camp cause" reached a climax was held November 14 to 16, 1966, at the Chateau Laurier in Ottawa. Camp had arranged to have the front seats of the hall packed with people, mostly youths, who were to show every discourtesy, scorn and insult possible to the former prime minister. They refused to stand when he entered the hall; they tried to shout him down when he spoke; they shouted, "We want Camp!" All of this in front of a national television audience. That weekend, it happened to be the Conservatives' turn to give a talk on a free-time political program on CBC television. Diefenbaker's office assigned me to this delicate task. I remember feeling that if I could just keep from making things worse, I would be doing very well. As a result I tried to be as non-controversial as possible, so my presentation probably made for dull television.

At the annual meeting, delegates re-elected Dalton Camp president of the party association by a narrow vote and passed a resolution calling for a leadership convention to be held before January 1968. Two months later, Diefenbaker himself called for a leadership convention at the earliest possible date. It was scheduled for September 1967.

When Robert Stanfield, then-premier of Nova Scotia, declared his candidacy, a delegation of Nova Scotia Conservatives came to the Island to try to convince me that, as a Maritimer, I should support Stanfield. At the time, I did not think Diefenbaker was going to run, so I probably would have voted for Stanfield — but only under certain conditions. "I can't support

Stanfield," I told the Nova Scotia Conservatives, "unless I can be assured that Dalton Camp will not have any special role under his leadership and that he will distance himself from Camp." Many Conservatives detested Camp at that time, and I think with some justification. It was not so much that he thought the party should have a new leader, it was the fact that he had used his position as president of the national Conservative association to undermine his leader. Most people, including me, felt that he should have been neutral and objective.

I went to the Conservative leadership convention in September 1967 intending to vote for Duff Roblin, the premier of Manitoba, for whom I had a high regard. We had been friends since the early days of the war, when we were both posted to the Fort MacLeod air force base. At the last minute, though, Diefenbaker announced that he was running for the leadership. I voted for him, not because I thought he had much chance of winning, but because I wanted him to get enough support so that he would not be completely humiliated. In the end, he dropped out after the second ballot, and Robert Stanfield became party leader. After his election, Stanfield gave a speech in which he made the unfortunate remark that he would "try to get along with that fellow Camp." This did not sit well with the Diefenbaker loyalists, and it reinforced a widespread notion that Stanfield was Camp's catspaw, which probably lost a few seats for the Conservatives in the next election.

Shortly after Stanfield took over the leadership, he visited the Island to give a talk at the University of Prince Edward Island. When he arrived at the airport, quite a few of us went out to meet him, including Bill Brown, a local party executive. Brown, who happened to be a well-known Charlottetown undertaker, drove Stanfield into town in his limousine. We were driving down Longworth Avenue, led by a police escort, when a pedestrian recognized Bill Brown and took off his hat. Then all the traffic stopped until the assumed funeral procession had passed. Some wit remarked afterwards that it was the first time he had ever seen the corpse sitting up beside the undertaker.

I thought Dalton Camp and the people from Toronto who wanted to get rid of Diefenbaker had used absolutely the wrong strategy. In his final years as leader, Diefenbaker told me more than once that he wanted to retire. "But I don't want to be pushed out," he said. That was typical of him. He was 71 in his last year as leader, and I am quite sure that if the party had taken the trouble to thank him publicly for the tremendous contribution he had made, he would have gladly and gracefully retired. The party would have been spared the conflicts that tore it apart, and he would have been spared the abuse to which he was subjected in those final months. But there was no banquet, no fanfare, no public acknowledgement for a job well done — just sniping and bickering and disloyalty.

The way Diefenbaker was treated in the end was absolutely contemptible. He had taken over the party when its fortunes were very low and had brought it to the point where it won the greatest election victory in its history. Under his leadership, we won three elections and made a credible showing in two more. As well, he gave this country pretty good government for six years. Even if he had been a totally inept leader, the methods used to replace him would have been completely unjustified. Nobody should be subjected to the treatment he endured from members of a party that had elected him in a democratic way for an open-ended term of office. It was a sad end to a troubled chapter in the party's history.

Against the backdrop of political infighting, there was one high point for me in 1967. That year I was president of the Canadian branch of the Royal Air Forces Escaping Society, an association of Commonwealth airmen who had escaped from prisoner-of-war camps or who had evaded capture in enemy territory in the Second World War. The society had been formed so that we airmen could express our gratitude towards European friends who had risked their lives to help us. As a Centennial project, the Canadian branch decided to invite 14 of these helpers from eight countries to Canada in September. I had the pleasure of drawing attention to their presence in the House of Commons, where they received thunderous applause from spectators in the public galleries. According to the rules of the House, spectators are not supposed to do this, but this time even the guards joined in the applause. Later, Veterans Affairs Minister Roger Teillet hosted a dinner for them, one of a number of meals at which they were special guests. At one of these dinners, I gave a talk in which I expressed our profound gratitude towards the helpers, paraphrasing the 25th chapter of Matthew — "I was hungry and you gave me something to eat; I was thirsty and you gave me a drink; I was a stranger and you took me into your homes." One of the helpers was Countess Geneviève de Poulpiquet of France. After she returned home, she wrote me a letter thanking me for my role in the visit. "I told you," she wrote, "that the first time I was near you at a lunch I thought, 'What an icy Englishman!' but day after day, I saw the ice melting till the day where even the men were crying hearing you. 'I was hungry, etc.' I never heard anything like that."

The Rise of
Pierre Elliott Trudeau

In the spring of 1968, I watched what I considered a national tragedy unfold on television: Pierre Elliott Trudeau was elected leader of the Liberal Party. To me, that event underlined my opinion that our political parties had moved to a foolish method of selecting their leaders. Before the Liberals started electing leaders in national conventions in 1919, party leaders were selected by caucus. The conventions were based on the idea that all constituencies, not just those that had elected MPs from the party, would be represented in choosing the leader. Unfortunately, these conventions have serious drawbacks. In a country the size of Canada, most delegates to national leadership conventions know very little about the people they are voting for. Watching that 1968 convention, the first one broadcast on television, I was struck by the fact that I knew the Liberal leadership candidates better than 95 percent of the delegates.

The public generally assumes that if someone is appointed a federal minister of the Crown, he or she must be stable, objective and mature, and that a party leader must be even more so. In my experience, the opposite is true. Anyone running for the leadership of a political party in our present system of national conventions has to be something of an egomaniac. You would certainly have to believe you were worth the million or so dollars a leadership campaign costs nowadays. Most of the prime ministers I knew were, at the very least, eccentric. Louis St. Laurent was the most stable and rational of the ones with whom I had any contact. In our modern system of selecting national leaders, image often triumphs over substance. Candidates are not promoted on the basis of experience, but thrust into a job for which they may have few qualifications. It is like appointing an inexperienced lawyer chief justice of the Supreme Court of Canada or making a dogcatcher chief of police.

Trudeau, in terms of suitability as a prime minister, languished at the bottom of my list. To me, he represented a disagreeable trend, promoted by some members of the media, in which it was considered fashionable to scorn traditional values such as patriotism, the obligations of good citizenship and the concept of individual restraint for the common good. Nevertheless, he projected an image that caught the imagination of the press and the public, and that stood him and the Liberal Party in good stead in the next election. When the election was called for June 25, 1968, he was riding high in the polls.

In the 1968 federal election campaign, I had to make one of the most difficult political decisions of my life. The previous year, redistribution had changed the names and boundaries of federal ridings. On the Island, instead of Kings, Prince and the dual riding of Queens, we now had Cardigan, Malpeque, Egmont and Hillsborough, all single-member ridings. Cardigan, in the eastern end of the province, now included my home community, but since Mel McQuaid also lived in Cardigan and was the incumbent, the logical place for me to run was Hillsborough, which took in much of my former riding. None of the four incumbents lived in Hillsborough. I was pretty sure that if I ran against Heath for the nomination there, I would win. But Heath was anxious to run in Hillsborough, which included Charlottetown and the university, and in past elections had produced by far the greatest part of our margins in Queens. If I ran against Heath, the person who lost would be a bit of an outcast and probably would not win a nomination anywhere else.

When the new party executive in Malpeque met, their first decision was that, even with their best efforts, they could not get Heath elected in that riding, even though his home was in Malpeque. Many people in Malpeque were still bitter about his support of Dalton Camp in the Diefenbaker debacle. The party workers decided they would have to recruit an entirely new candidate — unless I would run. I suppose this was a compliment to me, but a backhanded one that might easily result in my being defeated. Malpeque was the most difficult of the four ridings, and most people in the western end of the riding did not know me. After all, I would be two ridings away from my home. Malpeque included the western part of Queens, roughly the provincial ridings of First and Second Queens, and part of the old riding of Prince. Second Queens had usually given me a majority in previous federal elections, First Queens had tended to break about even, but Fourth Prince, which was now a part of Malpeque, had usually been strong Liberal territory. The Liberals knew they had a good chance of winning Malpeque and nominated a strong candidate there — Don Wood — who lived in the riding. He was regarded as a potential cabinet minister in what was expected to be another Trudeau government.

After a great deal of soul-searching, I agreed to run in Malpeque. Robert Stanfield was now the national party leader and would probably make substantial gains in the Maritimes. I felt it was vital that we hold all four seats on the Island. But it was a hard decision to make, because, for my family and me, this was no ordinary election. After nine elections and 17 years in the House of Commons, I would have almost no pension if I was defeated. In those days, MPs' pensions were grossly inadequate. Even former prime minister Louis St. Laurent received only $3,000 a year when he retired. An all-party committee of the House, of which I was the Conservative representative, had explored ways of improving the pension plan. The committee had prepared a bill, but Trudeau had called an election before the bill could be introduced in Parliament. Pension provisions in the bill were not retroactive, so any sitting members who were defeated would be out of luck.

So this election loomed as a huge risk for me and my family. Luckily, I never had better support from party workers. That support was harnessed and directed by a man of outstanding dedication and skill, my campaign manager, Wylie Barrett. As a first step, he arranged for the publication of campaign literature to introduce me to people in the Prince County part of the riding. The literature gave a condensed version of my life story, in words and photographs. The party also erected signs at the entrances to the riding that said: "You are now entering Malpeque, where people vote Angus MacLean."

At the start of the campaign, Wylie asked me what my policy was regarding the widespread Island custom of buying votes with five-dollar bills or bottles of rum. "Absolutely not," I told him. "If I can't get elected on my own merits, I will not be elected at all." Wylie told me later that one disgruntled voter complained that his father "always got a bottle of rum for his vote"; however, I do not think we lost any votes on account of our "dry" campaign. That had been my policy from the time I first ran alone for Parliament in the 1951 byelection, and I had never failed to get elected.

During the campaign, I refined some of the strategies I had employed in the past. My rule of thumb in canvassing was that it was better to go door-to-door alone; if you take another person with you, you multiply by two the chance of being unacceptable. I also suggested to party workers that they should try to end a canvassing session at a natural break such as a wood, river or open space, so that there would be no next-door neighbour to the last place of call — a neighbour who might take offence at being overlooked.

In my 1951 election campaign, one of my goals had been to improve our party rallies, which were usually held in poorly equipped country halls. I had a folding portable lectern made, equipped with a suitable light. We also had backdrops made for the stage and arranged for members of the Young Progressive Conservative Association to usher people to their seats. In Malpeque, I asked that the podium be solid to the floor so that even a shifting of a speaker's feet would not distract the audience. More important, perhaps, the speaker would not be distracted by wondering whether his fly was properly zipped. When Heath and I ran together in Queens, we hired some of the Maritimes' most outstanding musicians, including Catherine MacKinnon and members of the Don Messer band, to entertain the crowds. When I switched to Malpeque, we engaged local musicians to entertain between speeches.

When I spoke at political meetings, I never used the word "Liberal" to refer to our political opponents. I did not want to give offence to people who thought of themselves as Liberals but who might consider voting for me. This was not just wishful thinking. Years later, one old gentleman told me, in all seriousness: "I've been a Liberal all my life, but this will make eight times that I voted for you."

I also tried to inject some humour into my political speeches. Once, after a rally in Hunter River, a lady said to me, "I wasn't able to go to the meeting in Kensington last night, so I drove down here from Kensington, and you didn't tell the story you told in Kensington that everybody was telling me about." I told her I would try to do better from then on. As I recall, I had told the crowd that a certain statement made on behalf of the present government was not very convincing. I said it reminded me of the biology professor who was asked by one of his students whether a traumatic experience by a pregnant woman would affect her unborn child. "There is no scientific basis for such a notion," the professor replied. "Take me, for example. About a month before I was born, my mother was searching for something in the attic when she stepped on a couple of cracked gramophone records and took a terrible fall, and it didn't affect me, affect me, affect me."

The 1968 campaign was our first under the new Conservative leader, Bob Stanfield. Stanfield had a family connection to the Malpeque area: the Stanfield woollen mills had started in Tryon in the 19th century. Bob Stanfield's grandfather, Charles Edward Stanfield, had immigrated to Philadelphia from England, where he had been an apprentice in a woollen mill. In 1855, after meeting a ship owner from Prince Edward Island, he had sailed to the Island, where he established a woollen mill. He eventually owned a tannery, a general store, a hat factory and a farm. Before moving to Nova Scotia, he married an Islander.

I was determined to exploit the Stanfield connection. But when I phoned Ottawa to claim an hour of the leader's time at the location of the first Stanfield woollen mill, the party officials said this was impossible. Mr. Stanfield's itinerary was already set. He would be speaking in Kensington at 3:00 p.m. on his way to Charlottetown, and that was that. I suggested that he stop in Tryon instead of Kensington. No, the party people said. His speech in Kensington was very important because of all the media people travelling with him. I phoned Ottawa headquarters several times pointing out that I believed it was essential for Stanfield to stop at what was his grandfather's first mill in Tryon. Finally, the party officials relented. We would get 50 minutes of Stanfield's time in Tryon.

We decided to use our precious 50 minutes by taking Stanfield on a non-partisan, sentimental journey, back to the scene of the Stanfield business and the family's Island origins. We found the ideal person to organize this event — Norman Carruthers, a young Charlottetown lawyer who had grown up in Augustine Cove (he is now chief justice of the Prince Edward Island Supreme Court of Appeal). He advertised the event, had invitations sent to all of Bob Stanfield's relatives in the area, as well as to other prominent citizens, and asked a local historian to give a talk on the history of the mill. Stanfield's visit was a resounding success. He was in his element. He made a short, homey speech about his family's Island roots, which fascinated his audience. The event captured the fancy of the national media; as a result the party got favourable publicity across the country. I am sure I won some votes out of the visit, as well. In fact, I learned later that distant relatives of Stanfield's, who were Liberals, voted for me. After the election, the chair of the poll near Summerside told me that I won his poll with a fair majority, the first Conservative majority there since 1919.

I needed all the help I could get in the 1968 election, what with Trudeaumania, a new Conservative leader and the perils of running in a new riding. I ended up with a margin of 210 votes, a far cry from the comfortable margins I had enjoyed in Queens; however, we did manage to win all four Island ridings, so I had met my personal objective. Nationally, though, the results were dismal. The Conservatives were reduced to 72 seats, our worst showing since 1953, and the Liberals were returned to power with a majority government. Under Diefenbaker's leadership, we had never fared this badly.

Redistribution created some additional headaches for my office staff. My highly efficient secretary, Rosemary Trainor, had kept a master file of all my constituents, for the purpose of correspondence. Another master file listed correspondents who were not in the riding. After redistribution, people in the eastern end of my old riding had to be taken off the list and transferred to another file, and people from the western end of the new riding had to be added to the list. Rosemary delegated this task to Ensa Becchina, a young woman on our staff who had emigrated from Italy as a child and who had never been to Prince Edward Island, but imagined that it was a magical, mystical place that produced such people as Lucy Maud Montgomery's "Anne of Green Gables" and Rosemary Trainor. Naturally, Ensa was unfamiliar with Island family names. After she had spent several days at this tedious job, I asked her how it was going. "Not very well, Mr. MacLean," she said. "What's the problem?" I asked. "Oh, it's awful," she said, "just terrible, you wouldn't believe it." "What's so terrible?" "Well," she said, "we're losing all the Martins, and the Robins and the Jays, and the Cranes and the Drakes and the Swans, and we're not gaining anything but Pigeons."

Now that I was no longer a cabinet minister, and I had a much reduced salary — about $18,000 less a year — and much more freedom, it was time to think about going back to farming. I did not have to be in Ottawa when the House was not sitting. We had bought a house in Ottawa, but we decided we could rent it out, and I could live in an small addition at the back when the House of Commons was sitting. In 1969, three years after the death of my father, the family stayed in Lewis.

Gwen and I had been exploring the most practical and pleasing use of the farm. When I bought the land next to my father's farm after the war, it was growing up in white spruce and upland alders, having been uncultivated for several years. We noticed that low-bush blueberries, which are spread by birds, had started to grow on this land. Perhaps we could start cultivating blueberries. My friend Ken Yeo, who had worked closely with me on some of my campaigns, was one of the Island's blueberry pioneers. He happened to have a blueberry operation about three miles away from our farm. I sought his advice. He was (and is) a gold mine of friendly information and guidance, From his long experience he knows what works best in our area.

Armed with this information, and the knowledge that Ken had been successful, I concluded that we could develop much of our once-cultivated land for blueberry growing. Blueberries appealed to me for several reasons. First, they are indigenous to Prince Edward Island, which means that our acid soil does not have to be limed to grow the crop, as is the case for many crops of Old World origin. Second, the soil does not have to be tilled, so there is no need for huge tractors or heavy consumption of fossil fuels and the soil is in no danger of eroding. Third, blueberries need smaller amounts of pesticides than most crops, and fourth, the net value of the crop per acre is higher than that of many other crops, partly because blueberries are human food, not food that is fed to animals that then become human food. Blueberry fields take a few years to develop, but this development greatly enhances the value of the land, instead of eroding it. We began clearing land for blueberries in 1968 and have been growing them ever since.

In my next few years in Ottawa, I was given a number of responsibilities in addition to my constituency work, some of them involving extensive travel. I made several trips overseas as a representative of the Canadian Parliament. The first during that period was a fact-finding mission on defence spending. When Trudeau became prime minister, he gave many people the impression that he would make severe cutbacks in the armed forces. The suspicion was that Trudeau thought of the armed forces as a waste of money. The committee on defence, of which I was a member, was given the task of studying the matter. Shortly after the election, we visited our troops in Germany and Cyprus.

My least pleasant memory of that trip involved a painful accident in — of all places — the bathtub. It happened in my hotel room in Nicosia. Midway through my bath, I grasped the porcelain hand grip beside the tub. It came away in my hand and I lost a patch of skin off my arm on the razor-sharp stub of the hand grip. I was bleeding badly, so I wrapped my arm in a towel and knocked on the room next door, where a Liberal member of our committee was staying. He helped me get dressed and arranged for me to see a Canadian army doctor, who sewed up my wound. The doctor was quite disappointed that, in the confusion, I had neglected to bring along the two square inches of missing skin. By the time we flew to Germany, our next stop, I was in so much pain I had to lie down on the floor of the plane. In Germany, our delegation visited Canadian troops, and I recuperated in a senior officer's quarters. I had the stitches removed in Copenhagen, where we studied the military budget of Denmark, a country not in NATO. As a result of our trip, our committee recommended that the government make very little change in our defence arrangements, and in fact, it did not.

The next year, I represented Canada at a parliamentary course in London, England. Most of the participants were Africans, but there was also an MLA from Saskatchewan and an MP from Australia. We were given lectures on the British parliamentary system, its development, its traditions, its strengths and weaknesses. We were also given a talk on the city of London. In the course of the talk, the lecturer warned us that it was unsafe to cross the street unless we were on a "zebra" — the word for crosswalks in London. One of the black African MPs whispered to me: "Unfortunately, I haven't brought my zebra with me." On the Isle of Man, the finance minister gave a talk on his country's finance system. He kept comparing it with the system on "the surrounding islands." It took me a few minutes to realize that "the surrounding islands" were Great Britain and Ireland.

In November 1971, I was invited, along with two other MPs — Social Credit Leader Robert Thompson and Georges Lachance, Liberal MP for Lafontaine — to take a week's tour of South Africa. There were many aspects of the South African system that I did not agree with; our visit, however, confirmed my opinion that the world media had taken an unwarranted "holier-than-thou" attitude towards South Africa. In our own back yard, we have not treated aboriginal Canadians fairly — we have only to look at our system of Indian reserves that have lasted for generations. I am proud to have been a member of government when Diefenbaker gave Canadian Aboriginal people the right to vote. I wondered, however, whether we would have been so eager to give Canadian Aboriginal people this right if they had outnumbered us three or four to one, with the likely result that non-Aboriginals would seldom, if ever, have been elected to Parliament. Our smug, hypocritical attitude is possible only because of the bacteria that the Europeans brought to North America with them, which resulted in a form of unintentional genocide. Because native Americans had little resistance to Old World diseases, about 90 percent of most tribes died off within 10 years of their first contact with whites; the Aboriginal people in Newfoundland were wiped out entirely. I felt the Canadian feeling of moral superiority in this instance was due more to historical happenstance than actually having worked to attain moral higher ground.

In October 1972, we fought another federal election campaign. The Liberals won 109 seats to our 107, which placed them in a minority position. However, despite our strong showing nationally, we lost Cardigan to a Liberal, Daniel MacDonald, a war veteran who had been severely wounded in Italy. He was a popular and highly respected politician who had been a member of the provincial legislature for 10 years and had served as minister of Agriculture and Forestry.

Shortly after the 1972 federal election, I was a member of a delegation of three MPs to an inter-parliamentary conference on European Co-operation and Security in Helsinki, Finland. My daughter Jeannie travelled with us as far as England, where she planned to spend a working holiday. Because our delegation represented Parliament, and not the government, it was considered appropriate to appoint an Opposition member as leader, and I was chosen to head the delegation. It was an interesting conference, and I believe it helped relieve the tensions of the Cold War. As part of the entertainment, the Finnish government arranged a cruise on an icebreaker in the Gulf of Finland. This was a new and exciting experience for most of the delegates; for me, it was just a reminder of home. The next conference took place in Belgrade in 1974. I was again a member of the Canadian delegation, but Barnett Danson, the well-liked Liberal member for North York, led it. By this time, the Liberals had obtained a majority in Parliament through yet another federal election.

The Liberals were riding high in the polls in the 1974 election campaign. This time Wylie Barrett was not available to run my campaign, but I was fortunate to acquire the services of some hard-working and capable people, including Keith Harrington, a former MLA, who became my campaign manager, and Enid MacKay of French River, my constituency office manager and all-purpose staff of one. Both knew the riding extremely well. We opened our constituency office in 1973. Enid had been on our campaign staff in 1972, succeeding Dianne Taylor, and she was a tower of strength. She was well-informed politically and she had the right personality — outgoing and humorous — for the job.

In the 1974 campaign, we also received some help from an unexpected source. Conservative headquarters in Ottawa had asked John Diefenbaker whether he would speak on behalf of a few candidates of his own choosing. I was pleased, and a bit overwhelmed, to learn on fairly short notice that one of his choices was Malpeque. Kensington, the largest town in the riding, was the logical place for him to speak, but the day he was scheduled to visit happened to be the day of Kensington's high school graduation. Diefenbaker turned a potential problem into a plus by stopping off at the high school to speak to the graduating class before attending the main meeting in the rink.

The rally was a great success. Diefenbaker, then almost 79, was in top form, and a large, enthusiastic crowd attended, including some tourists staying on the North Shore. One man from Ontario was so impressed with Diefenbaker, he insisted on donating $100 to our campaign advertising fund. I have no way of knowing for sure how valuable that visit was, but I do know that, although my margin was 588 votes smaller than in 1972, Malpeque was the only Island riding where the Conservatives did better in 1974 than they had done in 1968. In Cardigan, the Liberal candidate, Dan MacDonald, increased his margin by more than 1,100 votes. David MacDonald and Heath Macquarrie both had reduced margins — David by more than 1,000 votes and Heath by more than 2,000 votes. It was the same story pretty well across Canada. The Liberals gained 32 seats, and we lost 12.

I think Bob Stanfield made a grave strategic error in the 1974 election campaign. A few months before the election, he announced in caucus that, since a poll had shown that inflation was the number one concern of Canadians, wage and price controls would be part of the Conservative platform. I was the lone voice of protest in the caucus. I considered wage and price controls a cure for inflation the way that decapitation is a cure for a headache. In any case, inflation is detrimental only to those who own wealth in the form of paper. People who owe money have their debt burden lessened by inflation. "I don't think this will wash,"

I told the caucus. "The majority of Canadians may think that inflation is the number one problem, but it doesn't follow that they believe wage and price controls should be used as a cure." Obviously, I did not succeed in changing Stanfield's mind. This was the only time I can recall him imposing a decision on caucus. It turned out to be a serious misreading of the Canadian public, and it probably deprived Canadians of an excellent prime minister.

My own political career reached the quarter-century mark a couple of years later. In June 1976, my riding association organized a dinner in Kensington marking the 25th anniversary of my first election to Parliament. There happened to be an air strike at the time, so people such as John Diefenbaker, Bob Stanfield and Joe Clark had to cancel plans to attend. However, Don McLarty drove from Ottawa to represent the Canadian branch of the Royal Air Forces Escaping Society; Joe Clark, who was then national Conservative leader, telephoned from Ottawa during the dinner; and friends and colleagues, including a couple of prominent Liberals — Paul Martin, Sr., and Dan MacDonald — sent dozens of messages of congratulation. During the dinner, it was pointed out that I had been elected to Ottawa more times, with bigger margins, than any other Island politician since Confederation.

By this time, I had decided not to push my luck. I have always considered running for Parliament a huge gamble, and I knew that one of the basic rules of successful gambling is to quit when you are ahead. I also felt somewhat guilty about my family. The youngest child was then 18, and I felt that my parliamentary duties had kept me from spending as much time with my children in their formative years as I would have liked, and had placed undue responsibility on Gwen — far more than most wives are required to bear. Taking all this into consideration, I decided to retire from Parliament when the next election was called. As it turned out, I left Ottawa earlier than that.

When I went home to the Island for the parliamentary recess that summer, groups of Conservatives started coming to our farm and to my office in Ottawa to urge me to run for the provincial party leadership. The leader, Mel McQuaid, had been appointed a Supreme Court judge, and a convention was to be held in September to elect his successor. I had not considered running provincially, but now the idea had some appeal. On the plus side, I would be able to live at home; my concerns would be mainly my home province; and I would be associating chiefly with Islanders, people with friendly and familiar faces. On the negative side, other competent people were willing and eager to seek the leadership. The party was in the doldrums. The Liberals had been in power for 10 years. In the 1974 provincial election, the Conservatives had won only six of 32 seats. And the party had no funds. I finally decided to take a run at provincial politics. I was 62 years old then, close to the age when most people are ready to retire, but I made a private commitment that if I won the leadership, I would devote five more years to politics and then spend the rest of my life enjoying my family, friends and farm.

I asked Horace Carver, a young Charlottetown lawyer, if he would take on the job of managing my campaign. He agreed, and a campaign committee was formed, including Marion Reid, Leone Bagnall, Enid MacKay, David Weale, Harry Baglole and Lowell Johnson. The only other candidate was Jim Lee, a realtor who had been elected to the legislature in a recent byelection and who had worked as a political organizer for many years and knew a huge number of people in the party. He also appeared to be running a professional, well-organized campaign. Early in the campaign, we read an item in the morning paper that outlined Lee's entire itinerary. Horace worried that our campaign looked amateurish by comparison. "What we have to do is turn a minus into a plus," I told him. "I've come home to run for the leadership. Maybe what we should consider doing is asking our supporters to hold 'at homes' across the province — informal teas in people's homes." We sent out written invitations to all kinds of people to come to the "at home with Angus" teas, and they turned out to be a big hit, much more successful, in fact, than the joint meeting we held with Jim Lee in Southport.

The convention took place at the Provincial Vocational Institute in Charlottetown on September 23. It was a sunny day in the middle of harvest season. An hour before the meeting started, Horace came to me and said, "Angus, I'm really nervous. A lot of our supporters haven't come because they think you're going to win anyway, and they need to work on the harvest. You're going to have to give the most powerful speech you can give." I went into a room by myself to work on my speech.

In my speech, I noted that the provincial Liberal government of Alex Campbell had come to power a decade earlier "with an image of youth, a promise for change, a hue and cry for development." I continued: "The vision they then saw has now turned out to be a mirage. Their youth has meant inexperience, and many needless and costly errors; their change has meant disruption, a preoccupation with change for the sake of change, an insensitive tampering with traditional ways of doing things; their development has meant the expenditure of vast sums of money, an ever-increasing dependence on Ottawa, an inability to be masters in our own house. The Liberal government has taken power from hundreds of school boards and given it to five consolidated school units; from small communities, and given it to regional service centres; from the people, and given it to planners and consultants; from you, and given it to someone else. Simply put, more and more people have now seen the future the Campbell government was selling us on 10 years ago. And it doesn't work."

We kept our campaign simple right to the finish line. Gwen and I were piped into the hall by a bagpiper, and a group of my young supporters showed up in MacLean tartan scarves, but that was about the extent of the hoopla on our end. When delegates cast their ballots, I won by a vote of 589 to 437. Jim Lee moved that the convention express unanimous support for my leadership, which it did. "Angus MacLean is still the number one Tory in the province," Jim announced from the platform.

After the convention, I received an avalanche of congratulatory letters and telephone calls, including many from former Conservative and Liberal colleagues in the House of Commons. These messages were heartwarming, but they also implied great expectations. I knew the road ahead would not be a smooth one. In the next few months, we had to prepare for four byelections, which might be called at any time. The party nominated George McMahon in Fifth Prince, Dr. George Dewar in Second Prince, Reginald Peters in First Kings and me in Fourth Queens.

In September, I had a few days' reprieve from politics: Gwen and I entertained four special guests at our house. Matthieu Beelen and Jane Pagie, two of the people who had helped me evade the Gestapo during the war, visited Prince Edward Island with their spouses. Matthieu Beelen had guided me across the border from Holland to Belgium; Jane Pagie's family had sheltered me on their houseboat. It was the first time I had seen either of them since being posted to Europe just after the war.

In October, I said my farewells in Ottawa with a mixture of feelings. I was happy to be going home, but I was sad to be leaving good friends, from both sides of the House. For some reason that is not obvious to me, people trust me. In a few of my early years in Parliament, I was the only Conservative among the four senators and four MPs from Prince Edward Island, and all of my so-called political enemies seemed to trust me — but not always each other. I used to be quite amused when some of them would take me aside and warn me in confidence about the others' personal flaws. In the House, and even on the political hustings,

I did not believe in a partisan reaction to everything the Liberals did. I also did not believe in condemning Liberals as a class. I believe that in any political party, 99 percent of its members belong in good faith, believing that they are doing what is best for the country. Of course, there is the occasional professional political parasite in every party.

In my final day in Parliament, leaders of all parties in the House spoke warmly about me and my career. The Liberal spokesperson, Allan J. MacEachen, president of the Privy Council, said a number of flattering things, including these comments on my performance in the House: "As a minister he performed exceedingly well, and following his departure from the ministry he has served as a member of the Opposition, on committees and in the House of Commons in an extremely effective way. However, I believe that all of us will remember Angus MacLean mostly for his personal qualities, his readiness to extend friendship and his high integrity."

New Democratic Party Leader Ed Broadbent, paying me similar compliments, concluded in his typically humorous fashion: "In expressing wishes for the continuing good health and personal happiness to the honourable member in the most genuine fashion on behalf of my colleagues, I, of course, want to make it abundantly clear that we do not extend those good wishes into the political domain … We wish him well as he returns to his native island. We hope the political success he confronts there is not at all commensurate with the 100 percent personal success we wish him."

Even the Speaker, James Jerome, took the unusual step of contributing to this sendoff by arranging for a farewell luncheon and making some remarks of his own in the House. This was partly because I was chair of a new all-party committee, the Management and Member Services' Committee, which decided what MPs were entitled to in terms of facilities, equipment and staff. This used to be the job of the Speaker and his small staff, but as the number of MPs grew, and as facilities allotted to them increased, the work became too much for the Speaker's office. In his remarks, the Speaker noted that this committee provided a service that potentially benefited all MPs. He continued: "For that committee to reach its maximum potential it really required in its infancy a chairman who ought probably to come from the Opposition side or at least have been able to demonstrate a very objective point of view, one who could bring to the post many years of experience both in and out of cabinet as well as a reputation for objective judgement and the respect of all his colleagues. At the same time, that person should enjoy a reputation for a sane and sensible hand on the throttle. I think we have all been deeply fortunate that we have found such a chairman in the Honourable Angus MacLean."

This sendoff was an unexpected pleasure for me; some MPs retire without a mention in the House. I was moved by the tributes my colleagues paid me, and I hoped that I was at least partly worthy of the attention. My 25 years as a parliamentarian had been rewarding ones. I had the privilege of meeting a wide array of interesting people around the world, the chance to speak out on issues that were important to me and the opportunity to make life a bit easier for many of my constituents. Nevertheless, when a newspaper reporter asked me at some point how I felt about retiring from the House, I said that, unfortunately, the country and the world were in worse shape than when I had first been elected. I hoped then — as I hope now — that this was despite my efforts, not because of them.

PART FOUR

Provincial Politics

Previous page:
*My provincial
Cabinet (front
row, left to right):
Lloyd MacPhail,
me, Leo Rossiter;
(back row, left to
right): Barry Clark,
Fred Driscoll,
George McMahon,
Horace Carver,
Pat Binns,
James Lee,
Prowse Chappell.
(1979)*

CHAPTER FIFTEEN

Island Politics

During my years in Ottawa, press gallery members of considerable stature wrote some complimentary things about me from time to time. In fact, the week I left Ottawa, an article in the *Montreal Star* claimed I had "no Commons peer as a respected MP." So it was quite a contrast to come back to the Island and find myself depicted by some of the local media as a country clown — an absolute hayseed. Some members of the media apparently could not understand how I could ever get elected to anything. "He looks agonized on public occasions," the local correspondent for the *Globe and Mail* wrote on one occasion. "He is the man who has stepped off the bus at the wrong stop — bewildered, vaguely embarrassed, uncertain where he is or how he got there, groping for words which might explain his predicament ... On the platform, he has all the charisma of another Prince Edward Island product, the potato." A reporter from the Charlottetown *Guardian* saw me as "unfathomable," "ponderous" and "uncommunicative." *Chatelaine* magazine described me as "a most unlikely politician, awkward, slow, hesitant. He has no easy clichés or show biz appeal."

I have never had any illusions about my degree of show biz appeal, but on the other hand, I had travelled a bit and rubbed shoulders with some interesting folks, and I had not realized I was such a bumpkin. Of course, this was the Trudeau era, in which a trendy image counted for a lot. I certainly was not trendy, and I did not want to be. I happened to be a blueberry farmer who lived on a clay road in a quiet rural community an hour's drive from Charlottetown. If that contributed to my hayseed image, I hoped it was an attitude that would change. I hoped that, as a public service to my province, I could help foster pride in our rural heritage — so that people would realize that, despite whatever current fads were being promoted by the media, the good life was not restricted to cities and towns. To ensure that country people could enjoy the good life, I wanted to try to revitalize the Island's rural communities, or at least to slow down their decline. I believed then, as I do now, that the devaluation and devastation of rural society is the greatest single misfortune that our country and our civilization have suffered in the past few decades. I am not sure who coined the term "rural renaissance," but that idea became an essential part of our provincial party's platform.

The Island that I went home to had changed drastically during the years I had been in Ottawa. On the plus side, programs such as rural electrification, put in place by the government of Alex Matheson, had made tremendous improvements in the lives of thousands of families. Paved roads throughout the Island now meant most people did not have to drive through mud up to the axles every spring. Other changes were not so agreeable. The old community spirit — the sense of pride in one's neighbourhood, the feeling of belonging to an extended family — had deteriorated badly. The watchword of the day was "amalgamation." The government seemed bewitched by the notion that "bigger" meant "better" — bigger farms, bigger schools, bigger public institutions. Tragically, this philosophy accelerated the demise of rural districts, which I have always believed are the cornerstone of any society. Farmers, told to "get big or get out," often invested heavily in big machinery to operate expanded farms — and lost their shirts in the process. The result was that, by the mid-1970s, the number of farms on the Island had declined significantly. The death knell of farming communities was sounded with school consolidation in the 1960s and 1970s, when the government closed down small schools and cut the heart and soul out of community life.

I had been preaching the "small is beautiful" philosophy ever since I had entered public life in the early 1950s. When I returned to the Island, I found that considerable numbers of Islanders shared my disenchantment with the government's attempt to urbanize and industrialize, so I was able to attract to the party a number of bright young men and women, either to work for the party or to run as election candidates. These people included Johnny Williams, Pat Binns, Marion Reid, Barry Clark, Leone Bagnall, Prowse Chappell, Rev. Bill MacDougall, Jim Larkin and Fred Driscoll; Jim Lee and Horace Carver were already active in the party.

From my own travels and activities I met and observed outstanding young adults who were well educated and devoted to our Island. When I asked such people if they would join me in trying to bring about a new government that would improve our Island's future, their response was enthusiastic. In areas of the Island that I did not know as well, I asked friends who knew the areas to recommend candidates to recruit. I even had one or two excellent people call me up and volunteer to run for me if I thought they were suitable. We set up an outstanding campaign committee to run the election campaign. Harry Baglole, David Weale and Leo Walsh were all towers of strength in this category. David Weale became my executive assistant after I became premier.

As a party, we had to work quickly. The four byelections had been called for November, including the one in which I was running for a seat in the legislature. The advance polls took place at the end of October. I asked Horace Carver to represent the Conservatives at the advance poll in my riding, held in Belfast at the home of a well-known Liberal family. When I dropped by the poll that afternoon, Horace told me that he had challenged two voters, one of whom had a summer cottage in the riding and a permanent residence in Charlottetown. I was disturbed by this news. "There's a trap here," I told Horace. "In this riding, a majority of the people consider themselves Liberals. For a Conservative to get elected, Liberals have to vote for him. If we take on the Liberal Party, and Alex Campbell appeals to the Liberals in this riding to uphold the honour of the party, I will lose. We can do nothing to antagonize people who consider themselves Liberals." We did not pursue the issue further, and in the end, I apparently did get some Liberal support: I won the byelection by 252 votes. We also elected Dr. Dewar in Second Prince and George McMahon in Fifth Prince. Reginald Peters was defeated by Liberal James Fay in First Kings.

In spite of our wins, the Campbell government remained as complacent as ever. Premier Campbell said there was no particular significance in the byelection results; voters had simply decided to strengthen the Opposition ranks. Morale in our party was rising, but the party was still deeply in debt and its organizational structure was rundown.

Walthen Gaudet, a lawyer who was a member of our party's three-person finance committee, had passed away some years earlier, and the vacancy had never been filled. The other members of the committee were Charlottetown lawyer Alan Scales and Reagh Bagnall of Hunter River, a fine man who had done outstanding work for many years as a poll chair and who was now running a motel near the airport. In looking into the operations of the finance committee, I found that Scales had been ignoring the regulations under which the committee was supposed to operate. I told him that was not good enough. He offered his resignation, which I quickly accepted. A new committee was formed, and with the advice of Reagh Bagnall, the party's financial situation quickly improved. Scales was also chair of an interim committee formed when Mel McQuaid, the former leader, was appointed to the bench. The committee was to look after the affairs of the party until a new leader was elected. This committee had been negotiating with advertising firms in Toronto in anticipation of the next election. I felt that we had to do a lot of work before we even thought about advertising; in any case, we should be using Island talent to create our advertising, since our party espoused the principle of self-sufficiency for Islanders in every possible way.

We spent the next year travelling across the province, recruiting good candidates for the next election. We attracted some outstanding people, including two members of the clergy, a university professor, a couple of lawyers, and several businesspeople, teachers, farmers and fishers. My political duties did not leave me much time to spend on my own farm. Gwen and I rented an apartment in Charlottetown and came home on weekends. Meanwhile, our children held the fort in Lewis. Rob took charge of the blueberry crop one summer, and Jeannie, who had been fascinated by sheep since she was a child, took over our flock after she graduated from agricultural college in Guelph.

In that era, many young people from other parts of North America were moving to rural Prince Edward Island, some of them taking over farms that had been deserted for years. I met one of our new neighbours through a manure spreader. A few years before, I had bought a half-share in a manure spreader from a neighbour who was giving up farming for health reasons. Then the owner of the other half of the spreader sold his farm to writer

Farley Mowat, who engaged someone to run the farm for him. One day I stopped by Mowat's farm to let the farmer know that I had a half-interest in the manure spreader. The farmer turned out to be Lindee Climo, a young woman from California. When I arrived, she was painting a picture with black stove polish, the only medium she had on hand. I thought she had a lot of talent, but since my education in artistic matters was limited, I asked Moncrieff Williamson, director of the art gallery at Confederation Centre, to come to the farm. He did and was impressed. Lindee went on to become one of the best-known painters in the region, and she and our family developed a warm friendship.

In the summer of 1977, Gwen and I took a break from our duties on the Island to encounter some ghosts of my past. The Comet Line Association, made up of survivors of the Comet Line, had invited members of the Royal Air Forces Escaping Society and their wives to go with them on a tour from Paris to San Sebastien — our old escape route — and then back to Brussels. This time, we travelled in comfort in two chartered buses, with no barbaric enemy to fear. In southwestern France, we met Florentino, the Basque guide who had led us through the Pyrenees on that unforgettable rainy night in 1942. We were happy to see him invested with the *Légion d'honneur* at a special ceremony.

Those of us who had escaped by the Comet Line went with Maria Goya and her husband to her childhood home where her late mother, Francia Usandizanga, had sheltered evaders and fed them before the perilous crossing of the mountains into Spain. It was here on January 15, 1943, that the Gestapo had caught Dédée and Maria's mother with three evading airmen, and had arrested all five in the presence of Francia's three children. They never saw their mother again, for she died under appalling conditions in the stinking corruption of Ravensbruk. We also went to the lonely spot on the Bidassoa River where I almost came to grief as we forded it in the pre-dawn darkness.

After our party disbanded in Brussels, Gwen and I went to Holland to visit some of my helpers there. Jane Pagie and her husband, Fons, drove us to the field where I had landed by parachute when my aircraft crashed, and to the place where the Pagie houseboat had been. We also visited Jane's brother and sisters and later spent some time with Matthieu Beelen and his wife and family in Weert. Jane and Fons took us to see another helper, Adriaan Ferdinand van Goelst Meijer, an artist and ex-army officer who was living at the old castle in Waardenburg. During the war, he had masterminded my escape from Holland to Belgium, and it was he who had sent my father the telegram from Switzerland confirming that I was still alive.

It was a glorious reunion with old friends. One memorable evening occurred in Biarritz, where we were guests of honour at a dinner given by the city. I happened to be sitting next to a woman I had not previously met. She was Baronne Bernadette Greindl, the widow of Baron Jean Greindl, whom I had known only as Nemo. During the war, he had managed the Belgian unit of the Comet Line. After he had questioned me in Brussels to make sure that I was not a Gestapo agent, I had given him my Masonic ring so that it would not incriminate me if I was caught by the Germans. His widow told me that when her husband was arrested, she and her father-in-law had buried the personal effects that airmen had given Nemo for safekeeping. When Belgium was liberated, her family dug up these items and sent them to their owners or next-of-kin. In a few cases, dampness had destroyed the names or addresses. One of the rings had no decipherable identification but "Canada" and the man's military number. "Would the number happen to be C1107?" I asked. Baronne Greindl did not remember, but she left me her address so that I could write to her. After I returned home, I sent her a copy of my discharge certificate. As we both found out, I was the owner of the Masonic ring. She immediately delivered my ring to the

Canadian embassy in Brussels. The Canadian ambassador at the time, Lucien Lamoureux, was a former Speaker of the House of Commons and knew me personally. He brought the ring back to Canada, and I picked it up in the Speaker's office. After 35 years, I had my ring back among my souvenirs.

Back on the Island, I resumed my duties as Opposition leader and continued the work of recruiting candidates for the next election, which was expected in the spring of 1978. On New Year's Day, I attended Premier Campbell's levee in Charlotte-town. When I reached the premier in the receiving line, I grasped his hand and said, "I wish you every blessing in the New Year, all of them well disguised." I was referring to my expectation — and hope — that he would be appointed to the Supreme Court. This eventually took place, but not before another provincial election. It was called for April 24, 1978.

By that time, we had all our candidates ready to go, and we met as a caucus frequently during the campaign. One strategy that I insisted on was that we would make no promises during the campaign. In previous elections, both parties had made many promises, which the winning side often found itself unable to fulfil. I did not want to be in that position. Instead of promises, we based our campaign on 10 principles: making the Island more self-reliant; strengthening the social and economic fabric of communities; reassessing the education program with a view to providing more parent and community involvement; revitalizing the rural economy by developing primary resources; creating more jobs by working with the private sector to establish industries appropriate to the Island; developing a balanced road, rail and water transportation system; decreasing dependence on imported energy by encouraging conservation and the development of renewable energy sources; providing sound fiscal management; enhancing Islanders' lifestyles by pursuing a humane social service policy, supporting preventive medicine and encouraging active participation in sports, recreation and the arts; and working with Islanders to protect and enhance the natural beauty of the Island and the character of its people. I also instructed our candidates that, during the campaign, they were to refer to the other side as "opponents" not as "Liberals," they were never to speak ill of an opponent and they were never to mention an opponent by name. Our motto, I told them, was "Mud slung is ground lost."

Mud was a concept that Islanders readily related to. That election campaign coincided with one of the worst mud seasons in years, which made it a bit inconvenient to call on people who lived on clay roads. The mud slowed me down sometimes, as well, because our farm was located a couple of miles from the nearest paved road. When the muck was really bad, Gwen and I used to park our car by the side of the paved road in Caledonia West. Heading for a political meeting, I would pull on a pair of overalls and drive the tractor to the car. One night, when I was scheduled to speak at a meeting in Murray River, my car got stuck. I went to a neighbour's house and phoned my son Rob, who rescued me with a four-wheel-drive vehicle. I was late getting to the meeting, and I explained why. I told the audience the incident reminded me of the young fellow from Caledonia who went to the States looking for work. At one workplace, a woman gave him a form to fill out. The information requested included place of birth. He wrote: Caledonia. The woman looked over the form and said, "Caledonia. What state is that in?" He replied: "It's in a hell of a state — mud up to your backside and no work."

On election night, the early returns appeared to bear out the Liberals' conviction that they would continue their decade-long winning streak; however, I knew that all the returning officers were Liberal appointees, and it was their custom to report quickly polls in which the Liberals were leading and to delay results unfavourable to them. When the final results were in, we found that we had 15 members in the legislature, seven more than before the election; the Liberals elected 17. That left the Liberals with a majority of one after electing the Speaker. Cecil Miller, the former Speaker, had been defeated by Horace Carver. (Miller was 82 at the time; Carver was 28. Some wit said they were really the same age, except that Miller was in Fahrenheit and Carver was in Centigrade.)

I was pleased that, since the results were so indecisive, we had not won by a majority of one. In that situation it would have been difficult to operate a government with so many inexperienced members. In any case, I believed that it was only a matter of time before we would win. Premier Campbell seemed stunned by the results. A reporter interviewed him late on election night, and he was quoted in the papers the next day as remarking that he was "in hiding until it's safe to come out." The federal Liberals were probably taken off guard, as well, as Trudeau had been expected to call a federal election shortly after the Island election.

The legislature sat for a little over a month in June and July of 1978 to pass routine legislation, such as a supply bill to provide for expenditures in that fiscal year. In September, Alex Campbell resigned as premier, and Bennett Campbell, a Kings County member of his cabinet, replaced him. Federally the Trudeau government had been in office four years and an election was due to be called at any time. Alex Campbell had been expecting a Supreme Court appointment, and time was now running out. During this interregnum, all kinds of rumours and speculations were rampant. One rumour was that Otto Lang, the minister of Transport and former minister of Justice, had persuaded Trudeau that the government was looking too partisan before an election and should appoint a Conservative to the bench. As it turned out, the federal election was not held until May 1979, when the Trudeau government was defeated, and a little before the provincial election, Alex Campbell got his appointment to the Supreme Court. This reduced the Liberals to 16 members, including the Speaker, making it difficult for the government to get through another session of the legislature. As a result, another election was called for April 23, 1979. This time, we won 21 seats to the Liberals' 11. On May 3, 1979, I was sworn in as premier. By the time the federal election was held in May, there were no provincial Liberal governments left in Canada.

Our election victory was almost anti-climactic. As the *Ottawa Journal* pointed out in an editorial, it is a political theorem that a party that almost wins in one election usually takes over in the next. I told a reporter that the Liberal government had done itself in partly with its attitude that officialdom knew what was good for Islanders better than the Islanders did themselves. My only surprise was that a couple more Liberal cabinet ministers had not been defeated.

One of my first acts was to choose a cabinet. I appointed Pat Binns to the Municipal Affairs, Environment and Labour portfolios; Horace Carver as attorney general, minister of Justice and minister of Public Works; Prowse Chappell to Agriculture and Forestry; Barry Clark as minister responsible for the Housing Corporation (a few months later, I named him minister of Tourism, Industry and Energy); Fred Driscoll to Education and Health; Jim Lee to Social Services, Tourism, Parks and Conservation; Lloyd MacPhail to Finance and Development; George McMahon to Highways, Industry and Commerce; and Leo Rossiter to Fisheries and as provincial secretary. I also formed a special three-person cabinet committee — consisting of Horace Carver, the government House leader, Jim Lee, and me — to go over every word of every line of every bill we planned to present to the legislature, before sending it to caucus. The committee was similar to one on which I had served when I was in the Diefenbaker cabinet. I nominated Dan Compton, my running mate from Fourth Queens and a distinguished veteran, as Speaker.

Marion Reid, newly elected from First Queens, became the first woman deputy Speaker.

I was fortunate enough to be able to rehire Rosemary Trainor as my secretary. Rosemary was a highly efficient, dedicated woman from South Melville who had started working for me when I became minister of Fisheries. She took care of the office work when I was MP for Queens. With Rosemary's help, constituency work was easy and rewarding. She continued as my secretary for 19 years. When I resigned from the House of Commons, she went to work for Egmont MP David MacDonald, but when I became premier, she moved from Ottawa to Charlottetown. She was always a special friend to Gwen and me, and we thought of her as almost being part of our family. (Later, when I resigned on her for the second time, she worked in the Executive Council office, and then as secretary to two lieutenant governors, Lloyd MacPhail and Marion Reid.)

As always, of course, Gwen provided unfailing support for my political career. Through the years, despite having to shoulder most of the load of raising our family, she joined me for formal social engagements, attended political rallies, befriended constituents and generally proved to be an invaluable asset. Maybe there is some significance in the fact that back in the days when I was single, I lost two of the three elections in which I ran, but after we were married I won every single one of the next 12!

In the summer of 1979, we held a session of the legislature, mostly to take care of routine business and to pass a budget for the year. But we also took care of two important issues. We declared a two-year moratorium on large shopping malls, and we promised to cancel an agreement the previous government had made to buy 5 percent of the power output of the new atomic power plant at Point Lepreau, New Brunswick. The previous government had sold this idea on the basis that this was cheap electrical power with no strings attached. In fact, what they did was to buy into 5 percent of the plant, which meant the Island government would be stuck with 5 percent of the cost of decommissioning it and 5 percent of the cost of any accidents. After the accident at the Three Mile Island nuclear power plant in the United States during the 1979 election campaign, we believed the risks involved were much too great for a small place like the Island, especially since no insurance company would insure anyone against the risks involved with nuclear power. (That decision has proved to be a wise one; to this day, people stop me on the street and congratulate me for having cancelled the nuclear power deal.)

While the legislature was sitting, John Diefenbaker came to the Island in July 1979 as a special guest at a Fathers of Confederation Building Trust Fund dinner. The next morning, he visited the legislature, and members gave unanimous consent for him to speak. Later, I invited him to my office for a lobster luncheon. After he went back to Ottawa he wrote a letter to Gwen and me. I treasure the letter, especially since he died 10 days later, on August 16, 1979.

> *House of Commons, Ottawa*
> *August 6, 1979*
>
> *It was a memorable couple of days that I spent in your province last week. Seeing you and Gwen again brought back memories of other days. Having an addiction to lobster added all the more to my enjoyment of the luncheon you gave me, and I want to thank you for it. Angus, I also want to thank you for the motion you moved in the Legislature, seconded by the Leader of the Opposition, which enabled me to express my appreciation on the floor of the Legislature. Watching the Legislature in action reminded me of the days when you, Angus, were a Minister. You are just as dominant today as you were then.*
>
> *With warmest regards, I am, Yours sincerely, John*

By this time, Joe Clark was prime minister. The federal Conservatives had defeated the Trudeau government in a general election in May. Clark had formed a minority government with 136 Conservative seats, 10 fewer seats than the combined Opposition. Clark was not my first choice as leader. One of my great regrets in politics is that Claude Wagner, the Quebec judge who later became an MP, was unsuccessful in his bid for the national Conservative leadership in 1976. I thought he would have made a fine prime minister. Perhaps my opinion was coloured by the fact that Wagner grew up in Charlottetown, where his father ran the Prince Edward movie theatre. In any case, we became friends in Ottawa and often had breakfast together, and I had a high regard for him.

I suspect that in some quarters Clark's popularity was not enhanced by the fact that his wife, Maureen McTeer, insisted on being called by her maiden name. Clark also handicapped himself after he was elected by the cabinet he appointed. It looked as though he did not want to appoint anyone more experienced than he was. Then he announced that he planned to govern the country as if he had a majority, which was like saying that he would fly off the Peace Tower as if he had wings. Predictably, the government was defeated on a budget motion. Had the Conservatives devised a strategy to avoid defeat until the New Year, Trudeau would have been gone. Instead, Trudeau led his party to a majority victory in February. The new Trudeau government, like his previous ones, continued to plunge the country deeper and deeper into debt. Trudeau also embarked on his mission of repatriating the Constitution.

The first of many federal-provincial talks on the Constitution took place in the summer of 1980. During that time, my respect for Quebec premier René Lévesque increased, and my regard for Trudeau shrank. Lévesque and I had a personal affinity, and at those meetings we developed a friendship that continued until his death. (After I left politics, he came to Charlottetown for a premiers' meeting and sent word that he wanted to see me. I went to the airport and saw him off, which seemed to please him.) I found Lévesque to be a reasonable person, not at all stiff-necked or rigid. I had the impression that if the federal politicians had had the kind of relationship with him that I did, we would have reached some sort of compromise on the Constitution. Trudeau was particularly antagonistic. Once, when the premiers met at the prime minister's residence, 24 Sussex Drive, Trudeau treated Lévesque with such scorn that I thought it was outrageous from the point of view of simple courtesy, if nothing else.

I am not a separatist, but I sympathized with the idea that the Constitution should be flexible enough to reflect the differences between the provinces in Confederation. I have always thought that it is a great pity that there is so much misunderstanding between Quebec and the rest of Canada, or more accurately, between French-speaking and English-speaking Canadians. During my service in the RCAF, I had many French-speaking officers and airmen under my command, and I was always impressed by their dedication and capability. The French-Canadian officers, NCOs and airmen who served with me in the Missing Research and Enquiry Unit in Europe after the war were especially outstanding, and in many cases became my lifelong friends.

I believe that some of the country's difficulties stem from the mistake that the Fathers of Confederation made in calling the new country "Canada," after two of its parts. The pre-Confederation stress between Upper and Lower Canada persists as a result, and the history and traditions of the old colonies that now are Atlantic Canada and British Columbia are often ignored, as if Canada had no history or traditions except that of Upper and Lower Canada. Perhaps relations between French and English Canada would have been smoother if certain politicians had come to power. For instance, I have always felt regret at the untimely death of Paul Sauvé, a Second World War veteran who served as premier of Quebec in 1959. Although he was in office only three months, he demonstrated such a spirit of co-operation with the federal government that he might have changed the course of history. I also suspect that some misunderstanding between the two language groups occurs because of bad translations by the news media. For example, the word *demand* in French is an innocuous term for asking a question; in English, of course, the word has a much harsher meaning.

Then, too, I think that English Canada is often far too rigid in its attitude towards Quebec. Perhaps we could learn from the United Kingdom, which considers itself a unitary state, but makes all kinds of accommodations to some of its parts. For example, the justice system in Scotland differs from that in England; the Channel Islands have their own legislatures and issue their own pound notes. We might also look to France and other European countries to learn how they deal with minority languages. France has many thousands of people who speak one of five languages other than French. And I believe that all Canadians should remember the benefits of co-operation and working together for our common benefit, rather than brooding over our few differences.

Trudeau's obsession with the Constitution stemmed, I suspect, from a yearning to make his mark in history. Diefenbaker had his Bill of Rights. Pearson had his flag. Now Trudeau wanted to be known for snipping the umbilical cord with the Mother Country. The Trudeau government also proposed entrenching a bill of rights in the Constitution and changing the amending formula without the consent of the provinces. Six provinces, including Prince Edward Island, decided to fight this unilateral action in the courts. Eventually Nova Scotia and Saskatchewan joined the six provinces in their opposition to Trudeau's unilateral decision to bring home the British North America Act.

Our government's position in the constitutional talks included a plea for more equitable economic treatment for poorer provinces such as ours. In my remarks to the constitutional conference in Ottawa in September, I reiterated a theme that I had been sounding for years in the House of Commons — that certain parts of the country, my own included, had to cope with built-in economic disadvantages, while Central Canada prospered. I asked, as an example, why the federal government argued that the national interest required a uniform price for gas and oil, but did not apply this argument to electrical power.

"We all know that the federal government has the power to treat electricity in a manner similar to oil and gas. Yet presently, Island producers and businesspeople pay from two to three times as much for their power as their counterparts in several of the other provinces. This is a crippling impediment to our whole provincial economy, and yet in a matter as fundamental as this, the federal government has done little to rectify the problem.

"Could it be that because of the nature of Parliament the central government has only responded to the interests of those large provinces whose interest in the matter of power generation might be affected? Could it be that the central government only responds 'in the national interest' when those who are asked to make concessions are minorities in the House of Commons, but never when those expected to make concessions are the numerical majorities? Could it be that if we had a truly federal state, in which all partners had a more significant voice, national policies might more truly reflect the interests of all provinces and hence the entire country?"

As the constitutional debate raged on, the *Toronto Star* began a series of profiles of the 10 provincial premiers taking part in the talks. In September, it published a full-page article on me in which I commented, among other things, about the importance of pride in one's heritage. I pointed out that Maritimers have a valuable way of life, which should not always be judged by the standards of others. The reporter then quoted me, correctly, as saying I was "an Islander first, a Maritimer second and a Canadian third." I added: "I am proud to be a Canadian but I think we make it hard for people to feel pride in the country because as a nation we have underestimated the importance of tradition, rituals and symbolism. We have to have a sense of special occasion to give some meaning to our brief span on earth." At the time of the interview — and after it was published — I had no inkling of the furore these seemingly innocent remarks would set off.

I soon found out. That fall, I was invited to appear on the television show *Front Page Challenge,* as the hidden guest on a segment featuring as its news headline the court challenge by the six provinces. After the panelists guessed the headline, I appeared on camera for the customary interview. To my astonishment, the panelists immediately attacked me. Pierre Berton was particularly hostile — not so much because of the constitutional issue but because of my audacity in admitting that I was "a Prince Edward Islander first, a Maritimer second and a Canadian third."

"Why in the heck in this country can't we call ourselves Canadians first?" he asked. I replied that my comment had come during a conversation pertaining to Maritime pride, and that my love for Canada and for the Island should not be subtracted from each other. "Arguing that because I love P.E.I. I am less a Canadian," I said, "is like arguing that because I love my wife I'm against the monarchy, because the Queen is a woman too."

Another panelist, Betty Kennedy, described the constitutional squabbling as "disgraceful" and asked whether I was concerned about my place in history. I replied that the provinces were rightfully objecting to unilateral changes in the Constitution by a prime minister who "can't change his mind and won't change the subject."

After the program was aired, people across Canada fired off hundreds of letters to the program's Toronto office and to Maritime newspapers, protesting that the panelists had treated me badly. "I was appalled by the rudeness displayed by members of the panel toward a very distinguished guest," a typical letter said. Some writers said the moderator, Fred Davis, should have kept the panelists in line. "Where was Fred Davis when Pierre Berton started to vilify the Hon. J. Angus MacLean, the great soldier, the honorable citizen and decent father of a family, with a lovely wife watching her husband being harassed by such thoughtlessness?" one writer asked.

This tempest in a teapot had almost died down when another *Front Page Challenge* panelist, Gordon Sinclair, revived it by writing to the Halifax newspapers, scoffing at "all that fuss because some Canadians thought a Canadian premier should be a Canadian before he's a parochial provincial chieftain." That brought another flood of letters, which did not let up for months. I received many letters as well, from every province and territory in Canada, and all supporting my point of view.

On the home front, we continued pressing forward with measures aimed at increasing the Island's self-reliance and revitalizing its smaller communities. Among other things, we provided extra funding for small schools and small farms, established a program to protect heritage roads, lobbied for a new veterinary college for the Island, embarked on projects to promote alternative energy sources and started a massive paving program. (I insisted, however, that my own road was not to be paved while I was premier; I did not want to be accused of obtaining special privileges.) As often as possible, I also continued to speak publicly on issues I felt strongly about, such as the need to protect our soil from erosion and the need to encourage small-scale farming.

One day after I had been premier for almost two years, I had to drive out to Eldon to keep a dental appointment with my dentist, Dr. Fortune, who is a Newfoundlander. He was in a cheerful mood and had just returned from vacation in Mexico. He had met another tourist there who said that his grandfather, surname Peters, had been premier in Prince Edward Island. Dr. Fortune asked me if this was possible. I told him that there had been two premiers of the Island who were named Peters and they were brothers. The doctor then asked me why some families produce so many politicians. I said, "Perhaps it's defective genes." The doctor thought this was very funny.

In August 1981, I decided it was time to quit politics permanently. The five years that I had committed to the provincial party were up, and I resigned as party leader. As one of my last official duties as premier, I travelled to Fiji in October to represent the Island legislature at the 27th Commonwealth parliamentary conference. After I returned home, Jim Lee was selected at a leadership convention in November to take my place. On November 17, 1981, I resigned.

In the two and a half years since I had become premier, we had achieved some goals and fallen short of others. Some of the situations I would have liked to rectify were the result of irreversible actions by previous adminstrations. For instance, I thought that the previous government had made a mistake with school consolidation. Some of the new schools were too big and the bus routes were too long. But the buildings were already in place, so there was not much we could do about it. Among the achievements that gave me most satisfaction were the construction of a new hospital in Charlottetown to replace the old P.E.I. and Charlottetown hospitals, and the decision to build the veterinary school in Charlottetown. I think our government also raised the morale of rural people on the Island. Small farmers who had been discouraged by the difficulty of making a living in an age of monster machinery started growing specialty crops that commanded high prices in the marketplace, proving that it is possible to make a living on a small farm.

I retained my seat as a private member until the summer of 1982, when the legislature was dissolved for the next election, to be held in September. I was then 68 years old, in good health and eagerly looking forward to a life in which I would be free to engage in interests I had had to postpone for more than 30 years. I still hoped to be of service to my home province and perhaps to the world outside it, but I also planned to devote much of my time to husbanding the land my ancestors had hacked out of the wilderness. My modest goal was to enhance one tiny corner of the world.

Retirement

Retirement Years

About a week before I stepped down as premier, I attended a meeting of the Council of Maritime Premiers. The other two Maritime premiers, John Buchanan and Richard Hatfield, held a dinner in my honour and presented me with two retirement gifts, a shepherd's staff and a rocking chair. In the next few years, I did not have the opportunity — or the inclination, for that matter — to wear out my rocking chair. I kept busy working on the farm, serving on community organizations and travelling.

At home, my major preoccupation was the blueberry crop. By the time I retired from politics, we had cleared about 50 acres of land that had grown up in white spruce and shrubs of various kinds, and stimulated the natural spread of wild blueberry plants. Over the next few years, we gradually cleared about 50 more acres, and our annual yield increased from a few thousand pounds to almost 200,000 pounds, enough to provide a slice of pie for about a million people.

One of the advantages of growing wild blueberries is that we do not have to plough or plant. The birds spread the seeds that grow new plants, and the existing plants spread through underground rhizomes. One year I noticed blueberry bushes springing up in a pasture field where we had grown hay and grain in previous years. I wrote to a blueberry expert at the agricultural research station in Kentville, Nova Scotia, to ask whether it would make sense to try to develop such a field, or whether it was better to clear the trees and shrubs from land that was already producing more berries. He suggested we give the cultivated field a try. The first year, that field produced only about 1,500 pounds of blueberries, but in the next decade or so the plants had spread so well, we were harvesting 80,000 pounds from that field.

To maintain the blueberry crop, we have to prune the bushes each year so that new foliage can produce berries the following year. We used to burn the fields, like most other growers, but there is always a danger that the fire will get out of hand. Now we use a flail mower, which clips the plants off close to the ground. I usually do the mowing in the fall, and then I go over a new area with a machine that grinds tree stumps down to the ground. In the spring, we apply herbicide to kill the weeds and grass. In the summer, there is not much to do besides watch for insect pests. Harvest time is late August. For the first 25 years or so, we hired pickers, mostly young people from the area, to harvest the berries with rakes. As our crops increased, we sometimes needed as many as 50 people for the 10 days to two weeks of the harvesting season. Now, we hire a contractor to harvest the berries by machine.

We still keep a flock of sheep, the descendants of the ewe that my great-grandparents received as a gift from a relative many years ago. Nowadays we attach tags to the ears of the sheep as a means of identification, but until about 1950, we carried on the traditional Scottish practice of marking sheep by cuts in the ear. That custom had its roots in the days when various flocks of sheep ran together in the hills in Scotland. The same distinctive cut would be made in the ears of all the sheep in one flock. When a flock was passed down from one generation to the next, the family member who inherited the flock, usually the eldest son, inherited the mark. Other members of the family — women, for instance, who were given sheep as dowries — would use the family mark but with the addition of another distinguishing mark. Someone who was knowledgeable about the system might be able to look at a sheep's marking and trace the owner's relationship with another sheep farmer. Our family's mark was two longitudinal cuts on the left ear and the tip cut off the right ear. A few years ago, I discovered that four sets of distant relatives on the Island whose ancestors kept sheep used that same family mark on the animals' left ears.

Although we have our busy spells on the farm, one of the advantages of keeping sheep and growing blueberries is that neither enterprise requires constant attention, the way a herd of dairy cows does, for instance. That means that I have had the freedom in my retirement years to follow other interests. One of the most memorable occasions for me was when I was asked to deliver a message at an ecumenical service in connection with the "Canada Remembers" commemorative event held at St. Peter's Bay, Prince Edward Island, on July 30 and 31, 1994. Here is part of my speech:

"Remembrance implies more than just remembering. It implies understanding and treasuring a great achievement. Canada is doing many things to mark this year, such as minting special coins; however, I am not going to talk about that. Instead, I am going to attempt to take you back to 1944 and speak for my generation from the viewpoint of 1944 — a tall order indeed.

"Then, we couldn't foresee or even dream of the many scientific and social changes that make modern life so relatively easy. We couldn't foresee the many advances in medicine, or universal medicare or the general availability of higher education. We could not imagine men walking on the moon, or modern computers or even television. Nor could we foresee the use of our armed forces for the worthy cause of peacekeeping. On the other hand, we could not foresee the past decade of greed when ostentatious materialism seemed to be the goal of many people. Neither could we imagine our country being plunged needlessly into paralyzing debt by incompetent leaders who had no personal experience with sacrifice.

"We never dreamed of the concept of the family being weakened and eroded, when the traditional family has been the chief means of passing on civilization from one generation to the next. We did dream, however, and sing, of love and laughter, and peace ever after. And bluebirds over the white cliffs of Dover, tomorrow, when the world is free.

"The hard-boiled wheeler-dealers of today probably think we were childishly naive. In some ways time has proven that we were. But we did not put our lives on the line for the sake of future generations lightly. For example, we aircrew in Bomber Command knew that on average we had just six months to live. However, we in the armed forces were not the only ones prepared to sacrifice our lives, if necessary, to achieve justice and freedom.

"Father Reiner Kloeg, a young Dutch priest who guided me from Zaltbommel to Weert in 1942, had this to say in a letter to his family:

> *Prison for Criminals*
> *Utrecht*
> *5 a.m.*
> *March 15, 1944*
>
> *Dearly beloved parents, brothers and sisters,*
>
> *When you receive this letter, I will be there where the goal is for all, with God.*
>
> *First I ask mother and father forgiveness for my lack of appreciation, in the light of all the things that you have*

*given me. If dying is not going to be easy, it is because I
know that this will cost you dearly. I die, or more precisely,
will try to die, according to the example that Jesus gave us
on the cross, praying for those who caused his death. Let us
pray for the well-being of our dear Homeland, for which
I believe I had to do something. Heartfelt greetings until
we soon meet again in Heaven.*

Your loving son and brother, Reiner

"Father Kloeg was executed by firing squad at 6:00 a.m. that same morning. His crime was helping me and others escape from the terror of Nazi-occupied Europe.

"Three of those who helped me in 1942 were later executed by firing squad. I always thank God that I was not the direct cause of any of them being captured by the Nazis.

"I think we should always strive to be worthy of the sacrifices made for us. We should treasure the gift of life. We should not break faith with those who died. We should hold high the torch of honesty, justice, decency, compassion and humility and be thankful for the good fortune bestowed on us by the sacrifices of the past."

After I retired from politics, I watched the political scene mainly from the sidelines. I was always happy to help out when asked, but I took the view that people in active politics probably did not want someone like me looking over their shoulders. I did not attend the 1983 national Conservative convention in Winnipeg, but I did keep a close eye on the proceedings in the media, and it was with some dismay that I watched Joe Clark walk into Brian Mulroney's trap. The convention held a leadership review. When 68 percent of the delegates gave Joe a vote of confidence, he decided that he needed a bigger vote to stay on as leader. I could not understand why he felt that 68 percent was not enough in Winnipeg, yet he was prepared to enter a leadership convention where he would be delighted to receive 50 percent plus one vote. One theory was that he wanted to leave politics but did not want to say so; another was that some of Mulroney's supporters had convinced Clark that 50 percent of 100 was 69.

I did go to the leadership convention in Ottawa a few months later, when the field of candidates included Joe Clark, Brian Mulroney, John Crosbie, Michael Wilson, Flora MacDonald and David Crombie. I voted for John Crosbie on the first ballot and then for Joe Clark. I thought Clark was a straightforward person who tried to do the right thing. The only problem was that his idea of what was right, in terms of political strategy, was sometimes off base; however, I think that with experience, he would have become a fine leader. Had Joe retained the leadership, I think he would have led the party to a majority victory in the 1984 election, and the party and the country would have been spared the Mulroney government.

When Mulroney was elected, he and his wife unfortunately created the image in the public mind of a pair that exhibited all the modesty, wisdom, maturity, good judgement and restraint of two three-year-olds who suddenly found themselves in charge of a candy store, and gave the impression that anything having to do with serving their fellow Canadians was well down their priority list. The Free Trade Agreement that Mulroney signed with the United States was justifiably unpopular in the Maritimes. It had little to do with tariffs and a lot to do with relinquishing sovereignty to trans-national corporations. That agreement also required replacing the manufacturer's tax with the goods and services tax, another unpopular move.

Maritimers had a gut feeling that the Free Trade Agreement would not be a good thing for Canada. When Nova Scotia and New Brunswick joined Confederation, their economies were melded with those of Upper and Lower Canada, whose economies were perhaps 10 times as large as that of the Maritimes. The result was that unemployment was always higher in the Maritimes than in Central Canada, with a resulting out-migration and a brain-drain to the rest of Canada and also to the United States of America. The Maritimes became the have-not provinces of Canada.

There are ominous signs that the melding of Canada's economy with that of the United States will create a repeat of the process on a much larger scale. In 1998 the unemployment rate in the U.S.A. is 4.7 percent, while the rate in Canada is 8.5 percent. It is estimated that 100,000 Canadians move to the United States annually. This causes a serious drain of highly skilled and highly educated people. For example, there are presently more than 17,000 nurses and 10,000 Canadian medical doctors working south of the border. My hope is that Canada, in spite of this, will not become the have-not country of North America.

It always struck me that Mulroney kept trying to out-Trudeau Trudeau. Like Trudeau, he was elected on the basis of image, not experience; most delegates to the leadership convention probably did not realize what they were getting when they voted for Mulroney. Like Trudeau, he appeared obsessed with the Constitution. And like Trudeau, he succeeded in plunging the country deeper and deeper in debt, and missed a great opportunity to cut down the deficit. If I had to rate the prime ministers that have been in power in my lifetime, Mulroney probably would lie near the bottom of the list, just above Trudeau. But Mulroney remained in power for almost a decade, and like many other Canadians, I could only observe the actions of the government from a distance. At one point, I scratched out a couple of limericks for the amusement of my family:

> Said Mulroney, I strongly desired
> To upstage the pact Pierre acquired
> But with Separatist germs
> And 10 cans of worms
> The whole wretched thing backfired.

and

> *Said Mulroney, as usual bragging,*
> *I've been feeding the Separatist dragon*
> *I'll have him so tame*
> *He'll think Tory's his name*
> *When I pat him, his tail will be waggin'.*

I may have been disappointed by the performance of the federal government of the day, but fortunately I had some pleasant duties ahead to occupy my mind. In the fall of 1985, Premier Jim Lee asked whether I would serve as the Island commissioner for Expo 1986, which was to be held in Vancouver. The job carried no salary, but paid all expenses for Gwen and me. By that time, I already had a lot on my plate: I was a member of the P.E.I. Energy Corporation, on the Senior Advisory Board of the Maritime Provinces Education Foundation and on the consultative committee of the National Museum of Natural Sciences. In addition, Gwen and I had planned to spend the winter in a warmer climate. Both the premier and my MLA, Wilbur Mac-Donald, insisted I could still do the job at Expo and urged me to take it on. In the end, I accepted, gladly.

Gwen and I spent about three months enjoying the sun in Portugal. When we arrived home in early April 1986, we found the Island in the middle of an election campaign. The Liberals, led by Joe Ghiz, won that election, with 21 seats to the Conservatives' 11. On April 22, the day after the election, I went to see Joe Ghiz and offered to bow out as the Island's Expo commissioner. He would not hear of it, so I left for Vancouver that day and spent most of the next five and a half months there. Jim Clark, my capable deputy commissioner, did most of the administrative work. Gwen and I spent much of our time representing the Island at various functions in connection with the special days of other provinces, states and countries, and we had a wonderful summer.

I was interested to notice that when a meal was served at one of these functions, the main dish was usually lamb or mutton, the only red meat that is acceptable to all religions of the world.

At home, I served on a number of boards, including that of the Island Nature Trust and the P.E.I. Museum and Heritage Foundation, and filled a number of speaking engagements. During the protracted debate on the fixed link to the Island, I made a presentation to a Senate committee as part of a delegation questioning the wisdom of building the link, and I was pleased to learn that some of the senators changed their minds because of my arguments. My opinion about the bridge was that proponents were confusing change with progress, and they had never showed that the changes brought by the link would actually improve life on the Island. If a link to the mainland were all that it took to bring about prosperity, I argued, Cape Breton would be booming. Subsequent events have not changed my opinion; however, the bridge is now a fact of life, one of those irreversible decisions that we now have to make the best of.

Since my retirement from politics it seems to me that the government of Prince Edward Island has been on a pretty steady course; regardless of which party is in power, there has not been a drastic change in policy or management. The provincial Liberals, however, do seem to have the mentality that they are born to rule and that it is abnormal for them to be out of power. They did form the government in 1986, defeating Jim Lee, who in my estimation was a hard-working premier. Perhaps the time had come for another hard-working generation of leaders. I regarded Joe Ghiz highly — he was an objective person who tried to do as good a job as he could. His successor, Catherine Callbeck, had been a minister in the Campbell government, and I always felt that she was very competent. Recruited to take over when Ghiz retired, Callbeck also happened to be the right sex at the right time, or at least that is how I saw it — the Liberals deemed the time right for a woman to be premier — it was not absolutely necessary but it was timely.

When I left provincial politics, I was happy to see some of the people I recruited into the Conservative party continue with community involvement. When I resigned as premier, Jim Lee became premier and all the cabinet members continued on in the government he led. Horace Carver is one of the leading lawyers in Charlottetown. Pat Binns engaged in the sponsoring of growing beans on the Island and processing them for human consumption in a plant near Kilmuir. He, for a time, was the MP for Cardigan and then returned to the provincial scene, where he is now premier. Prowse Chappell retired after a distinguished career in agriculture, including several years as minister of Agriculture. Fred Driscoll returned to the University of Prince Edward Island as professor of history. Lloyd MacPhail became lieutenant governor of the province and has since passed away. Leo Rossiter became chair of the Worker's Compensation Board and has since passed away. George McMahon is now retired after a distinguished career in law. Barry Clark returned to the United Church ministry and is now in the Far East. Former MLAs Leone Bagnall and Marion Reid both took on leadership roles; Mrs. Reid, in fact, became the Island's first female lieutenant governor. Pat Mella, who did an exceptional job as the only Opposition member in the legislature when the Liberals were in power, is doing an equally competent job as treasurer in the present government.

The bright spots of my retirement years included a number of honours that I received. In 1982, I was made an officer of the Order of St. John of Jerusalem; in 1985, I received an honorary doctor of laws degree from the University of Prince Edward Island; and in April 1992, I went to Rideau Hall, where the Governor General invested me in the Order of Canada. In 1990, the Island Nature Trust presented me with that year's Natural

Areas Award for my role in preserving the Acadian forest my family has owned and protected for a century and a half. This is a 150-acre plot that includes centuries-old white pine, and hemlocks that are hundreds of years old. For generations, my family has practised selective cutting in this woodlot. Nowadays we carefully harvest firewood for our own use but not lumber; the living forest is worth far more to me than any price tag one could put on it.

Another family tradition that we have carried on is that of veterinary medicine. About the turn of the 18th century, two of my father's great-grandfathers, Duncan MacLeod, a practical veterinarian, and Duncan Matheson, a farrier, worked as a team to provide services to owners of animals in parts of the Hebrides. Descendants of the two Duncans settled in Lewis, and two of them — Duncan MacLean, my grandfather, and George MacLean, my father — kept up the tradition of providing practical veterinary services to their neighbours at no cost for almost 100 years, from 1863 to 1956. And when the Atlantic Veterinary College opened in the fall of 1986, its first class included my daughter Jeannie and my grandniece Michelle Nicholson. Michelle graduated in 1990; Jeannie forfeited one year from study to bring her daughter Jessica into the world and graduated in 1991. If the two Duncans could have known about it, I am sure they would have been as proud as I was.

My ancestral roots have been important to me for most of my life, and my retirement years gave me some extra time to foster friendships with distant relatives in the old country. One of the connections I made in Scotland was with a fourth cousin, Sorley MacLean of Skye, a school headmaster who was considered the greatest Gaelic poet of his age. (At one point, he received the Queen's gold medal for poetry, the only time it was won in a language other than English.) Over the years we have enjoyed several trips back and forth between Prince Edward Island and the Isle of Skye visiting our MacLean relatives. Sadly, Sorley passed away in late 1996, but Renée, his gracious wife, is still in

Skye. Sorley had four brothers and two sisters. They were all brilliant scholars. One of the brothers, Dr. Alasdair MacLean, has retired to Skye; his sister, Mary, recently retired there from Edinburgh. Sorley's other sister, Ishbel, and her husband, John, live on the nearby Island of Raasay. Last year we had the pleasure of a visit from one of Sorley's daughters, Ishbel MacLean MacKay, her husband, Allan MacKay, their young son and one of her nephews. It pleases me that we have contact with two more generations of MacLeans from Scotland.

I first wrote to Sorley in the 1960s, when I began trying to track down relatives in Scotland. My older relatives on the Island knew nothing about the branch of the family in Scotland, but they did tell me that an uncle of mine, who had just passed away, had served in the Canadian Forestry Corps in Scotland during the First World War and that he had visited relatives there. I had been told that a man named Sam MacLean (who usually went by his Gaelic name, Sorley), who had grown up in my ancestral home, Rasaay, was a likely source of information. He wrote back, telling me that he thought I must be related to another group of MacLeans in Rasaay because as far as he knew, none of his ancestors had left Scotland as early as my great-grandfather had come to Prince Edward Island.

Then it occurred to me that when my uncle had visited relatives in Scotland, he probably had written to his father about it, and my grandfather probably would have kept such a letter. At the time, a first cousin of mine lived in our grandfather's house in Wood Islands North. The house had been vacant or rented to various people for several years. I asked my cousin whether it was possible that there was anything left in the house belonging to our grandfather. He told me there was an old chest in the attic. When we examined the contents of the chest, we found some photographs and a packet of letters that apparently had been undisturbed for 46 years. The first letter proved to be what I had hoped for: dated 1918, it was from my uncle in Scotland to my grandfather, and it provided the key to many of my questions about the family tree. The next day, I read in the paper that my grandfather's house, with all its contents, had burned to the ground — just hours after I had rescued this precious (to me) old letter. I sent a copy of the letter to Sam (Sorley) MacLean in Scotland, and everything fell into place. The letter revealed to him that we were fourth cousins, and we were able to find out exactly how we were related. This correspondence started the special friendship that lasted until Sam's death.

I engaged in another bit of detective work to find the Australian branch of the family. I knew that my great-grandaunt and her husband, Norman MacLeod, had emigrated to Australia in 1836, the same year my maternal grandfather had arrived in Prince Edward Island with his parents. My great-grandmother and the sister who had emigrated to Australia had corresponded for 60 years, but the only remnant of this correspondence I could find was a photograph of a young man named Angus Brens, probably taken in the 1890s by a photographer in Warrnambool, Australia. I wrote a letter to the newspaper in Warrnambool, asking whether any of its readers could identify Angus Brens.

A few weeks later, I received a shower of letters from Australia, mostly from distant relatives, who informed me that Angus Brens was the father of Bill Brens, the mayor of Melbourne. In 1965, after attending a Commonwealth Parliamentary Association conference in New Zealand, I decided to take a side trip to Australia. Bill Brens met me at the airport in Melbourne and told me that the descendants of my great-grandaunt, Mrs. MacLeod, had held a family reunion every year for many years, but had not met for about 10 years. Because of my visit, he had decided to revive the custom. A few days later, I met about 30 of my distant cousins and their spouses in Warrnambool. It was a most enjoyable day.

In the past two decades I have also kept in touch with old friends in Europe. Many of the brave people who helped me and other airmen during the war came to Canada as guests of the Royal Air Forces Escaping Society. When the annual meeting of the Escaping Society took place in Charlottetown in 1981, the guests included Baronne Bernadette Greindl, the widow of the man I knew only as Nemo, and her daughter, Claire Greindl. In 1984, the society met in Winnipeg. Elvere Morelle, who ran the Comet Line house in Paris, was among the guests from Europe. The next year, when we met at Niagara-on-the-Lake, I was delighted to see Peggy van Lier, the young woman who had guided me across Brussels to my hiding place. Other guests over the years included Count Georges d'Oultremont, my guide from Brussels to Paris; and Maria Goya, the daughter of Francia Usandizanga, who had fed us before we crossed the Pyrenees. Although I had visited with Dédée in Europe in 1947 and 1977, unfortunately, we never had the pleasure of having her as our guest in Canada. After she was freed from the concentration camp and regained her health, she spent her working life as a nurse in leper colonies, first in the Belgian Congo and then in Addis Ababa. By the time she returned to Belgium, her health had deteriorated so badly she was unable to make the trip to Canada.

In 1988, Gwen and I took part in a reunion in Europe with some surviving members of the Resistance. I had received a letter from the Dutch Association of Allied Aircrew Helpers, asking me to support a request to the city of Rotterdam to name a new street after Father Kloeg, the young Dutch priest who had guided me from Zaltbommel to Weert. In my letter to the city fathers of Rotterdam, I noted that his assistance had made it possible for me to eventually escape to Gibraltar. I added: "I believe that it is very fitting that a new street in Rotterdam should be named Frater Kloeg Straat as a tribute to this gallant clergyman and as a reminder to present and future citizens of the supreme sacrifice made on their behalf by Frater Kloeg."

The city council granted this request. As a result, members of the Canadian branch of the Royal Air Forces Escaping Society were invited to Holland as guests of the Dutch helpers in May 1988. We had a glorious 10 days in Holland, a trip that included a visit to the royal palace, where we were warmly received by Queen Juliana and Prince Bernhard. Our visit also included a dinner at a restaurant in Waardenburg, which was about five miles from the field where I had landed in Holland 46 years earlier. One of my helpers, Sir Adriaan Ferdinand van Goelst Meijer, and his wife were our special guests. He was 96 at the time, but he stayed for a couple of hours, becoming caught up in the nostalgia of reuniting with old wartime friends and enthralling us with a witty speech in perfect English. One of his lines was: "I did not realize what I started when I supplied a fishing pole for Angus MacLean to carry on his way to Zaltbommel railway station, to help disguise him as a local. The next time I heard of him, he was minister of Fisheries for Canada."

The main event took place one afternoon in Rotterdam. The Canadian guests met in a hall with surviving members of the Dutch wartime underground and their next of kin to unveil the names of four streets named for citizens who had lost their lives because of Resistance work. Two of Father Kloeg's brothers were there, as were representatives of the Canadian embassy. Among the Dutch underground survivors at the ceremony were Nel Lind and Joke Fulmer. Nel Lind had taken over Father Kloeg's duties after the Gestapo caught up with him, and when she too was arrested, Joke Fulmer had succeeded her. They had helped dozens of people escape capture by the Gestapo, but eventually Joke was arrested, and she and Nel were sentenced to death. In the case of women arrested by the Gestapo, Hitler reserved the right to either approve of a death sentence or grant a pardon. In the confusion of the last months of the war, Nel Lind and Joke Fulmer were moved so often that Hitler's approval of their death sentence never caught up with them and the Russians liberated their concentration camp before the Nazis got around to executing them. At the ceremony, Matthieu Beelen and I had the honour of unveiling the name of the street named for Father Kloeg.

When the horrors of war overtake friends and associates, one's realization of the evil and stupidity of war becomes vivid indeed. The First and Second World wars, with their huge scale and use of modern technology, are among the greatest calamities ever to beset humankind. In every nation involved in the Second World War, a large percentage of the cream of my generation lost their lives. This was a loss that civilization could ill afford, for it took the brightest, healthiest and best educated to operate the modern machines of war. Thus modern warfare is the negation of one of nature's basic laws for improvement: the survival of the fittest.

My own experience with war changed the course of my life and my attitude towards life. When I think of the sacrifices made by the men and women who served in the war, thus making possible many of the benefits we enjoy today, I become disgusted with people who fail to appreciate those sacrifices, and who try to reap where they have not sown by practising questionable methods of business or politics. I also continue to have a sense of wonder about my own life. The question in my mind, and I think perhaps in the minds of all aircrew who survived, has always been, "Why me? Why am I so lucky? Why have the fates decided that one particular person should survive when so many have not?" In the minds of evaders, the question often is, "Why should I be so fortunate as to find help from a stranger who had to put his or her life on the line?" I have never been able to answer these questions. All I know for sure is that I have been left with a profound sense of gratitude towards my helpers and an enduring appreciation of the gift of life on borrowed time.

Many years ago, when Horace Carver and I were in the middle of my first provincial election campaign, we were driving in the country one day when he remarked, "Angus, you always seem to be so much at peace with yourself. You're never in a rush." I told him that my wartime experiences had marked me forever. "My attitude is that every day is a wonderful day," I said, "and I'm not going to fritter it away."

Island Life

But ask the beasts, and they will teach you,
The birds of the air, and they will tell you.
Or the plants of the earth, and they will teach you
And the fish of the sea will declare to you.
Who among these does not know
That the hand of the Lord has done this?
In his hand is the life of every living thing
And the breath of all mankind.

—— The Book of Job, chapter 12, verses 7 - 10

For many years, Gwen and I have been hanging hummingbird feeders on the verandah of our house every summer. Hummingbirds are marvels of creation. They migrate each fall down through Florida and Cuba and sometimes across the Caribbean Sea, more than 3,000 miles non-stop to South America. In the spring they migrate back to the very spot in which they spent the previous summer — in this instance, to our farm in Lewis, a place that even some of our best friends have trouble locating. All of this magic is bound up in about one-third of an ounce, the weight of one penny.

The hummingbirds usually return to our verandah about May 20 every year. One year when I was seldom home and preoccupied with other matters, I forgot to put up the feeders. While I was home briefly one Sunday afternoon, I thought I heard some high-pitched squeaks. I looked out the window to see two hummingbirds buzzing around where the feeders ought to have been. The high-pitched squeaking was hummingbird language for "What a lousy homecoming — all the way from South America, and not even a snack!"

This homing instinct is not something that is merely imprinted, or learned, or just force of habit. It is deeper and more fundamental than that. It is an instinct that is carried on in the genes of fish and birds, and probably in our own genes as well. One of the deepest needs of mammals, including humans, and of birds and fish, and probably of all forms of life, is a knowledge that they belong in a certain corner of the universe, and that it belongs to them. It is to declare that they have adopted a chosen spot that songbirds sing. For the same reason dogs and wolves mark out their territory in a less attractive way. It is this strange longing that causes birds to migrate a quarter of the way around the world in fall and return, as the hummingbirds do to our farm, to the very same spot that was home the year before.

When I was minister of Fisheries, one of the problems my department tried to solve was the depletion of salmon stocks. Salmon runs had been wiped out in some rivers in British Columbia that previously had been productive. Landslides and logjams prevented the migration of salmon up the rivers to spawn. Some scientists in the department believed that if the obstructions were removed, salmon would again migrate up these rivers. This was done at considerable expense. No salmon appeared. The Fisheries biologists then suggested that spawn from salmon in other rivers be transplanted to the headwaters of the barren rivers to hatch and live and eventually migrate out to sea. This was done, and the young salmon were marked so that they could be identified on their return three years later from the far expanses of the Pacific Ocean. The salmon returned in large numbers, but about 10 percent did not go back to the rivers where they had hatched and where they had spent the first months of life, but to the rivers where their ancestors had migrated from time immemorial. There was something in their genes that indicated that the river of their ancestors had a special meaning for them.

It may be for the same reason that every time I travel to the Hebrides off the coast of mainland Scotland, I feel singularly at home, as though I belong there in a special way. This may be merely an intellectual thing — the knowledge that for many centuries my ancestors toiled and danced and sang and wept, and often suffered, but fell in love, married and raised children, and lived and died in those islands — but it may well be more than that. It may well be that we still have in us the vestiges of some primeval instinct that we once shared with Pacific salmon and hummingbirds that, for each one of us, some particular spot is special.

The need to belong is one of our deepest needs. Perhaps, after the urge to mate and procreate, it is the instinct that shapes our lives more than anything else. In all cultures, after love songs, I think more songs are written and sung about home and longings for home than about any other subject: "Home on the Range," "Home Sweet Home," "My Old Kentucky Home," "My Heart's in the Highlands." My ancestors lived for centuries in their special corner of the universe, the Hebrides. One hundred and sixty-five years ago they were forced to leave their natural habitat because of the pressure of overpopulation and the notion that they were less important, in themselves, than solving the problem of feeding the teeming cities of the British Isles. The business and political leaders of the day thought that sheep for mutton and wool for the cities had a higher claim on the land than mere country people did. As a result of the process known to historians as the Highland Clearances, thousands of Scots were cleared from the Highlands and islands of Scotland to make room for sheep.

These Scots, along with people from other areas who were experiencing a similar fate, became the pioneer settlers of the New World. For a while they were able to live as independent small farmers on their own land. But not for long. For the last century, the farmers and country people of this Island and beyond have been waging a losing battle. Today, farming people have been reduced to less than 5 percent of the population. In recent years, this process has accelerated. The development of monstrous farm machinery, the emergence of large, vertically integrated agricultural corporations and the prevailing emphasis on producing cheap food for urban dwellers have reduced the farming population perilously close to the vanishing point. In other words, for the past century, we country people have been suffering a more subtle but radical version of the Highland Clearances, and in the crowded world of today there is nowhere else to go and start anew.

It has often been observed that all societies of the past collapsed when they became highly urbanized. I believe that civilizations decay when, through over-urbanization, people lose sight of the fact that we humans are merely part of the intricate web of life, and that if we damage that web, we do so at our own peril. We who are custodians of this small Island must treat it with care, so that we can hand it on to future generations. Despite trends of the recent past, there still remain on the land a substantial number of small-scale and part-time farmers who continue to exist despite government neglect and in the face of conventional economic theory that suggests they should not be there. In fact, for a growing number of people, the fascination and allure of the urban lifestyle is less powerful than the prospect of earning either all or part of their living on the land. People realize that in the country, they can now have modern conveniences once available only in the city. In addition, they can have more security. They can produce some of their own food, and in many cases, their own housing and fuel. Perhaps more important, they can develop a much-needed sense of belonging.

I have always felt attached to the countryside in which I live, and to the Island as a whole. I guess it was my own sense of belonging that compelled me to tell a reporter 20 years ago that I was "an Islander first," thus inadvertently setting off a nation-wide controversy on television and in the newspapers. Now my children are taking over the farm in Lewis, and I am pleased that they share my love for this corner of the earth. Gwen and I live in the house in which I was born. Most of my siblings had passed on by the early 1990s. As I write this, only Effie, who lives in Halifax, and Murdoch, in Moncton, are still alive. But our old farm kitchen, still warmed with the wood range my parents bought in 1938, is a favourite gathering spot for a new genera-tion of children. The youngest grandchild, Sophie Christina MacLean, was born to Rob and his wife, Melissa, on October 28, 1997. Rob and Melissa manage the blueberry operation and oversee the selective woodcutting in the woodlot. Mary, who works in Montreal as a computer programmer, and Allan, who lives in Charlottetown, come back to the farm for frequent visits. Jeannie lives just up the road from us. Her two daughters, Jessica Robin Sutton, born in January 1987, and Sarah Sue Sutton, born in September 1991, now play in the fields that their great-great-grandfather hacked out of the forest a century and a half ago. As for me, I am grateful to be able to spend my years of retirement here, as a temporary custodian of the fields and woodlands that my ancestors called home.

I believe it was Rudyard Kipling who said it best:

> God gave all men all earth to love,
> but since our hearts are small,
> Ordained for each one place would be
> Beloved over all.

Important Dates

1914, May 15	John Angus MacLean born in Lewis, Prince Edward Island
1920 - 30	Attends elementary school in Lewis until the end of grade 9
1930 - 31	Attends grade 10 at West Kent School, Charlottetown
1931 - 32	Works on family farm in Lewis
1932 - 33	Attends grade 11 at Mount Allison Academy in Sackville, N.B.
1933 - 34	Works on family farm in Lewis
1934 - 35	Attends grade 12 at Summerside High School
1935 - 36	Attends Mount Allison University
1936 - 37	Attends the University of British Columbia in Vancouver
1937 - 38	Returns to Mount Allison University
1938 - 39	Works on family farm in Lewis; completes final university course by correspondence
1939, May	Graduates with a bachelor of science in industrial chemistry
1939, Sept. 8	Joins Royal Canadian Air Force
1939, Sept. 9	Canada declares war
1939, Nov. 5	Completes elementary flying course in Halifax, Nova Scotia
1940, Feb. 24	Completes ground school in Trenton, Ontario
1940, Apr. 6	Completes intermediate flying training at Camp Borden, Ontario
1940, May 15	Completes advanced flying training in Trenton, Ontario
1940, July 19	Graduates from Central Flying School in Trenton as flying instructor
1940, July 29	Posted to No. 1 Service Flying Training School at Camp Borden
1940, Sept. 9	Posted to No. 4 Service Flying Training School in Saskatoon, Saskatchewan
1941, Jan. 25	Posted to No. 7 Service Flying Training School in MacLeod, Alberta
1942, Jan. 21	Posted overseas

1942, Mar. 17	Posted to No. 27 Operational Training Unit in Litchfield, England
1942, Apr. 16	Posted to 405 RCAF Squadron, Pocklington, England
1942, May	Starts flying bombing operations
1942, June 8	Shot down over German-occupied Holland while on night bombing raid
1942, Aug. 20	Reaches British embassy in Madrid, Spain
1942, Sept. 10	Reaches Gourock, Scotland
1942, Oct.	Receives Distinguished Flying Cross from King George VI
1942, Oct. 6	Attends crash course on chemical warfare
1942, Oct. 13	Posted to No. 20 Maintenance Unit, Aston Down, England
1942, Nov 13	Posted to No. 8 Maintenance Unit, Little Rissington, England
1942, Nov. 17	Posted to No. 39 Maintenance Unit at RAF Station Colerne, England
1943, May	Returns to Canada
1943, June 10	Posted to the Repatriation Centre in Rockcliffe, Ontario
1943, June 24	Posted to Test and Development Establishment at Rockliffe
1943, July 26	Promoted to Officer Commanding the Test and Development Establishment
1943, Nov. 25	Nominated to run for the Conservative Party in the federal riding of Queens, Prince Edward Island
1944, March	Promoted to rank of Wing Commander
1945, June 11	Finishes third in first federal election
1945, Aug. 15	Second World War ends
1945, Oct.	Posted to Europe as Officer Commanding the No. 2 Missing Research and Enquiry Unit
1947, Sept.	Returns to Canada
1947, Nov. 15	Demobilized
1947	Returns to Lewis and expands family farm
1949, June 27	Finishes third in second federal election
1950, Aug. 23	Mother dies
1951, June 25	First elected to Parliament; moves part-time to Ottawa

1951 - 57	Member of the air force reserve
1952, Oct. 29	Marries Gwen
1953, Aug. 10	Re-elected to Parliament to be returned in every federal election until resignation from federal politics in 1976; re-elected in Queens 1957 - 58, 1962 - 63, 1965 and after redistribution in Malpeque, 1968, 1972, 1974
1953, Aug. 15	Daughter Jean born
1954, Dec. 15	Son Allan born
1955, Jan.	Appointed Deputy Opposition Whip
1956, June 23	Daughter Mary born
1957, June 21	Sworn in as minister of Fisheries; retains cabinet position until defeat of Diefenbaker government in 1963
1958, May	Receive LLD from Mount Allison University
1958, Sept. 29	Son Rob born
1959, July	Minister in attendance to the Queen and Prince Philip during royal visit to Prince Edward Island
1963, Apr. 22	Returns to backbenches
1966, Mar. 15	Father dies
1969, July	Family moves to farm in Lewis; begins blueberry farming
1976, Sept. 23	Elected leader of the Progressive Conservative Party in Prince Edward Island
1976, Oct. 20	Resigns from Parliament
1976, Nov. 8	Elected to the Prince Edward Island Legislature in Fourth Queens; re-elected Apr. 4, 1978; Apr. 23, 1979
1979, May 3	Sworn in as Premier of Prince Edward Island
1981, Nov. 17	Retires as premier
1982, Aug. 31	Retires from politics
1982, Oct.	Awarded the Order of St. John of Jerusalem
1985, May	Receives LLD from the University of Prince Edward Island
1986, Apr.	Officiates as P.E.I. Commissioner to Expo 86 in Vancouver
1990	Presented with Island Nature Trust Natural Areas Award for family's woodlot
1992, Apr. 29	Receives Order of Canada

Index